D0843396

# Custom, Power and the Power of Rules

*International Relations and Customary International Law*

This book sets out to explain the most foundational aspect of international law in international relations terms. By doing so it goes straight to the central problem of international law – that although legally speaking all States are equal, socially speaking they clearly are not. As such it is an ambitious and controversial book which will be of interest to all international relations scholars and students and practitioners of international law.

MICHAEL BYERS is a Fellow of Jesus College, Oxford and Visiting Fellow, Max-Planck-Institute for Comparative Public Law and International Law, Heidelberg.

# Custom, Power and the Power of Rules

*International Relations and Customary International Law*

Michael Byers

PUBLISHED BY THE PRESS SYNDICATE OF THE UNIVERSITY OF CAMBRIDGE
The Pitt Building, Trumpington Street, Cambridge CB2 1RP, United Kingdom

CAMBRIDGE UNIVERSITY PRESS
The Edinburgh Building, Cambridge, CB2 2RU, UK http://www.cup.cam.ac.uk
40 West 20th Street, New York, NY 10011-4211, USA http://www.cup.org
10 Stamford Road, Oakleigh, Melbourne 3166, Australia



First published 1999

Printed in the United Kingdom at the University Press, Cambridge

Typeset in Plantin 10/12 pt [SE]

*A catalogue record for this book is available from the British Library*

ISBN 0 521 63289 7 hardback
ISBN 0 521 63408 3 paperback

It is true that politics are not law, but an adequate notion of a body of law cannot be gained without understanding the society in and for which it exists, and it is therefore necessary for the student of international law to appreciate the actual position of the great powers of Europe.

John Westlake, *Chapter on the Principles of International Law* (Cambridge: Cambridge University Press, 1894) 92

Law is regarded as binding because it represents the sense of right of the community: it is an instrument of the common good. Law is regarded as binding because it is enforced by the strong arm of authority: it can be, and often is, oppressive. Both these answers are true; and both of them are only half truths.

Edward Hallett Carr, *The Twenty Years' Crisis* (2nd ed.) (London: Macmillan, 1946) 177

# Contents

# Foreword

The subject of customary international law as a general phenomenon is hardly more suitable for graduate research students in international law than Fermat's last theorem used to be for their counterparts in mathematics. The central puzzles of a discipline, which generations of its senior professionals have failed to solve, are usually better approached from the edges, and indirectly. Light may thus be shed on the centre, but there is less risk of complete failure. So when Michael Byers came seeking to work on custom it seemed sensible to look not frontally at the 'problem' as such, but at a number of examples of different kinds of custom in transition, at different contexts where, we could be relatively sure from the *communis opinio*, a particular customary rule existed and had changed. What were the factors that had produced the change; how had they interrelated; what influence did the 'structure' of the particular problem exercise – for example, what difference did it make on the evolution of a particular institution or custom that the issue characteristically arose in one forum (national courts in the case of state immunity, foreign ministries in the case of the breadth of the territorial sea)? At least it was a starting point.

It says much for the energy and initiative of its author that the resulting book tackles these particulars within the framework of a study seeking to show the ways of international lawyers to the scholars of international relations. Of course international relations has been studied within the disciplines of history, ethics and law for as long as those disciplines have existed. But there was a particular point in focusing on 'international relations'. As a self-conscious academic discipline it is of recent origin and has its own special history and orientation. The history is tied up with the failure of idealism, legalism and the League of Nations. So far as international law is concerned, its orientation is, or at least was, strongly influenced by the fact that early exponents such as Hans Morgenthau were versed in the subject and saw themselves as reacting from it – not so much in its lower reaches, those parts of the routine conduct of diplomatic and inter-state relations which the first generation scholars rarely reached, and which could safely be left to be 'influenced' by international law, but in the great affairs of state, and in particular in relation to the use of force. There was tension between the claim of international law, as embodied in the Charter and in decisions of the International Court, to regulate the use of force and the assertions of certain most powerful States, and of certain of their scholars, that force could be used in international relations as a matter of policy on any sufficient occasion, and that the language of diplomacy on those occasions was merely cosmetic. A further feature of the international relations literature has been its dominant focus in and on the United States. True, the involvement of the United States as superpower in any case can always be presented as involving a difference of kind, and it may indeed do so. But the combined emphases on the use of force and on the United States produced, at least until recently, a view of the world amongst international relations scholars which had a quite different feel – as if arising from a studied determination to grasp only one part of the elephant.

For a variety of reasons this situation is changing, and more balanced appraisals of the links between international law and international relations are becoming possible. Dr Byers' study is one such appraisal; but it also makes a contribution to an understanding of the process of international law, a process which is something more than a flux. While doing more than he started out to do, it also demonstrates, on modest assumptions as to the underpinnings of international law, its distinct character and power – though not by any formal proof. One result is to suggest a need to recast the tradition of realism itself in more realistic, that is to say in more comprehensive and representative, terms.

JAMES CRAWFORD
*Whewell Professor of International Law*
*Lauterpacht Research Centre for International Law*
*University of Cambridge*

# Preface

At the beginning of his or her career, every international lawyer has to grapple with the concept of customary international law, with the idea that there are informal, unwritten rules which are binding upon States. This is because there remain important areas of international law, such as the laws of State responsibility and State immunity, where generally applicable treaties do not exist. And despite the lack of an explicit, general consent to rules in these areas, no international lawyer doubts that there is a body of law which applies to them.

I stumbled into the quagmire of customary international law very early in my legal career, in the autumn of 1989. It was during the second year of my law studies when, as a member of McGill University's team in the Jessup International Law Moot Court Competition, I was assigned to write those sections of our memorials that concerned customary international law. Having written what I thought was a thorough analysis of '*opinio juris*' (i.e., subjective belief in legality) and State practice concerning the issue of maritime pollution in the Antarctic, I was struck by how difficult it was to explain this 'law' to my teammates. They, quite rightly, were concerned about how to present our arguments in a convincing manner, and theoretical discussions of subjective belief seemed far too amorphous to take before judges. In the end, we decided to focus on what States had actually done – i.e., State practice – rather than what States may or may not have believed they were required to do. Not surprisingly, this incident left me convinced that there was something wholly unsatisfactory about traditional explanations of customary international law.

At the same time, the problems of customary international law seemed related to a more general problem that I had already encountered. Having come to the study of law after a degree in international relations, I soon began to identify the distinction between '*opinio juris*' and 'State practice' with the distinction between international law and international politics, between what States might legally be obligated to do, and what they actually did as the result of a far wider range of pressures and opportunities. Moreover, the lack of interest in international law among most of the international relations scholars I had encountered, combined with the apparent lack of interest among most international lawyers in the effects of political factors on law creation, suggested to me that there was something unsatisfactory in this area as well.

In the intervening decade, thinking about the relationship between international law and international politics has advanced significantly, to the point where interdisciplinary studies now constitute an important part of both academic disciplines. Relatively few international relations scholars still doubt whether international law actually exists. Instead, they are increasingly interested in regimes, institutions, the processes of law creation, and in why States comply with rules and other norms.

International lawyers, for their part, are demonstrating an increasing interest in international relations theory. Regime theory and institutionalism, in particular, are now being applied by a number of legal academics in their work on international law. Yet, though a vast amount has been written about customary international law, relatively few writers have examined the relationship between law and politics within this particular context. In an area of law that is constituted in large part by State practice, and which would therefore seem particularly susceptible to the differences that exist in the relative affluence or strength of States, this would seem to be a serious omission. Fortunately, calls are now being made to remedy the situation, with Schachter, among others, writing that the 'whole subject' of the 'role of power in international law . . . warrants empirical study by international lawyers and political scientists'.[1]

The time may be particularly ripe for such an investigation of the role of power in customary international law. The international situation has changed profoundly in recent years, not only as a result of the end of the Cold War, the disintegration of the Soviet Union and the demise of most command economies. The earlier process of decolonisation, the acquisition by non-industrialised States of a numerical majority in many international organisations, and the economic resurgence of Western Europe and the Pacific Rim have all contributed to reducing and rearranging relative power advantages and disadvantages. As a result of these new power relationships, new ideas such as the concept of democratic governance in international law are appearing, and the extreme politics of East–West, North–South confrontation have at last given way to a more complex situation which may be more conducive to objective academic analysis.

These dramatic changes may also be at least partly responsible for the increasing interest that many international relations scholars have in international institutions and international law. Numerous new interna-

[1] Schachter (1996) 537.

tional institutions are appearing at the same time that many old institutions are becoming more effective. The international system is, arguably, becoming more refined, complex and less dependent on applications of raw power. As we reach the turn of the century, international relations scholars clearly find themselves having to address such new complexities.

Within this new environment, this book seeks to provide a balanced, interdisciplinary perspective on the development, maintenance and change of customary international law. By doing so, it hopes to assist both international lawyers and international relations scholars better to understand how law and politics interact in the complex mix of '*opinio juris*' and 'State practice' that gives rise to customary rules.

This book is a substantially revised version of a PhD thesis that was submitted to the Faculty of Law at the University of Cambridge on 1 May 1996. The thesis was supervised by Professor James Crawford and examined by Dr Vaughan Lowe and Professor Bruno Simma in Munich, Germany on 16 July of that same year. An earlier attempt at expressing some of the ideas developed in the thesis was published in November 1995 in the *Michigan Journal of International Law*. That article, entitled 'Custom, Power and the Power of Rules: An Interdisciplinary Perspective on Customary International Law', represented an early state of my thinking on the interaction of law and politics within the context of customary international law. Many of my ideas have changed since that article was published and my thesis submitted: some have been developed further, several have been abandoned and a few have been replaced. This book is also a much more extensive treatment of the issues.

MICHAEL BYERS
*Jesus College, Oxford*

# Acknowledgments

The writing of a doctoral dissertation and its subsequent modification is often portrayed as a lonely experience, as much a test of one's fortitude in dealing with intellectual seclusion as a test of academic ability. Fortunately, this has not been my experience. I benefited greatly from the assistance, encouragement and friendship of many individuals, only a few of whom I am able to thank here.

During the course of writing my dissertation and in subsequently seeking to improve upon it my work received much needed criticism from the following people: Philip Allott, Blaine Baker, Ian Brownlie, Bob Byers, James Crawford, Deborah Cresswell, Anthony D'Amato, Anne Denise, Carol Dixon, Emanuela Gillard, Peter Haggenmacher, Benedict Kingsbury, Martti Koskenniemi, Heike Krieger, Claus Kress, Susan Lamb, Vaughan Lowe, Susan Marks, Frances Nicholson, Georg Nolte, Geneviève Saumier, Jayaprakash Sen, Bruno Simma, Stephen Toope, Thomas Viles and Arthur Weisburd. I thank them all.

Of these individuals, several deserve special mention. First and foremost, James Crawford provided everything a doctoral student could want from a supervisor. In particular, I wish to thank him for his patience during my first year and a half in Cambridge, when I had little idea as to where my work was taking me.

In addition to James Crawford, I wish to thank Philip Allott, Blaine Baker and Peter Haggenmacher for being outstanding role models. Their commitment to excellence in teaching and scholarship is humbling.

Stephen Toope deserves special thanks for directing me to Cambridge, and for his belief that a PhD was something I could do, and would enjoy doing.

Jayaprakash Sen provided friendship and intellectual stimulation. I benefited greatly from his brilliance.

Frances Nicholson was not only a critical and imaginative editor, but also a forgiving and compassionate housemate.

Jochen Frowein, Georg Nolte and Andreas Zimmermann were gracious hosts during many visits to Heidelberg, while Katharine Edmunds,

Sylvie Scherrer and Geneviève Saumier have been particularly good friends.

Although I never asked him to comment on my work, Venkata Raman allowed me to read his own doctoral thesis on customary international law and to test my amateurish lecturing skills on his students.

I also wish to thank the many people who participated in the graduate seminar on the History and Theory of International Law in the University of Cambridge from 1992 to 1995, as well as my undergraduate and graduate students in Cambridge from 1994 to 1996, and in Oxford since then. They have taught me a great deal.

Last but not least, Vaughan Lowe and Bruno Simma were critical yet constructive examiners whose many suggestions have, I hope, enabled this book to be an improvement on the thesis. The same may be said of the international lawyers and international relations scholars who anonymously reviewed the manuscript for Cambridge University Press.

I am grateful for the financial or logistical support provided by the British Secretary of State for Education and Science, the Cambridge Commonwealth Trust, Cambridge University's Faculty of Law, the Canadian Centennial Scholarship Fund, Jesus College (Oxford), the Kurt Hahn Trust, the Max-Planck-Institut für ausländisches öffentliches Recht und Völkerrecht, McGill University, Queens' College (Cambridge), and the Social Sciences and Humanities Research Council of Canada.

This book is dedicated to my parents, Brigitte and Bob Byers, with love.

# Table of cases

# Table of treaties

# Abbreviations

| | |
|---|---|
| AC | *Appeal Cases* |
| All ER | *All England Reports* |
| CTS | *Canada Treaty Series* |
| DLR | *Dominion Law Reports* (Canada) |
| F. 2d | *Federal Reports* (United States of America), Second Series |
| F. Supp. | *Federal Reports* (United States of America), Supplement |
| FAO | United Nations Food and Agriculture Organisation |
| FSIA | Foreign Sovereign Immunities Act (1976, United States of America) |
| GAOR | United Nations *General Assembly Official Records* |
| GATT | General Agreement on Tariffs and Trade |
| ICJ | International Court of Justice |
| ILA | International Law Association |
| ILC | International Law Commission |
| ILM | *International Legal Materials* |
| ILR | *International Law Reports* |
| Keesing's | *Keesing's Contemporary Archives* (now *Keesing's Record of World Events*) |
| LNTS | *League of Nations Treaty Series* |
| Moore | Moore, *A Digest of International Law* |
| NAFO | North Atlantic Fisheries Organisation |
| NZLR | *New Zealand Law Reports* |
| PCIJ | Permanent Court of International Justice |
| QB | Court of Queen's Bench (England) |
| S. Ct | *Supreme Court Reports* (United States of America) |
| SC | *Statutes of Canada* |
| SCR | *Supreme Court Reports* (Canada) |
| Stat. | Statutes |
| UKTS | *United Kingdom Treaty Series* |
| UNGA | United Nations General Assembly |
| UNHCR | United Nations High Commissioner for Refugees |

| | |
|---|---|
| UNTS | *United Nations Treaty Series* |
| USC | *United States Code* |
| Whiteman | Whiteman, *A Digest of International Law* |
| WLR | *Weekly Law Reports* |

# *Part 1*

# An interdisciplinary perspective

# 1 Law and power

The International Court of Justice has observed that international law is not a static set of rules, that it undergoes 'continuous evolution'.[1] The evolution of international law is a subject that has absorbed international lawyers for centuries, for, among other things, the way in which law develops and changes clearly determines the rules that are applicable today.[2] This book addresses one particular characteristic of the evolution of international law, namely that it does not occur in a legal vacuum, but is instead circumscribed and regulated by fundamental rules, principles and processes of international law. One such process is the process of customary international law, which is also referred to here as the 'customary process'. This process governs how one particular kind of rules – rules of customary international law – is developed, maintained and changed.[3]

Unlike treaty rules, which result from formal negotiation and explicit acceptance, rules of customary international law arise out of frequently ambiguous combinations of behavioural regularity and expressed or inferred acknowledgments of legality. Despite (or perhaps because of) their informal origins, rules of customary international law provide substantive content to many areas of international law, as well as the

[1] *Barcelona Traction Case (Second Phase)* (1970) *ICJ Reports* 3, 33.

[2] For an historical overview, see Wilhelm Grewe, *The Epochs of International Law* (trans. Michael Byers) (Berlin: Walter de Gruyter, 1999).

[3] On the distinction between custom as process and custom as rules, see, e.g., Sur (1990) 1er cahier, 8; and pp. 46–50 below. This book focuses on the customary process as it operates in respect of generally applicable rules. The process may operate in a similar but more restricted manner in respect of rules of special customary international law. Special customary international law involves rules which apply among limited numbers of States, often as exceptions to rules of general customary international law. States within such a limited group remain governed by any generally applicable rule in their relations with any States outside that group. Special customary international law is sometimes referred to as 'regional customary international law' because it often develops among States which are in geographical proximity to one another. However, issues which are particular to limited numbers of States and therefore likely to attract special customary rules are not always confined to single regions. For explanations of special customary international law, see Cohen-Jonathan (1961); Guggenheim (1961); D'Amato (1969); Akehurst (1974–75a) 28–31; and Sur (1990) 2e cahier, 3 and 12–13.

procedural framework within which most rules of international law, including treaty rules, develop, exist and change. Customary rules are particularly important in areas of international law, such as State immunity and State responsibility, where multilateral treaties of a general scope have yet to be negotiated. They are also important in areas, such as human rights, where many States are not party to existing treaties nor subject to the relevant treaty enforcement mechanisms. Finally, customary rules would seem to exist alongside many treaty provisions, influencing the interpretation and application of those provisions, and in some cases modifying their content.[4]

The customary process and other fundamental rules, principles and processes of international law are, in terms used by Keohane, 'persistent and connected sets of rules . . . that prescribe behavioral roles, constrain activity, and shape expectations'.[5] In other words, they are normative structures which regulate applications of what international relations scholars usually refer to as 'power'. This book examines the relationship between international law and power, in its most general sense, within the confines of the process of customary international law. Still more specifically, it focuses on the interaction, within that process, between certain principles or basal concepts of international law, such as jurisdiction and reciprocity, and non-legal factors, such as the differences in wealth and military strength which exist among States.

In examining the relationship between law and power within the process of customary international law, this book adopts an interdisciplinary perspective which seeks to combine aspects of the history, theory and practice of international law with certain elements of international relations theory and methodology. There are four reasons why such a perspective seems desirable. First, both international relations scholars and international lawyers are concerned about the relationship between power and normative structures, although they characteristically adopt different approaches to that relationship, and the subject of power. Secondly, a study of the role of power in customary international law transcends any distinction between the two disciplines, in part because of the particular expertise of international relations scholars in the study of power, and that of international lawyers in the rules, principles and processes of international law. Thirdly, although it may be relatively easy to make a distinction between the politics of law-making and the legal determination of rules when dealing with legislatively enacted, executively decreed, or judge-made law, the linkages between these activities

[4] See pp. 166–80 below. On the continuing importance of customary international law, see generally Danilenko (1993) 137–42.

[5] Keohane (1989b) 3.

would seem to be much stronger in custom-based legal systems like the process of customary international law. Customary law is constantly evolving as the relevant actors, whether States or ordinary individuals, continually engage in legally relevant behaviour.[6] As a result, change in these systems is often gradual and incremental, whereas legislatively enacted or executively decreed law tends to change less often, and, when it does change, to do so more abruptly. Finally, inequalities among actors may have a greater effect on customary law-making than on law-making in other areas due, in part, to the lack of formalised procedures in this area and to the central role played by behaviour in the development, maintenance and change of customary rules.

In examining the role of power in its most general sense, this book considers power to involve the ability, either directly or indirectly, to control or significantly influence how actors – in this case States – behave. In an attempt to avoid reductionism, this book does not put forward a precise definition of power. However, it does emphasise that there is an important distinction to be made between non-legal power and the rather more specific kind of power that resides in rules.

Power may be derived from a variety of sources. For example, power derived from military strength gives some States the option of using force to impose their will, and the ability to resist the efforts of others to impose theirs. Similarly, power derived from wealth gives some States the capability to impose trade sanctions and to withstand them, to withhold Most Favoured Nation status or not to care whether that status is granted. Power derived from wealth may also enable States to support effective diplomatic corps which can monitor international developments and apply pressure, based on all the various sources of power, in international organisations such as the United Nations.[7] These different sources of power would seem to be important within the customary process because they determine, either separately or cumulatively, whether and to what degree different States are able to contribute to the development, maintenance or change of customary rules.

Power derived from military strength and wealth is clearly not the only kind of power at work in international society. For example, power might also devolve from moral authority, which could be defined as the ability to appeal to general principles of justice. In the human rights field it is possible that the existence of a high degree of moral authority in support of some customary rules has discouraged States which might otherwise have

[6] They are, in this sense, both creators and subjects of the law. On this '*dédoublement fonctionnel*' see Scelle (1932/34) 2ème partie, 10–12; and Scelle (1956).
[7] See Franck (1995) 481.

opposed those rules from so doing. It might also have discouraged them from openly engaging in violations of those rules, and from admitting to concealed violations.[8] Power devolved from moral authority, and an associated shift in international society's perceptions of justice, may also have played a role in the process of decolonisation.[9]

The legitimising and constraining effects of the international legal system are less noticeable than power derived from military strength, wealth or even moral authority, although they are perhaps equally important. They are important because States pursue their self-interest in a variety of ways. States will occasionally apply raw, unsystematised power in the pursuit of a particular, often short-term goal. However, the application of raw power through the direct application of military force or economic coercion tends to promote instability and escalation. It is neither subtle nor, in many cases, particularly efficient. More frequently, States will apply power within the framework of an institution or legal system. States seem to be interested in institutions and legal systems because these structures create expectations of behaviour which reduce the risks of escalation and facilitate efficiency of action. Institutions and legal systems promote stability, thus protecting States which recognise that, in future, they could find themselves opposing any particular position they currently support, and *vice versa*.[10]

However, a legal system such as the international legal system does more than simply create expectations and promote stability. It also fulfils the essentially social function of transforming applications of power into legal obligation, of turning 'is' into 'ought' or, within the context of customary international law, of transforming State practice into customary rules. Legal obligation represents a society's concerted effort to control both present and future behaviour.[11] International society uses obligation to confer a legal specificity on rules of international law, thus distinguishing them from the arbitrary commands of powerful States and ensuring they remain relevant to how States behave.

[8] The prohibition against torture is probably the best example of such a rule. See Rodley (1987) 63–4. See also the discussion of Burma's reservation to Art. 37 of the 1989 Convention on the Rights of the Child, note 35, p. 136 below.

[9] On the history of decolonisation, see, e.g., Fanon (1991). For a philosophical examination of moral authority as a source of power, see Nietzsche (1913).

[10] This latter insight is generally attributed to Rawls: see Rawls (1971). See also Franck (1995) 99. The creation of institutions and legal systems by States would thus seem to be motivated by long-term calculations of self-interest. On the creation of institutions, see generally Keohane (1989d); and Young (1989) 1–6. For further discussion of the benefits offered by institutions, see: pp. 107–9 below.

[11] On the distinction between legal obligation and other forms of obligation, see generally Finnis (1980) 297–350.

In many instances obligation will also provide correlative rights to apply power within certain structures using certain means. For example, in international society the obligation not to exercise military force against another State except in self-defence serves to legitimise, at least to some degree, the use of force by a State against insurgents within its own territory.[12]

Within the process of customary international law, States apply power in order to develop, maintain or change generally applicable rules, or even to cause such rules to lose their legal character.[13] In doing so they may also be acting to protect and promote established sources and means of applying power from the pressures of an ever-changing world or, conversely, to challenge those very same sources and means of application.

Numerous attempts have been made to identify the basis of obligation in international law.[14] And from these attempts, one thing appears clear: that the basis of obligation is located anterior, not only to individual rules of international law, but even to the processes that give rise to those rules. As Triepel wrote in 1899:

> Immer und überall wird man an den Punkt gelangen, an dem eine rechtliche Erklärung der Verbindlichkeit des Rechtes selbst unmöglich wird. Der 'Rechtsgrund' der Geltung des Rechts ist kein rechtlicher.[15]

It would therefore seem that the question of how applications of power can generate obligation cannot be answered by international lawyers operating strictly within the confines of their own discipline. Instead, this question would seem to require international lawyers to consider non-legal factors and non-legal relationships, to regard international law as but one part of a larger international system, and to apply concepts and methods which, although familiar to other disciplines, are largely alien to their own.

However, instead of exploring the basis of obligation in international law, this book assumes that States are only bound by those rules to which they have consented. This consensual or 'positivist' assumption is not as narrow as it might seem, for it admits that consent may take the form of a general consent to the process of customary international law, of a diffuse

[12] On the use of force, see generally Brownlie (1963).

[13] Higgins ((1994) 19) has written: 'To ask what is evidence of practice required for the loss of obligatory quality of a norm is the mirror of the evidence of practice required for the formation of the norm in the first place.'

[14] See generally Brierly (1958).

[15] Triepel (1899) 82. My translation reads: 'One will always invariably arrive at the point where a legal explanation of the obligatory character of the law becomes impossible itself. The legal basis of the validity of the law is extra-legal.' For an attempt to locate the basis of obligation *within* processes of law creation, see Schachter (1968).

consensus rather than a specific consent to individual rules. In other words, by accepting some rules of customary international law States may also be accepting the process through which those rules are developed, maintained or changed, and thus other rules of a similar character.[16]

This consensual assumption does not in itself raise the question of the basis of obligation in international law, for as Fitzmaurice explained:

> [Consent] is a *method* of creating rules, but it is not, in the last resort, the element that makes the rules binding, when created. In short, consent could not, in itself, create obligations unless there were already in existence a rule of law according to which consent had just that effect.[17]

This book focuses on identifying and explaining the customary process through which *individual* rules and principles acquire obligatory character, and on exploring how principles of international law qualify applications of power within that process. That said, if the customary process is an integral part of international society, it would seem likely that the basis of obligation in international law also lies within the social character of inter-State relations.

International relations scholars have traditionally had little time for such questions. Instead, they have regarded international law as something of an epiphenomenon, with rules of international law being dependent on power, subject to short-term alteration by power-applying States, and therefore of little relevance to how States actually behave.[18] International relations scholars have tended to focus on the ability of States to control or influence *directly* how other States behave, through factors such as wealth, military strength, size and population.

However, some international relations scholars have more recently observed that certain applications of power may give rise to normative structures, and that these structures in turn sometimes affect State behaviour. Some of these same scholars have also concluded that these normative structures are in some way related to international law. The work of these particular international relations scholars is considered in some detail in chapter 2 of this book, which concludes that most of them have yet to take the additional, necessary step of recognising that the obligatory character of rules of international law renders those rules less vulnerable

[16] See Lowe (1983a); Raz (1990) 123–9; Allott (1990) 145–77; Sur (1990) 2e cahier, 5 and 10; and pp. 142–6 below. For particularly clear statements as to the consensual approach to customary international law, see *Lotus Case* (1927) PCIJ Reports, Ser. A, No. 9, 18, quoted at p. 142 below; *Nicaragua Case (Merits)* (1986) *ICJ Reports* 14, 135 (para. 269); Corbett (1925); van Hoof (1983) 76ff; Sur (1990) 2e cahier, 4–5; and Wolfke (1993a). For consensual ('contractual') language from international relations scholars, see Keohane (1993); and Kratochwil (1993).

[17] Fitzmaurice (1956) 9, emphasis in original.

[18] See pp. 21–4 below.

to short-term political changes than the other, non-legal factors they study.[19]

Not surprisingly, the idea of obligation as a control on power has not only arisen with regard to international law. Hohfeld, for example, developed the idea of 'legal powers' in the context of private law.[20] For Hohfeld, a legal power was the ability of one actor to rely on existing law to change or use a legal relationship with another actor to his own benefit. Although a legal power of this kind was held by an individual actor or group of actors, by implication it was based upon another kind of power, that of obligation residing in rules.

Weber, despite placing an emphasis on 'commands' and 'office', used the concept of 'legitimacy' in a manner which underlined the special character of rules and the processes by which they are created. He wrote: 'Today the most common form of legitimacy is the belief in legality, i.e., the acquiescence in enactments which are formally correct and which have been made in the accustomed manner.'[21]

Hohfeld's use of 'legal power' and Weber's use of 'legitimacy' may be contrasted with the use that Franck has made of the concept of 'legitimacy' in international law. Franck considered legitimacy to be derived, not only from the processes of rule creation, but from a number of other factors as well. These factors include 'internal coherence', which is inherent in rules themselves, and 'ritual and pedigree', which are associated with, but not an intrinsic part either of rules or of the processes of rule creation.[22]

When Franck discussed rule creation he did so using modified versions of Hart's concepts of secondary rules and rules of recognition.[23] According to Franck: 'A rule has *greater* legitimacy if it is validated by having been made in accordance with secondary rules about lawmaking.'[24] In addition, 'there is widespread acceptance by states of the notion that time-and-practice-honored-conduct – pedigreed custom – has the capacity to bind states'.[25] This 'rule of recognition' is part of a larger 'ultimate rule of recognition',[26] which in turn is but one of several ultimate rules. These rules, which are 'irreducible prerequisites for an international concept of right process'[27] and *not* derived from any *legal*

[19] See also Byers (1997b). It is also this distinction between the non-legal power wielded by States and the obligation that resides in rules that enables this book to avoid a risk that may be inherent in any general definition of a potential causal factor in international relations, i.e., of losing sight of the causal factor amongst its potential results.

[20] See Hohfeld (1913–14) 44–5; and Hohfeld (1923) 50.

[21] Weber (1954) 9. See also Weber (1968) 31–6; and Allott (1990) 133–66.

[22] Franck (1990). See also Franck (1995) 30–46.

[23] See Hart (1961).

[24] Franck (1990) 193, emphasis added.

[25] Franck (1990) 189.

[26] Franck (1990) 189.

[27] Franck (1990) 194.

process, are the sole source of legitimacy within the process whereby particular, primary rules are created.

This book agrees that legitimacy may originate from many sources. However, it adopts a narrower approach than Franck and focuses on the legitimising effects of the customary process as such, on the effects of that process in transforming applications of power into obligation in the form of customary rules.[28] In doing so this book takes the additional step of examining how four principles of international law qualify applications of power *within* the customary process, in order to determine whether some rules of customary international law have more-or-less independent causal effects on the efforts of States to develop, maintain or change other customary rules. This book does not address the larger issue of the effects of customary international law on State behaviour more generally.

The term 'principles' is used to indicate that the rules under examination are rules of a general character. As the Chamber of the International Court of Justice in the *Gulf of Maine Case* explained:

> [T]he association of the terms 'rules' and 'principles' is no more than the use of a dual expression to convey one and the same idea, since in this context 'principles' clearly means principles of law, that is, it also includes rules of international law in whose case the use of the term 'principles' may be justified because of their more general and more fundamental character.[29]

Yet such principles are not, in Danilenko's words, 'just broad ideas formulated by abstract reasoning and logical constructions'.[30] Instead, they 'find their specific expression in a number of technically more precise norms' and remain 'rules of conduct having all the essential qualities of law'.[31]

Chapters 4 to 7 of this book explain how the principles of jurisdiction, personality, reciprocity and legitimate expectation affect the application of power by States as they seek to develop, maintain or change rules of customary international law. Although these four principles are too general in character to impose specific normative requirements on States, they nevertheless constitute a firmly established framework within which other, more precise customary rules may develop, exist and change. As a framework within which rules of international law evolve, they affect how States are able to participate in the customary process, both in terms of

[28] It will later become apparent that this focus is consistent with this book's suggestion that even the principles which provide a framework for the international legal system are derived from the customary process, and are not external to it. See pp. 159–60 below.

[29] *Gulf of Maine Case* (1984) *ICJ Reports* 246, 288–90 (para. 79). On the chamber procedure within the ICJ, see Art. 26 of the Statute of the International Court of Justice; Schwebel (1987); Oda (1988); and Ostrihansky (1988).

[30] Danilenko (1993) 8.

[31] Danilenko (1993) 8.

how they may apply non-legal power, and in terms of their effectiveness in so doing.

Chapter 4 begins by considering the principle of jurisdiction. It suggests that this principle may either facilitate or hinder the application of power within the customary process, depending on whether that power is applied within, or in close proximity to, the territory of the power-applying State. Chapter 5 considers how the principle of personality may qualify the application of power by limiting the range of potential participants in the customary process, and by increasing the scope of State interests and the range of legally relevant behaviour through the mechanism of diplomatic protection. Chapter 6 considers the operation of the principle of reciprocity within the process of customary international law. In doing so it focuses on the role of claims, such as claims to persistent objector status, and the effect that the principle of reciprocity has upon those claims. Lastly, chapter 7 considers various ways in which the principle of legitimate expectation may act to prevent or retard the development or change of customary rules.

The principles of jurisdiction, personality, reciprocity and legitimate expectation are singled out for examination because they represent important points of State interaction. For example, boundaries, State and diplomatic immunities and extraterritorial applications of national laws all involve issues of jurisdiction.[32] Nationality, diplomatic protection, human rights and the rights and obligations of international organisations all involve issues of personality.[33] Reciprocity is an important aspect of the law of treaties, of persistent objection and other issues of opposability, and of the process of customary international law generally.[34] Legitimate expectation is involved in the doctrines of *pacta sunt servanda* and estoppel and provides the basis for the law of State responsibility.[35] That said, this book does not presume that these four principles are the only principles which qualify applications of power within the process of customary international law. There may be other such principles and even the principles identified here may themselves change over time.

These four principles also play an important role in defining or characterising a central concept of international law, which is statehood. According to this concept, States have jurisdiction and full international legal personality, the combination of which gives them the competence to control their territory and to represent themselves and their nationals in international law. As a result of their full international legal personality States are also formally equal. This 'sovereign equality' entitles them all

[32] See pp. 53–74 below. [33] See pp. 75–87 below. [34] See pp. 88–105 below.
[35] See pp. 106–26 below.

to the same general rights and subjects them all to the same general obligations, as ensured by the principle of reciprocity. The principle of legitimate expectation, which subsumes both explicit and inferred consent, ensures that States are not subject to the application of rules of international law unless they consent.[36]

Given their role in defining or characterising statehood, these four principles may well be necessary prerequisites of modern international society. They may, as 'a set of norms for ensuring the co-existence and vital co-operation of the members of the international community',[37] be 'dictées par les exigences de la coexistence entre Etats'.[38] However, this does not mean that the source of these principles is necessarily different from that of other customary rules. As the International Law Commission has observed:

> [I]t is only by erroneously equating the situation under international law with that under internal law that some lawyers have been able to see in the 'constitutional' or 'fundamental' principles of the international legal order an independent and higher 'source' of international obligations. In reality there is, in the international legal order, no special source of law for creating 'constitutional' or 'fundamental' principles.[39]

It is entirely possible that international society could have developed differently from the way that it in fact did, with a correspondingly different, or modified, set of principles.[40] Notwithstanding, since States recognise that these principles, like the concept of statehood, are necessary to the current system, they almost always behave in a manner which is supportive of them.

There is, however, a distinction to be made between these principles and *jus cogens* rules which, as will be explained in chapter 10, are also reflective of important State interests.[41] As Thirlway explained:

> [T]he concept of *jus cogens* is roughly the equivalent on the international plane of *ordre public*, whereas [these principles concern] not whether it is in the interests of the international community that States should be permitted to agree to a certain

[36] For an extensive analysis of the requirements of statehood, see Crawford (1979), especially 32–3.

[37] *Gulf of Maine Case*, 299 (para. 111). The Chamber (at 300, para. 113) referred to one such necessary prerequisite, namely 'that [maritime] delimitation, whether effected by direct agreement or by the decision of a third party, must be based on the application of equitable criteria and the use of practical methods capable of ensuring an equitable result'. This rule, in turn, might be seen as falling within the scope of the principle of legitimate expectation. See generally pp. 106–26 below.

[38] Sur (1990) 2e cahier, 1. My translation reads: 'dictated by the demands of co-existence among States'. Lowe ((1983a) 211) has written of a 'logical necessity which demands that, if a legal system exists at all, some basic rules must be admitted'.

[39] (1976) 2(2) *Yearbook of the International Law Commission* 85–6.

[40] See Thirlway (1972) 30.

[41] See Lowe (1983a) 211; pp. 183–95 below.

end, but what are the concepts of international law which exist so undeniably that States cannot agree to ignore them . . . In short, derogations from principles of the class we are considering are not permitted, not because they are matters of *jus cogens*, nor because they enshrine some sort of *jus naturale*, but because they are such that derogation from them implies a denial that they are *jus*, with consequences for the whole international community.[42]

## Some working assumptions

In selecting the principles of jurisdiction, personality, reciprocity and legitimate expectation for examination, this book makes several assumptions. These assumptions, which are based in part upon the relationship of these principles to the concept of statehood, are made in order to impose manageable limits on this book's exploration of the interaction of power and obligation in the development, maintenance and change of customary rules. The first of these assumptions is a statist one, in that this book assumes that States are the principal actors in the process of customary international law.

Clearly, States are not the only actors of importance on the international stage. International organisations, transnational corporations, currency speculators, insurgents, criminals, terrorists and human rights groups are all able to influence other international actors, including States, in important ways. Yet, as Higgins has explained: 'States are, at this moment of history, still at the heart of the international legal system.'[43] States are the only holders of full international legal personality, and as such it is they which are principally responsible for the behaviour that makes and changes international law, however much that behaviour may itself be influenced by the activities of non-State actors.[44]

Thus, one particular consequence of the statist assumption is that it precludes consideration of those non-State actors that operate entirely within individual States, influencing what those States perceive and manifest their interests to be. The way that competing interests are balanced at the national level in order to determine which interests are expressed internationally is clearly relevant to understanding why States behave the way they do. Yet an examination of the role of such internal non-State

[42] Thirlway (1972) 29–30. [43] Higgins (1994) 39.

[44] See pp. 75–87 below. In the context of customary international law, see Villiger (1985) 4. For similar statist positions adopted by 'realist' international relations scholars, see, e.g., Morgenthau (1954); Schwarzenberger (1964) 13–15; and Waltz (1979) 93–7; for commentary, see Rosenberg (1994a) 10–15. For examples of non-statist 'realist' approaches, which are only just beginning to appear, see Strange (1988); and Haufler (1993) 94. For an author who considered the behaviour of non-governmental organisations relevant to the process of customary international law, see Gunning (1991).

actors would involve a level of analysis very different from that adopted here, for this book focuses on how the customary process transforms *external* expressions of State interest into rules of customary international law. It assumes, at least initially, that individual State interests have already been determined within the State, in any variety of possible ways.[45]

The second assumption made by this book has already been mentioned above: it is a consensual or 'positivist' assumption to the effect that States do not in general become subject to legal obligations without their consent. However, this consent may take the form of a general consent to the process of customary international law, of a diffuse consensus rather than a specific consent to individual rules.[46]

The third assumption is a classic 'realist' assumption, namely that States act in more-or-less self-interested ways and that the primary way in which they promote their self-interest is through applications of power.[47] In fact, all three of these assumptions coincide with fundamental assumptions made by that dominant school of international relations scholarship which is referred to as 'realism',[48] with the statist and consensual assumptions also being important aspects of many modern conceptions of international law.

These coinciding assumptions reflect this book's effort to keep its initial examination of the relationship between power and obligation within the confines of traditional conceptions of international relations and international law. A consideration of some possible implications of more recent theoretical developments is left to the later stages of this book. The assumptions are thus analytical aids which may later need to be discarded or modified in order to accommodate further complexities or changes in international society, or in our understandings of it – but only once the essential aspects of the relationship between power and obligation in the customary process are understood.

At this point, three additional assumptions should perhaps also be made explicit. This book assumes that an international legal system exists, that most States and scholars are in general agreement about many aspects of that system, and that these generally agreed aspects may be relied upon for the limited purpose of facilitating a study of the interac-

[45] Some legal scholars, such as those making up the 'New Haven School' and more recent 'liberal' authors, have sought to break down the divide between the determination of interests nationally and internationally. See, e.g., Lasswell and McDougal (1992) vol. 1, 417–25; Reisman (1992) 122; Slaughter Burley (1993); Slaughter (1995); Koh (1996); and Koh (1997). Some international relations scholars have sought to do likewise. See, e.g., Nye (1988); Cowhey (1993); Knopf (1993); Risse-Kappen (1994); Powell (1994); as well as the literature on epistemic communities, note 58, p. 141 below.

[46] See p. 142–6 below.

[47] See, e.g., Carr (1946) 85–8; Morgenthau (1954) 5–8; and, more recently, Keohane (1989d).

[48] See pp. 21–4 below.

tion of power and obligation in the process of customary international law. Although it is possible that some international relations scholars may find these latter three assumptions disconcerting, within the confines of this book it would be impractical to establish a basis for each and every one of the many rules or principles to which reference is made.

## Power and the study of international law

Apart from the possible relevance of this book to the work of international relations scholars, it is also hoped that its general conclusion – that the outcomes which result from the customary process reflect the ability of legal obligation, in certain situations, to qualify or condition the application of non-legal power by States – will encourage international lawyers to pay more attention to non-legal factors, as well as to the work of their colleagues in the discipline of international relations.

Most international lawyers assume that international law affects how States behave. As a result of this general assumption, they tend to have a somewhat more extended understanding of power than most international relations scholars. From an international lawyer's perspective, rules of international law have a certain 'power' of their own, which is necessary to constrain or facilitate State action. Yet international lawyers have not given much consideration to the possible connections between obligation and the non-legal forms of power traditionally studied by international relations scholars. Indeed, most of them have seemed reluctant to investigate how power might affect obligation, and, more precisely, how it might affect processes of law creation.[49] It is possible that such a focus on 'law as rules' may be a necessary aspect of their work.[50]

This book accepts that it is difficult and perhaps undesirable for international lawyers to consider the effects of non-legal power when determining the existence and content of rules. However, it argues that international lawyers would nevertheless benefit from a broader perspective on the legal system within which they operate, and that consideration of the effects of non-legal power would in no way undermine the inherent stability and determinacy of international law. This book thus seeks to develop one way in which the disciplines of international relations and international law might together explore and conceptualise the functional character of power within international society generally – even though it restricts its own examination of power to the context of customary international law. And for this reason, this is not a book about customary international law in the strict, normative sense. This book does not put

[49] See pp. 35–40 below. [50] See pp. 46–50 below.

forward a theory of customary international law as that law is dealt with by international courts and tribunals. Instead, it steps back from the examination of customary law as rules and considers the ways in which the interaction of power with normative structures affects how customary rules are developed, maintained and changed. That said, it is hoped that this somewhat different perspective will cast some light on a few of the more traditional theoretical controversies which bedevil this particular area of international law.

An additional argument in favour of such an approach is that international lawyers are sometimes required to perform tasks which are not strictly legal in character. For example, an international lawyer may be called upon to advise a State on its long-term policy in respect of an issue of legal concern. As chapter 6 will seek to demonstrate in its discussion of the principle of reciprocity, in such instances an understanding of the processes which give rise to international law may be as important as an expertise in legal rules themselves.

Despite the apparent reluctance of many international lawyers to investigate the role of non-legal power, some international lawyers have certainly sought to defend the 'relevance' of international law against realist international relations scholars and other sceptics.[51] Moreover, debates about the role of non-legal power constitute an important, although rarely acknowledged part of the discourse of modern international law.[52] Chapter 3 examines how the discipline of international law has dealt with the issue of non-legal power, while at the same time considering how and why most international lawyers remain unaccustomed to thinking about how such applications of power might generate international law.

Of the relevant developments within the discipline of international law, perhaps the most interesting involves the fact that a small but growing number of international lawyers has recommended the adoption of interdisciplinary approaches so that non-legal factors may be incorporated into explanations of the international legal system. For instance, Henkin has commented:

> Lawyer and diplomat . . . are not even attempting to talk to each other, turning away in silent disregard. Yet both purport to be looking at the same world from the vantage point of important disciplines. It seems unfortunate, indeed destructive, that they should not, at the least, hear each other.[53]

[51] See, e.g., Fried (1968); Henkin (1979); D'Amato (1984–5); Boyle (1985); and Brownlie (1988). [52] See pp. 40–6 below..

[53] Henkin (1979) 4. It may be noted that Henkin assumed that diplomats operate strictly within the sphere of 'international relations', and that they are therefore synonymous with traditional international relations scholars. However, many diplomats are international lawyers by training, and most deal regularly with aspects of international law.

Similarly, Slaughter Burley has written:

Just as constitutional lawyers study political theory, and political theorists inquire into the nature and substance of constitutions, so too should two disciplines that study the laws of state behavior seek to learn from one another. At the very least, they should aspire to a common vocabulary and framework of analysis that would allow the sharing of insights and information. If social science has any validity at all, the postulates developed by political scientists concerning patterns and regularities in state behavior must afford a foundation and framework for legal efforts to regulate that behavior . . . From the political science side, if law – whether international, transnational or purely domestic – does push the behavior of States toward outcomes other than those predicted by power and the pursuit of national interest, then political scientists must revise their models to take account of legal variables.[54]

Unfortunately, neither Henkin nor Slaughter Burley have applied this suggested interdisciplinary approach to the processes of international law creation, or, more specifically, to the process of customary international law.

An attempt has been made by Setear to apply game theory to the law of treaties, and to treaties generally.[55] In doing so he helped to clarify the linkages between game theory and a new area of international relations theory called 'institutionalism', as well as the linkages between game theory and international law. Setear also derived several useful insights into how treaty law is developed and changed, for example, that the progressively increasing degrees of interaction and obligation which are sometimes apparent in the different phases of treaty-making may be explained on the basis of multiple plays of a 'game'.[56]

However, Setear's general conclusion – that treaties, and by implication all rules of international law, are based on the calculations of States that their long-term interests are best served through the co-operative creation of such normative structures – was not surprising. Most international lawyers have long accepted that States are not only the subjects, but also the creators, of international law, that international law is consequently not imposed on States but is, instead, the result of co-ordinated or at least (in large part) common behaviour, and that rules of international law therefore reflect the long-term interests of most, if not all, States.[57]

Setear failed to recognise that the central point of consent-based theories of international law is that a State, by consenting, binds itself to behave in a certain manner *even if* it subsequently changes its mind about the desirability of that behaviour. He argued that a rule acquires

[54] Slaughter Burley (1993) 205–6. [55] Setear (1996). [56] Setear (1996) 193–201.
[57] See, e.g., Oppenheim (1905) 4–18; Scelle (1932/34) 7–14; and Dahm (1958) 7–14.

predictive force through 'iteration', i.e., by being the focus of repeated interactions. He did not consider the role that might be played by legal processes, and the international legal system as a whole, in giving rules of international law an obligatory character and thus a unique ability to qualify the short-term behaviour of States.[58] Nevertheless, his article represents an important step forward in the interdisciplinary effort to explain how international law is made, and the role that it plays in international relations more generally.

Bodansky has posed a number of important questions about the customary process which clearly call for the adoption of an interdisciplinary approach. He asked:

> [W]hat economic, social, psychological, and political processes explain the emergence of customary norms? To what extent, for example, do customary norms emerge as a result of calculations by states of rational self-interest? To what extent are they imposed by powerful states [?][59]

This book attempts to answer some of these questions, to reach beyond the confines of the discipline of international law, and to do with the process of customary international law what Henkin and Slaughter Burley have suggested should be done generally, and what Setear has attempted to do in the different context of treaty law. As Bodansky has indicated, there is a need 'to ascertain . . . not merely what international lawyers think about the concept of custom, but how custom actually operates'.[60]

## Opinio juris, the customary process and the qualifying effects of international law

The central aspect of this book's explanation of the way in which power and obligation interact within the process of customary international law concerns the element of *opinio juris*. It is argued here that *opinio juris* is the key element in the transformation of power *into* obligation – or in traditional terminology, of State practice into rules of customary international law. However, *opinio juris* is far more difficult to identify and define than general, framework principles of international law. Although most international lawyers agree that *opinio juris* plays a role in transforming State practice into rules of customary international law, they have not been able to agree on its character, nor to resolve many theoretical problems associated with it. Chapters 8, 9 and 10 review the more important of those theoretical problems as well as some of the attempts that have been made to

[58] For a more detailed critique, see Byers (1997b).
[59] Bodansky (1995) 668.
[60] Bodansky (1995) 679.

resolve them. In doing so they advance an alternative explanation of *opinio juris*, and thus of the process of customary international law.

According to this explanation, *opinio juris* itself represents a diffuse consensus, a general set of shared understandings among States as to the 'legal relevance' of different kinds of behaviour in different situations. In short, only that behaviour which is considered legally relevant is regarded as capable of contributing to the process of customary international law. This diffuse consensus, these shared understandings of legal relevance, would seem to be based on the general acceptance by States of the customary process, as signalled by their reliance on customary rules and their acknowledgment of the potential validity of claims made by other States based on similar rules. And, although these shared understandings apply generally to all State behaviour, they are not static, but instead undergo subtle modifications as the international system evolves.

This book goes on to argue that the customary process operates to maximise the interests of most if not all States by creating rules which protect and promote their common interests. In effect, the customary process measures the legally relevant State behaviour which has occurred in respect of any particular issue in order to determine whether a particular interest is widely shared. This measurement is made possible by the fact that States generally behave in accordance with their own perceived interests, in so far as they are able to manifest them. In other words, States either support, are ambivalent towards, or oppose potential, emerging or existing customary rules and usually behave accordingly. Anything a State does or says, or fails to do or say, therefore has the potential to be considered legally relevant, and thus to contribute to the development, maintenance or change of a rule of customary international law.

Since the customary process involves a measurement of the State behaviour which has occurred in respect of particular issues, it might seem that those States which are capable of engaging in more behaviour than others will have an advantage in developing, maintaining or changing customary rules to protect and promote their own particular interests. But though this may be true to some degree, the effect of disparities among States is qualified in this context by fundamental principles such as those of jurisdiction, personality, reciprocity and legitimate expectation. This qualification is able to occur because one result of the measurement of legally relevant State behaviour in respect of potential or existing customary rules is that those rules which have attracted relatively more supporting, and relatively less opposing, behaviour are generally more resistant to change than other customary rules. These relatively more resistant rules include the principles that are singled out for examination here. It is these principles' relatively high degree of resistance to change that enables them to qualify applications of power in the development, maintenance and change of other, usually less resistant customary rules, and thus to promote the general stability of the international legal system. And it is these principles' relatively high degree of resistance to change – and the very real effects that it has on applications of non-legal power – which leads this book to suggest that international relations scholars and international lawyers would both benefit were they to devote more attention to this and other aspects of the interface between international politics and international law.

# 2 Law and international relations

International relations as an academic discipline seeks to explain those political developments which occur outside the confines of the nation-State. Although its intellectual roots extend to Antiquity and the Renaissance, international relations is generally considered to be a relatively young academic discipline which grew out of a split between two groups of Anglo-American international lawyers during the 1930s and 1940s. The split occurred as a result of attempts by some lawyers to move away from positivism, which defined international law as a set of objectively determinable rules which were devoid of moral content and applicable to States solely on the basis of their consent, towards more inclusive conceptions of international law.[1]

The move away from positivism during the inter-war and early post-war periods towards an approach, often referred to as 'legal-moralism', was notably influenced by President Wilson of the United States and bore overtones of earlier conceptions of natural law. This new approach envisaged international law as a tool for the achievement of world peace through the operation of international organisations, systems of collective security, free trade and processes such as disarmament and national self-determination.[2]

It was, however, strongly rejected by some writers, such as Carr and Morgenthau, as a misplaced idealism. From the perspective of these 'realists', States were self-interested actors engaged in a ruthless struggle for power, considered as the ability of a State or States to control or influence directly how other States behaved, through factors such as wealth, military strength, size and population. Morgenthau wrote:

> Power may comprise anything that establishes and maintains the control of man over man. Thus power covers all social relationships which serve that end, from

[1] On positivism, see generally: Ago (1984). Positivism itself had replaced natural law as the dominant approach to international law during the late nineteenth and early twentieth centuries. On natural law, see generally Verdross and Koeck (1983).

[2] See Wilson's 'Fourteen Points', in Scott (1918) 359–62. See also Barker (1918); Laurence (1919); Lansing (1921); Lauterpacht (1933).

physical violence to the most subtle psychological ties by which one mind controls another. Power covers the domination of man by man, both when it is disciplined by moral ends and controlled by constitutional safeguards as in Western democracies, and when it is that untamed and barbaric force which finds its laws in nothing but its own strength and its sole justification in its aggrandizement.[3]

Like Morgenthau, Schwarzenberger was a German-trained international lawyer who rejected the idealism of much of post-war international law.[4] He wrote:

*Power* is the mean between influence and force. All three are different ways of establishing a social nexus on a footing regarded as desirable by the active agent in such relations. Power distinguishes itself, however, from *influence* by reliance on external pressure as a background threat, and from *force* by preference for achieving its ends without the actual use of physical pressure. Thus, *power* may be defined as capacity to impose one's will on others by reliance on effective sanctions in case of non-compliance.[5]

Waltz, a leading figure in what might be considered the second generation of post-war international relations scholars, added:

To define 'power' as 'cause' confuses process with outcome. To identify power with control is to assert that only power is needed in order to get one's way. That is obviously false, else what would there be for political and military strategists to do? To use power is to apply one's capabilities in an attempt to change someone else's behavior in certain ways . . . Power is one cause among others, from which it cannot be isolated. The common relational definition of power omits consideration of how acts and relations are affected by the structure of action.[6]

These three definitions of power differ widely. Yet realist scholars agreed on one thing. For them, international law as it existed at that time was something of an epiphenomenon, dependent on power and therefore subject to short-term change at the will of power-applying States.[7]

Even those early realists who dealt with international law were sceptical of its efficacy. Morgenthau explained that the decentralised character of international law left its definition and enforcement, and thus the entire

[3] Morgenthau (1954) 8.

[4] Morgenthau and Schwarzenberger's German origins are relevant in this context because the development of the discipline of international relations in the middle of the twentieth century was not the first time that such an idealist/realist split had occurred. In Germany a similar debate about the 'Rechtsnatur des Völkerrechts' (legal nature of international law) may be traced back at least as far as Hegel. See Hegel (1821) especially paras. 330–40. For an historical overview see Dahm (1958) 7–14. Although writers from the United States have dominated the discipline of international relations in the second half of the twentieth century, the role played by these German-educated scholars, and others such as Hoffmann and Gross, indicates the existence of a connection with that earlier debate.

[5] Schwarzenberger (1964) 14 (emphasis in original).

[6] Waltz (1979) 191–2.

[7] See, e.g., Carr (1946) 170–207; and Morgenthau (1954) 249–86.

international legal system, at the mercy of sovereign States. He wrote that '[g]overnments . . . are always anxious to shake off the restraining influence that international law might have upon their foreign policies', and that 'the lack of precision, inherent in the decentralized nature of international law, is breeding ever more lack of precision, and the debilitating vice that was present at its birth continues to sap its strength'.[8] Morgenthau was highly critical of the absence of an effective international judicial system,[9] and of what he perceived as serious weaknesses in international law's enforcement system. Concerning the latter he wrote:

> There can be no more primitive and no weaker system of law enforcement than this; for it delivers the enforcement of the law to the vicissitudes of the distribution of power between the violator of the law and the victim of the violation. It makes it easy for the strong both to violate the law and to enforce it, and consequently puts the rights of the weak in jeopardy.[10]

Schwarzenberger, who despite his realist views continued to work as an international lawyer, wrote:

> In a society in which power is the overriding consideration, the primary function of law is to assist in maintaining the supremacy of force and the hierarchies established on the basis of power, and to give to this overriding system the respectability and sanctity law confers.[11]

Notwithstanding this initial scepticism concerning international law, it soon became apparent to some twentieth-century international relations scholars that law was something which they needed to incorporate within their realist conceptualisations of international relations. Hoffmann, Kaplan and Katzenbach, for example, attempted to account for the existence of international law on the basis of systems theory.[12] For these systems theorists law was a part, as well as a product, of any political system seeking to regulate itself. However, in their evaluation the international system, unlike national systems, had not established sufficient consensus to allow the creation of truly independent, binding rules. In short, States were not yet prepared to allow international law to play an autonomous role.[13] Although international law existed, that law

8 Morgenthau (1954) 255. 9 Morgenthau (1954) 261–9.

10 Morgenthau (1954) 270–1.

11 Schwarzenberger (1964) 199. Part of Schwarzenberger's scepticism concerning the neutrality of international law was based on his view that self-help was the only means of law enforcement available within the system. He did, however, acknowledge that reciprocity played an important role in encouraging States to conform voluntarily to rules of international law. He wrote ((1964) 211) that 'a legal order based on reciprocity can safely rely on the penalties inherent in its social machinery: the unwillingness of participants to jeopardise the enjoyment of the benefits derived from participation in the legal régime in question'. 12 See Hoffmann (1968a); and Kaplan and Katzenbach (1961).

13 See Hoffmann (1968b); and Kaplan and Katzenbach (1961) 350.

remained entirely dependent upon the evolving power relationships among States.

Structural realism, largely associated with the work of Waltz and sometimes referred to as 'neo-realism', also sought to explain international relations in a systemic manner. However, it was considerably less favourable towards international law. Structural realists considered systems theory to be unsatisfactory because it involved the regulation of actors through systems which those actors had themselves created. They favoured instead what was in effect a new systems theory which focused on the larger system, or structure, within which actors operate. For Waltz, this larger structure included an ordering principle, the specification of functions of differentiated units, and the distribution of capabilities across those units.[14] Although it is conceivable that Waltz could have included international law among those structural elements which determine how actors in the international system behave, he argued instead that unequal States engage each other in a system, the defining structural aspect of which is anarchy. Anarchy – the absence of an overarching sovereign – was by definition incompatible with law.[15]

Waltz's rejection of international law as a structural element within the international system might be regarded as a step away from a possible reconciliation between the disciplines of international relations and international law.[16] Nevertheless, the idea of structural or systemic controls on the exercise of unequal power did leave open the possibility of incorporating international law into a more sophisticated realist conception of international relations. Although the absence of an overarching sovereign is clearly an important aspect of modern international society,[17] it is not evident that the absence of an overarching sovereign should imply the absence of normative controls.

## Regime theory and institutionalism

Regime theorists elaborated upon the ideas of the system theorists and structural realists by developing the concept of structural control in terms of the structural characteristics of 'sets of implicit or explicit principles, norms, rules, and decision-making procedures around which actors' expectations converge in a given area of international relations'.[18] Regime

[14] See Waltz (1979) 88–101. [15] Waltz (1979) 102–28.

[16] See, e.g., Slaughter Burley (1993) 217 ('[Waltz] left no room whatsoever for international law'). [17] See generally Bull (1977).

[18] The definition is taken from Krasner (1983) 2. This book's interpretation of the relationship between structural realism and regime theory thus differs from that initially put

theorists were, in short, international relations scholars who recognised the difficulties involved in attempting to explain all relations among States solely on the basis of relative degrees of power and short-term calculations of self-interest. Instead, they argued that sets of rules and procedures developed by and between States acquire a life of their own, controlling, or at least qualifying, the day-to-day application of power by the States involved, as well as by other States. To an international lawyer this phenomenon sounds like international law by another name – with the important distinction that regime theorists, unlike most international lawyers, were directly concerned with the relationship between power and sets of rules or procedures.[19]

Regime theorists, like most political scientists, were operating at a different level of analysis from most legal writers. Political scientists are interested in how groups of human beings organise themselves and, broadly speaking, interact with one another. At the national level, they examine the political processes which, among other things, give rise to legal rules. Most legal writers, on the other hand, have a more restricted focus. They are concerned with determining the existence, meaning, scope of application and effect of legal rules, and not so much with understanding the processes through which those rules are created.[20]

To a regime theorist, power and the rules and procedures which result

forward by Slaughter Burley. However, Slaughter Burley later acknowledged the connection between structural realism and regime theory, referring to regime theory at one point as 'modified Structural Realism': Slaughter Burley (1993) 221; see also 219. For support of this view see Young (1989) 92, note 41; and Keohane (1989b) 7–8. There is nevertheless an ongoing debate between structural realists and regime theorists (and their successors) about what Wendt ((1992) 393) describes as 'the extent to which state action is influenced by "structure" (anarchy and the distribution of power) versus "process" (interaction and learning) and institutions'. See Grieco (1988); Nye (1988); Keohane (1989e); Wendt (1992); and Powell (1994).

19 See Chayes and Chayes (1993) 195, note 64. Indeed, sceptics ask the same questions about regimes as they ask about international law: 'Does the absence of centralized political authority force states to play competitive power politics? Can international regimes overcome this logic, and under what conditions? What in anarchy is given and immutable, and what is amenable to change?': Wendt (1992) 391 (explaining the debate between structural realists and institutionalists). International relations scholars have yet to examine the relationship between different 'regimes', focusing instead on the relationship between particular regimes and States. This book goes further by considering how pre-existing treaties affect the subsequent development of customary rules, and how the subsequent development of customary rules affects pre-existing treaties. See pp. 166–80 below. See also 'Problems Arising From a Succession of Codification Conventions on a Particular Subject' (1995) 66(1) *Annuaire de l'institut de droit international* 15, especially Sinclair, 'Provisional Report' 195, 202–5.

20 It may therefore be that international lawyers do not *need* to understand the process of customary international law. Nevertheless, and as chapter 3 will explain, there are several reasons why they should seek to do so. See pp. 35–52 below.

from patterns of interdependence 'are closely related – indeed, two sides of a single coin'.[21] This is because interdependence is often asymmetrical; despite their dependence on each other some States remain more powerful than others.[22] Since interdependence is both the reason for and the result of regimes, rules and procedures necessarily reflect the frequently asymmetrical character of inter-State power relationships.[23]

Regime theorists have not written much about informal rules and procedures, although some have recognised that regimes 'may be more or less formally articulated, and . . . may or may not be accompanied by explicit organizations'.[24] For example, Young has written:

> Some writers have fallen into the habit of equating regimes with the agreements in terms of which the regimes are often expressed or codified. In practice, however, international regimes vary greatly in the extent to which they are expressed in formal agreements, treaties, or conventions . . . As in domestic society, moreover, it is common for informal understandings to arise within the framework established by the formal structure of an international regime. Such understandings may serve either to provide interpretations of ambiguous aspects of the formal arrangements . . . or to supplement formal arrangements by dealing with issues they fail to cover . . . Though it may be helpful, formalization is clearly not a necessary condition for the effective operation of international regimes. There are informal regimes that have been generally successful, and there are formal arrangements that have produced unimpressive results.[25]

Young, however, gave no example of an informal regime which has been 'generally successful'.

Regime theorists have instead focused on multilateral treaties and international organisations, around or within which informal rules or procedures may develop, but, if they do develop, will fulfil only supplementary roles. Regimes are said to operate in 'issue areas' (whether environmental protection, telecommunications, human rights or the law of the sea),[26] and most regime theorists have, for one reason or another,

[21] Keohane and Nye (1987) 730.

[22] See generally: Keohane and Nye (1977) 10–11; Keohane and Nye (1987) 728, and citations therein.

[23] According to the regime theorists it is because States seeking to further their self-interest recognise the benefits of co-operation that they create rules and procedures at the international level. Realist premises are thus central to the entire project of regime theory. See Keohane (1984); Keohane (1989a); pp. 107–9 below. Presumably, a higher degree of interdependence between States or within groups of States will result in some States having an interest in a greater number and scope of transnational rules and procedures. See the writings of 'liberal' theorists of international law, e.g., Slaughter Burley (1993); Slaughter (1995); and Koh (1996).

[24] Young (1989) 13.

[25] Young (1989) 24, see also 15 (note 11) and 214.

[26] Young has written ((1989) 13): 'International regimes . . . are . . . specialized arrangements that pertain to well-defined activities, resources, or geographical areas and often involve only some subset of the members of international society.' Specific regimes, and

focused on issue areas of a commercial character, such as trade, monetary management and technology transfer.[27] There is little sense in their work of any 'regime' of these regimes, in the sense of systems which are not issue-specific but which instead provide larger, encompassing structures.[28]

Regime theory has developed into an area of international relations thought referred to as institutionalism.[29] Its two leading proponents have been Keohane and Young, although the ideas of these two scholars differ in important ways. For Keohane, the concept of institutions was far more comprehensive than that of regimes. It included all 'persistent and connected sets of rules (formal and informal) that prescribe behavioral roles, constrain activity, and shape expectations'.[30]

Keohane divided institutions into three groups on the basis of their differing degrees of organisation or formality. First, there are 'formal intergovernmental or cross-national nongovernmental organizations'. Secondly, there are 'international regimes', which Keohane defined as 'institutions with explicit rules, agreed upon by governments, that pertain to particular sets of issues in international relations'; regimes are, in short, 'specific contractual solutions'. Thirdly, there are 'conventions', which Keohane defined as 'informal institutions, with implicit rules and understandings, that shape the expectations of actors'.[31]

Keohane elaborated somewhat on his idea of conventions, writing that they 'enable actors to understand one another and, without explicit rules, to coordinate their behavior' and that they 'are especially appropriate for situations . . . where it is to everyone's interest to behave in a particular way as long as others also do so'. States conform to these conventions because 'non-conformity to the expectations of others entails costs'. Keohane provided two examples of conventions: first, '[t]raditional diplomatic immunity' before it was codified in the 1961 Vienna

the issue areas they regulate, are often 'nested' in larger and more general regimes which address larger and more general issue areas. Consequently, regimes build on, and rarely conflict with, one another. Young (1989) 14. See, e.g., Young (1977); Haas (1979–80); Donnelly (1986); Cowhey (1990); Krasner (1993); Money (1993); and Haas (1993).

[27] This focus on commercial issues was perhaps partly due to Keohane's use of a market-forces analogy to explain the 'demand' for international regimes. See Keohane (1989d). See also Cooper (1975); Ruggie and Haas (1975); Haas (1979–80); Finlayson and Zacher (1983); and Aggarwal (1985).

[28] However, see Buzan (1993) 350, where he suggested that international society 'might be seen as a regime of regimes' and that this would add 'a useful element of holism to the excessively atomized world of regime theory'.

[29] It is again worth noting that continental European scholars had already covered much of this ground. For what can only be described as early institutionalist thought, see the work of Hauriou, Renard and Delos (translated and analysed in Broderick (1970)) and Schmitt (1934). See as well, in the context of international law, Scelle (1932/34).

[30] Keohane (1989b) 3. [31] Keohane (1989b) 3–4.

Convention on Diplomatic Relations and in the 1963 Vienna Convention on Consular Relations and, secondly, reciprocity.[32]

Initially, Keohane's definition of conventions would seem to encompass both the process of, and individual rules of, customary international law. Like many customary rules, Keohane's conventions are 'temporally and logically prior to regimes or formal international organizations' and '[i]n the absence of conventions, it would be difficult for states to negotiate with one another or even to understand the meaning of each other's actions'.[33]

Unlike customary rules, however, none of Keohane's conventions appear to be legally binding.[34] He seems to believe that these conventions are not part of international law. Thus, he emphasised the formal nature of international law, writing (here using the word 'conventions' in a different sense, to refer to multilateral treaties) that 'all formal international regimes are parts of international law, as are formal bilateral treaties and conventions'.[35] Although his informal conventions are, like regimes and organisations, voluntary constructs of States, nonconformity with such a convention merely imposes efficiency costs and does not constitute a breach of legal obligations. This is presumably because these conventions, unlike the explicit rules involved in regimes and organisations, are not 'contractual' in character.

For example, Keohane explained reciprocity as involving 'exchanges of roughly equivalent values in which the actions of each party are contingent on the prior actions of the others in such a way that good is returned for good, and bad for bad'.[36] He distinguished between 'specific reciprocity', where two parties 'exchange items of equivalent value in a strictly delimited sequence', and 'diffuse reciprocity', where exchanges occur within a group of parties, with the co-operative behaviour of one party frequently being rewarded in another situation, at some other time, by a party which did not benefit directly from that first specific instance of co-operative behaviour.[37] Keohane's concept of diffuse reciprocity was an advance on previous discussions of reciprocity by international relations scholars, where it was assumed that the degree of trust or obligation nec-

[32] Keohane (1989b) 4. The two treaties may be found at (1964) 500 UNTS 95 and (1967) 596 UNTS 261, respectively. An international lawyer cannot help but consider this is a curious conjunction in that diplomatic immunity is a rather specific rule, whereas reciprocity is a much more general principle. On the distinction, see p. 10 above. It is also noteworthy that Keohane did not discuss the possibility of 'conventions' continuing to exist after codification. Compare: the discussion of parallel customary and treaty rules, at pp. 166–80 below.

[33] Keohane (1989b) 4.

[34] Keohane (1989e) 163.

[35] However, Keohane expressly acknowledged that informal or implicit, but nevertheless legally binding rules, exist at the national level, noting that 'some very strong institutions, such as the British constitution, rely principally on unwritten rules' (Keohane (1989e) 163).

[36] Keohane (1986) 8.

[37] Keohane (1986) 4.

essary to support such non-specific exchanges does not exist between States.[38] However, although Keohane based his explanation of diffuse reciprocity on 'a widespread sense of obligation' among the members of a group,[39] he did not consider the connections between that sense of obligation, reciprocity and law. The furthest he went was to state that 'actors recognize that a "veil of ignorance" separates them from the future but nevertheless offer benefits to others on the assumption that these will redound to their own advantage in the end'.[40]

An additional problem with Keohane's approach results from his general conception of international law as itself unstable and indeterminate. In short, the unequal application of power is not substantially checked by the existence of obligation. Although Keohane's institutions 'affect the incentives facing states, even if those states' fundamental interests are defined autonomously',[41] they are defined by power-maximising States and are subject to redefinition at their will, or at least at the will of the most powerful among them. For instance, Keohane posited that 'changes in the relative power resources available to major states will explain changes in international regimes'.[42] He explained that '[i]n modern international relations, the pressures from domestic interests, and those generated by the competitiveness of the state system, exert much stronger effects on state policy than do international institutions, even broadly defined',[43] and that his theory 'emphasizes the pervasive significance of international institutions *without denigrating the role of state power*'.[44] Keohane thus accepted that law remains vulnerable to sudden shifts in the power relationships among States, even in cases where redefinition does not occur because of the benefits derived from the institution in question, or because of the widespread consensus which such a redefinition might require.[45]

The same is true of the institutions which Young has described. For Young, all social institutions, including international institutions, were

[38] See, e.g., Axelrod (1984) 3–20. [39] Keohane (1986) 20.

[40] Keohane (1986) 23. This book, in contrast, considers reciprocity not only as a general social concept which recognises the benefits of specific and diffuse co-operation, but also as a principle of international law which plays an important role in qualifying applications of power in the development, maintenance and change of customary rules. See pp. 88–128 below. [41] Keohane (1989b) 5. [42] Keohane (1989c) 75.

[43] Keohane (1989b) 6. [44] Keohane (1989b) 11 (emphasis added).

[45] See generally Keohane (1984) 85–109. See also pp. 107–9 below. It should be noted that Keohane assumed that each State has engaged in some sort of internal political process in order to balance competing interests within the State and determine a unified State 'interest'. Young (see p. 30 below) made a similar assumption, as does this book (see pp. 13–14 above). Some 'liberal' international relations scholars, in contrast, have sought to break down the divide between the study of national and international politics, as have some legal writers the divide between national and international law. See the citations in note 45, p. 14 above.

created as a result of 'the conjunction of behavioral regularities and convergent expectations'.[46] This conjunction:

> commonly produces identifiable social conventions, which actors conform to without making elaborate calculations on a case-by-case basis . . . international regimes, like other social institutions, typically acquire a life of their own in the form of clusters of widely accepted social conventions.[47]

Yet like Keohane's institutions, Young's institutions may still undergo rapid changes as a result of evolving power relationships. They have no truly independent force. Although Young pointed out that '[i]nstitutions change in response to an array of political, economic, technological, sociocultural, and even moral developments',[48] it is these developments which affect the relative interests and power of different States, which in turn change international institutions. Young was writing about how different developments concerning different sources of power affect States, how they choose to behave, and what they are able to create or modify in the international institutional sphere.

Young and Keohane have ascribed great influence to institutions. They are, in this respect, very different from what Young has referred to as the '[o]rthodox students of international relations' who '*assume* that international institutions, including regimes of various sorts, are mere surface reflections of underlying forces or processes, subject to change with every shift in the real determinants of collective outcomes'.[49] However, neither of them has gone on to demonstrate that any international institution, whether an organisation, or a treaty or customary rule, is to any significant degree independent from the power relationships which exist among States.

Young, to his credit, has recognised this omission. He wrote:

> One of the more surprising features of the emerging literature on regimes is the relative absence of sustained discussions of the significance of regimes, or, more broadly, social institutions, as determinants of collective outcomes at the international level.[50]

The result, he concluded:

> is something of an analytic vacuum. The ultimate justification for devoting substantial time and energy to the study of regimes must be the proposition that we can account for a good deal of the variance in collective outcomes at the interna-

[46] Young (1989) 81. [47] Young (1989) 82 (footnote omitted). [48] Young (1989) 205.

[49] Young (1989) 58 (emphasis added). Young ((1989) 58, note 2) cited Strange (1983) as an example of the orthodox international relations reaction to regime theory.

[50] Young (1989) 206. Young cited Krasner (1983) 5–10 and Ruggie (1983) especially 462–5 as partial attempts which have been made. See also Biersteker (1993); and Breitmeier and Wolf (1993).

tional level in terms of the impact of institutional arrangements. For the most part, however, this proposition is relegated to the realm of assumptions rather than brought to the forefront as a focus for analytical and empirical investigation.[51]

In short, regime theorists and institutionalists have not, for the most part, demonstrated that regimes and institutions actually make a difference; that they qualify the application of power in some significant way. Nevertheless, these scholars clearly sense that normal State behaviour does give rise to legal obligation, that some regimes and institutions represent a transformation of power of the kind that they have traditionally studied, into another kind of power – and that this other kind of power, 'the power of rules', subsequently affects what States say and do. Consider, for example, the following thoughts expressed by Young in a panel discussion:

Why is it that an actor acquires and feels some sense of obligation to conform its behavior to the dictates or requirements of a regime or an institution? There are a number of reasons, and for the most part we have conflated them. For example, I think that there are differences in being obligated to do something because of a moral reason, a normative reason and a legal reason.[52]

### The 'English School'

The English School of international relations theory, of which scholars such as Manning, Wight, Bull and Watson have been leading figures, has long recognised that there is some sort of connection between the international society of States and the binding force of international law.[53] According to Wight:

[International society] is manifest in the diplomatic system; in the conscious maintenance of the balance of power to preserve the independence of the member communities; *in the regular operations of international law whose binding force is accepted over a wide though politically unimportant range of subjects*; in economic, social and technical interdependence and the functional international institutions established latterly to regulate it. All these presuppose an international social consciousness, a world wide community sentiment.[54]

Bull elaborated upon the connection between this conception of international society and international law, writing:

[51] Young (1989) 206–7. See also Hurrell (1993) 53: 'The central problem . . . for regime theorists and international lawyers is to establish that laws and norms exercise a compliance pull of their own, at least partially independent of the power and interests which underpinned them and which were often responsible for their creation.'

[52] Young (1992) 175.

[53] See, e.g., Manning (1962); Wight (1966); Wight (1977); Bull (1977); Bull and Watson (1984); and Watson (1992).

[54] Wight (1966) 96–7 (emphasis added).

A *society of states* (or international society) exists when a group of states, conscious of certain common interests and common values, form a society in the sense that they conceive themselves to be bound by a common set of rules in their relations with one another, and share in the working of common institutions.[55]

More recently, Hurrell might also be described as a member of the English School. Yet he has adopted a position which would satisfy many international lawyers, in that he recognised the importance and unique character of legal obligation. He began by advancing a view of international society similar to those advanced by Wight and Bull, such that international law is an instrument used by States to achieve both short- and long-term common goals:

Once states see themselves as having a long-term interest in participating in an international legal system, then the idea of obligation and the normativity of rules can be given concrete form and can acquire a degree of distance from the immediate interests or preferences of states. Within this society, law exists but is no longer seen to depend on the command of the sovereign. Law is rather the symbol of the idea of being bound and voluntarily accepting a sense of obligation. It is not based on external sanctions or the threat of them but is based rather on the existence of shared interests, of shared values, and of patterned expectations.[56]

Hurrell then took the additional step of recognising the special character of international law, the legal specificity which distinguishes it from the other factors studied by international relations scholars:

Being a political system, states will seek to interpret obligations to their own advantage. But being a legal system that is built on the consent of other parties, they will be constrained by the necessity of justifying their actions in legal terms. It is for these reasons that it is important to make a clearer distinction than is common in regime theory between specifically legal rules and the workings of the legal system within which they operate on the one hand, and the wide variety of other formal and informal norms and rules and the processes of negotiation, bargaining, or imposition that underpin them on the other.[57]

Even more recently, Beck, Arend and Lugt have pulled together a variety of perspectives on 'international rules' from across the disciplines of international relations and international law. Yet despite the undeniable value of their contribution, these authors have, unlike Hurrell, done little to demonstrate or indeed argue that rules of international law are in any way independent of the power relationships which exist among States. Consider Arend's assertion that:

For a putative international rule to be an international *legal* rule, it must possess two elements: authority and control. First, the rule must be controlling of state

[55] Bull (1977) 13 (emphasis in original). [56] Hurrell (1993) 60.
[57] Hurrell (1993) 61. See, in this context, the discussion of the distinction between law as 'norm' and law as 'fact': at pp. 46–50 below. See also Buzan's attempt to connect the work of the English School to structural realism and institutionalism: Buzan (1993).

behaviour. This is simply another way of saying that it must be reflected in state practice. Second, it must be perceived by states to be authoritative. That is, the decision-making elites in states must regard the rule to be law; they must regard it to be obligatory. In the language of international law, the rule must have *opinio juris*.[58]

This assertion, in itself, seems to be consistent with mainstream conceptions of customary international law, as epitomised by Article 38(1)(b) of the Statute of the International Court of Justice.[59] However, later on the same page Arend asked:

[H]ow does one measure authority and control? Unlike barometric pressure or relative humidity, authority and control do not admit of precise measurement. It is, however, reasonably clear what one looks at to determine if a putative rule has authority and control. A rule is controlling if international actors comply with the rule. To determine compliance, a scholar would examine the behavior of the international actor to whom the rule is addressed. If, for example, one were to explore the rule of diplomatic immunity, one would examine all those cases where diplomats had been implicated in a crime. If the rule were completely controlling, the investigator would expect to find no case where the diplomat, once his or her status had been established, was arrested and tried.[60]

A international rule, in other words, is only a rule if it is never – or hardly ever – violated. By simply repeating the traditional bipartite conception of customary international law as constituted of State practice and *opinio juris*, without acknowledging that conception's inherent limitations, Arend expresses an understanding of international law that would not seem to extend to the reality of, for example, the prohibitions on torture and aggression, where many international actors do not actually comply with what are generally regarded as fundamental rules. It is a conception that admits of no real distinction between what States do and what they are legally obligated to do, and for that reason requires further elaboration.

This book is – in part – an attempt to provide such elaboration, to help fill the analytical vacuum that Young described, to demonstrate that rules, principles and processes of international law are not, at the relevant level of analysis:

epiphenomena whose dictates are apt to be ignored whenever actors find it inconvenient or costly to comply with them and whose substantive provisions are readily changeable whenever powerful members of the community find them cumbersome or otherwise outmoded.[61]

Rather, this book argues that the customary process is a power-transforming, and thus power-qualifying, institution of the kind Young and

[58] Arend (1996) 300. [59] See pp. 129–65 below. [60] Arend (1996) 300–1.
[61] Young (1989) 208. For other attempts to demonstrate the normative independence of international law see, e.g., Fried (1968); Henkin (1979); D'Amato (1984–85); Boyle (1985); and Brownlie (1988).

many other international relations scholars have been seeking. As Kratochwil has indicated:

> Actors are not only programmed by rules and norms, but they reproduce and change by their practice the normative structures by which they are able to act, share meanings, communicate intentions, criticize claims, and justify choices. Thus, one of the most important sources of change, neglected in the present regime literature, is the *practice of the actors* themselves and its concomitant process of interstitial law-making in the international arena.[62]

But rather than examining the effect of customary rules on State behaviour generally, this book focuses on the effect that some of those rules have within a rather more confined context. In short, it studies the effects of four principles of international law on how States behave, and what they are able to accomplish, when they seek to develop, maintain and change other rules of customary international law. And to the extent that this book draws upon developments in international relations theory while conducting this interdisciplinary exercise, it focuses on the work of the regime theorists, institutionalists and the theorists of the English School that has been canvassed in this chapter, for it is they who have made the greatest efforts to explore the interface between politics and international law.

[62] Kratochwil (1989) 61 (emphasis in original); see also at 14. For other acknowledgments of the need for international relations scholars to address the issue of customary international law, see Kratochwil (1993) 84–93; and Beck (1996) 19.

# 3 Power and international law

In the absence of an overarching sovereign in the international system, States are not only subject to, but also create, international law.[1] States also vary greatly in their wealth, military strength, size and population, and therefore in their ability to apply the kinds of power traditionally studied by international relations scholars. Inequalities among States and their relative abilities to apply power would therefore be expected to have some effect on the development, maintenance and change of rules of international law.

Most international legal scholars, however, have devoted little energy to considering *directly* the effects of State inequalities, or international relations-type power relationships, on the processes of international law creation.[2] Studies of treaties, customary international law, general principles of law and the 'subsidiary' sources of international law (i.e., judicial decisions and scholarly writings) usually give short shrift to the possibility that relative power differences among States might affect the development, maintenance and change of rules.[3] Many international lawyers have assumed, to varying degrees, that international law is the result of processes which are at least *procedurally* objective and in that sense apolitical. It is possible that this relative lack of interest in the role of power, and the associated assumption of procedural objectivity, are based, in part, on an overly broad conception of sovereign equality.

The concept of sovereign equality has been part of international legal thought for more than two centuries.[4] It is representatively expressed in

[1] See Scelle (1932/34) 2ème partie, 10–12; and Scelle (1956).

[2] Exceptions include Schwarzenberger (1964) 198–212, but see 506–9; Lasswell and McDougal, see e.g. (1992), vol. 1, 399–452; and, to some degree, Stern (1981). For other recent exceptions, see Wright (1993); and Fidler (1996). For a discussion of how this book relates to the work of Lasswell and McDougal, see pp. 207–10 below.

[3] On the different sources of international law, see Art. 38(1) of the Statute of the International Court of Justice; Brownlie (1990) 1–31; Danilenko (1993); and Dinh *et al.* (1994) 111–390.

[4] In 1758 Vattel wrote: 'A dwarf is as much a man as a giant is; a small Republic is no less a sovereign State than the most powerful Kingdom' (Vattel (1916), Introduction, section 18).

Article 2(1) of the 1945 Charter of the United Nations, which states that '[t]he Organization is based on the principle of the sovereign equality of all its Members'. It has been articulated repeatedly in resolutions and declarations of the United Nations General Assembly[5] and is regarded as axiomatic by judges of the International Court of Justice.[6] There is, however, an important difference between the notional or formal equality of States and social equality.[7]

The concept of sovereign equality is, in some respects, an essential element of the international legal system. All States are entitled to participate in the system because they are formally equal holders of full international legal personality.[8] The principle of reciprocity has the legal effects it does because all States are formally entitled to the same general rights and subject to the same general obligations.[9] In terms of law creation, the concept of sovereign equality would seem to be particularly important in respect of treaties, in that it allows States to enter into these agreements with reasonable assurance that the obligation of *pacta sunt servanda*, the rules of treaty interpretation and the duty to make reparation in the event of a breach will be applied on an equal basis.[10]

Nevertheless, just as contract law in national legal systems allows for the application of 'bargaining power' while at the same time regulating the interaction of economically interested parties, so the rules governing international treaties accommodate disparities in negotiating strength and the ability to impose effective retaliatory sanctions in the event of a breach.[11]

[5] See, e.g., Declaration on Principles of International Law concerning Friendly Relations and Co-operation among States in accordance with the Charter of the United Nations, UNGA Res. 2625 (XXV) (1970). Note, however, the creation of special rights for the permanent members of the Security Council in Chapter V of the Charter and the weighting of votes in, for instance, the World Bank and International Monetary Fund. See Art. 5(3)(a) of the 1944 Articles of Agreement of the International Bank for Reconstruction and Development (World Bank), 2 UNTS 39, 134, 606 UNTS 266; and Art. 12(5)(a) and (b) of the 1944 Articles of Agreement of the International Monetary Fund, 726 UNTS 266.

[6] See, e.g., the separate opinion of Judge Shahabuddeen in the *Nauru Case (Preliminary Objections)* (1992) *ICJ Reports* 240, 270; and the individual opinion of Judge Anzilotti in the *Danzig Legislative Decrees Case* (1935) PCIJ Reports, Ser. A/B, No. 65, 39, 66.

[7] See Crawford (1989) 284–7. The difference between formal and social equality is also relevant to national legal systems. See, e.g., Wilkinson (1979); Morris and Nott (1991); and Bacchi (1992). For theoretical discussions see, e.g., Rawls (1971) 60–90; and Dworkin (1977) 179–83 and 223–39.

[8] See pp. 75–87 below.

[9] See pp. 88–105 below.

[10] On the international law of treaties, see generally the Vienna Convention on the Law of Treaties, 1155 UNTS 331, reproduced in (1969) 8 ILM 679; McNair (1961); and Reuter (1995).

[11] See Jennings (1981) 68; and Pellet (1992) 42–5. International treaties are still considered valid even if they have been entered into under duress, unless that duress has involved an unlawful use of force. This is not the case with contracts in most national legal systems. See Dawson (1947). Power would thus seem to be even less constrained by the law of treaties than it is by most national laws of contract.

However, these rules do provide an essential element of procedural consistency without which the enormous expansion in treaty relations which has occurred in the latter half of the twentieth century would have been greatly constrained.

The concept of sovereign equality may be less useful in respect of the process of customary international law which, in Schachter's words, 'gives weight to effective power and responsibility'.[12] The customary process involves patterns of legally relevant behaviour rather than contractual agreements, with these patterns of behaviour only developing into rules if they are largely unopposed. As Danilenko has explained:

> By contrast to the elaboration of [an] international treaty, which requires formal negotiations, custom is created by conduct of members of the international community which constantly 'negotiate' with each other by means of actual deeds, statements and other acts.[13]

Although all States are equally entitled to participate in the customary process, in general, it may be easier for more 'powerful' States to behave in ways which will significantly influence the development, maintenance or change of customary rules. Such States may also have more opportunities than less powerful States in which to do so. De Visscher, noting that the 'slow growth of international custom has been compared to the gradual formation of a road across vacant land', wrote:

> Among the users are always some who mark the soil more deeply with their footprints than others, either because of their weight, which is to say their power in this world, or because their interests bring them more frequently this way.[14]

Among other things, powerful States generally have large, well-financed diplomatic corps which are able to follow international developments globally across a wide spectrum of issues. This enables those States to object, in a timely fashion, to developments which they perceive as being contrary to their interests. If more than oral or written objection is required, powerful States also have greater military, economic and political strength which enables them to enforce jurisdictional claims, impose trade sanctions and dampen or divert international criticism.

The importance of the relational character of inter-State power was perhaps implicitly recognised by the International Court of Justice in its judgment in the 1969 *North Sea Continental Shelf Cases*, where it wrote:

[12] Schachter (1989) 721. His sentence continues: 'whereas multilateral treaty-making . . . treats all States as equally capable'. See also Schachter (1987) 158; Schachter (1991) 26–32; and Schachter (1996).

[13] Danilenko (1993) 75; see also 119. See also Thirlway (1972); Akehurst (1974–75a); Wolfke (1993a); pp. 147–65 below.

[14] de Visscher (1957) 149.

> [I]t might be that, even without the passage of any considerable period of time, a very widespread and representative participation in the convention might suffice of itself, *provided it included that of States whose interests were specially affected.*[15]

As de Visscher noted, powerful States, given the broader range and greater frequency of their activities, are more likely than less powerful States to have interests which are affected by any particular legal development. They are therefore more likely to be 'specially affected' by the development or change of a customary rule. Danilenko has written:

> In the absence of a clear definition, the notion of 'specially affected' states may be used as a respectable disguise for 'important' or 'powerful' states which are always supposed to be 'specially affected' by all or almost all political-legal developments within the international community. However, while as a matter of policy the traditional importance of the views of a few preponderant states in custom formation is widely acknowledged, there is no indication that their special status in customary law-making is recognized as a matter of law.[16]

The passage from the Court's judgment in the *North Sea Continental Shelf Cases* may, however, be of greatest relevance in terms of what it says about the role of *interests* in the customary process, i.e., that the process seeks to measure and balance interests, and therefore pays particular attention to the interests of specially affected States, regardless of how powerful they might be.

The ability of powerful States to participate more effectively in the customary process may be partly concealed by the fact that States sometimes choose not to participate in that process in respect of particular rules. Even the most powerful of States often acquiesce to the development, maintenance or change of customary rules. If the world's most powerful States are ambivalent in respect of a potential, emerging or existing rule and do nothing, the power relationships among less powerful, but more interested, States may determine the outcome.[17] That said, a powerful State's decision not to participate actively in respect of a particular rule may in some situations also constitute an application of power having effects of its own. A good example of such a situation may have been the refusal of powerful States either to support or to oppose the efforts of some Latin American States to develop a customary rule giving themselves control over the geostationary orbit.[18]

[15] *North Sea Continental Shelf Cases* (1969) *ICJ Reports* 3, 42 (para. 73) (emphasis added).

[16] Danilenko (1993) 96, footnote omitted; see also 236. On the latter point, see pp. 75–87 below.

[17] A similar phenomenon may occur with respect to the negotiation of some multilateral treaties, in situations where the more powerful States are less interested than some less powerful States in the outcome of the negotiations. Those less powerful States may then assume leading roles.

[18] See Goedhuis (1978) 590–1; Gorove (1979) 450–5 and 460; and Theis (1986) 229–31.

Sometimes there will be no disagreement among States as to the desirability of a particular rule and therefore no opposition. Power relationships will probably play a different and less important role in these situations. Examples of such situations may include the development of the prohibition against genocide, of rules concerning the use of outer space and celestial bodies, and of coastal State jurisdiction over the continental shelf.[19] In these situations power may be most important in creating conditions favourable for consensus, which in turn may allow customary rules to develop very quickly.[20] Although such situations may be quite common, they would rarely be noticed because the existence of consensus greatly reduces the possibility that a potential, emerging or existing rule will become the subject of dispute.

Many international lawyers have glossed over the possibility that inter-State power relationships may affect the development, maintenance or change of customary rules, or have made unpersuasive attempts to explain such effects away. D'Amato, for example, acknowledged that some States are better at publicising their actions and related legal opinions than others, and consequently are more effective in shaping customary international law.[21] However, he assumed that the customary process offers States a level playing field. He claimed that:

> all nations have the same set of entitlements; that each entitlement has equal legal standing *vis-à-vis* other entitlements; that international law strives to preserve the equilibrium that equal entitlements create by permitting retaliation by nations whose entitlements have been violated.[22]

As a result 'the customary rules that survive the legal evolutionary process are those that are best adapted to serve the mutual self-interest of *all* states'.[23] D'Amato did not consider whether the degree to which a State participates in the process – the degree to which it protects its 'entitlements' – might relate to its relative power *vis-à-vis* other States.[24]

Schachter is one writer who has recognised that power is a factor in the development and change of customary rules. He has recently written:

> As a historical fact, the great body of customary international law was made by remarkably few States. Only the States with navies – perhaps 3 or 4 – made most of the law of the sea. Military power, exercised on land and sea, shaped the customary law of war and, to a large degree, the customary rules on territorial rights and principles of State responsibility. 'Gunboat diplomacy' was only the most obvious form of coercive law-making.
>
> Economic power, like military power, is applied often through implicit, if not

[19] See respectively Shaw (1989); Cheng (1965); and pp. 90–2 below.
[20] See pp. 160–2 below. [21] D'Amato (1971) 96–7. [22] D'Amato (1982) 1112.
[23] D'Amato (1987a) 104 (emphasis added).
[24] For a view similar to that of D'Amato on this point, see Akehurst (1974–75a) 23.

open, threats in support of claims over a broad range of inter-State action. The more powerful the economy, the greater the presence of its government and nationals in international transactions. Trade, foreign investment, and technical know-how emanate disproportionately from the advanced economic powers; they carry with them, as a rule, the political views of their respective States, together with social attitudes bearing on international relations. Moreover, for these reasons the affluent States are objects of attention by others. Their views and positions are noticed and usually respected. Their official legal opinions and digests of State practice are available along with international law treatises that influence professional opinion and practical outcomes. In De Visscher's words, 'the great powers after imprinting a definite direction upon a usage make themselves its guarantors and defenders.'[25]

Yet despite these and other acknowledgments that power plays a role in the process of customary international law, relatively few international lawyers have explored that role in any detail.[26] It therefore comes as something of a surprise that power is a central, if frequently unacknowledged, aspect of at least several other, related debates within the discipline.

## Power and the debate about whether resolutions and declarations constitute State practice

An important debate continues in respect of whether, in what way and to what degree the resolutions and declarations of international organisations – especially of the United Nations General Assembly – actually contribute to the development, maintenance and change of customary rules. The traditional position is reflective of a period in which the international system had far fewer members than it does today, with those members being predominantly Western, developed States. This position considers that resolutions and declarations can only contribute to the customary process in so far as they are expressions of *opinio juris*, the subjective element of customary international law.[27] Some scholars have even expressed doubt as to this function, suggesting that resolutions and declarations cannot constitute reliable expressions of *opinio juris* because State representatives frequently do not believe what they themselves say.[28]

The latter half of the twentieth century has seen a proliferation in the number of States, with most new States being non-industrialised, former colonies. This increase in numbers has given the new, relatively

[25] Schachter (1996) 536–7, quoting de Visscher (1957) 155. See also Fidler (1996).

[26] For other, limited acknowledgments of the importance of power in the customary process, see, e.g., Baxter (1970) 66; Raman (1976) 388; Stern (1981) 494–9; Degan (1981/82) 549; Reisman (1987) 144; Sur (1990) 1er cahier, 19–20; Pellet (1992) 44; and Sur (1995) 246–9.

[27] See, e.g., Abi-Saab (1968) 100; and Dupuy (1974) 83–4. On *opinio juris*, see pp. 130–3, 136–41 and 147–51 below.

[28] See, e.g., Arangio-Ruiz (1972) 455–9; and Schwebel (1979).

less powerful States an important advantage over established, industrialised States: a numerical majority in international organisations, such as the United Nations General Assembly, which are based on the principle of 'one State – one vote'. It is possible that this principle had qualifying effects on traditional sources of power even before less powerful States achieved numerical majorities, by giving those States a better means of expression and raising the possibility that this expression could have law-creating effects. However, its potential consequences were only fully appreciated once numerical majorities within those organisations were achieved.

The newly independent non-industrialised States found themselves in a legal system which had been developed primarily by relatively wealthy, militarily powerful States. They consequently sought to change the system. They used their numerical majorities to adopt resolutions and declarations which advanced their interests.[29] They also asserted, in conjunction with a significant number of legal scholars (and perhaps with the International Court of Justice) that resolutions and declarations are instances of State practice which are potentially creative, or at least indicative, of rules of customary international law.[30] It is true that in respect of some customary rules, such as those rules concerning human rights, resolutions and declarations have clearly had law-creating effects.[31]

Powerful States, for the most part, along with some scholars from powerful States, have resisted these developments. They have emphatically denied that resolutions and declarations can be State practice.[32] Elsewhere, in organisations such as the World Bank and the International Monetary Fund, the dominant position of powerful States is secured by weighted voting systems.[33] In the United Nations Security Council the

[29] In some cases the non-industrialised States nevertheless recognised the necessity of having the powerful States on their side. A good example of this occurred during the negotiation of the 1982 United Nations Convention on the Law of the Sea, UN Doc. A/CONF. 62/122 (1982), reproduced in (1982) 21 ILM 1261. See Caminos and Molitor (1985).

[30] See, e.g., Higgins (1963) 5–7; Asamoah (1966) 46–62; Castaneda (1969) 168–77; Jiménez de Aréchaga (1978) 30–4; Gupta (1986); Brownlie (1990) 5; *Nicaragua Case (Merits)*, note 16, p. 8 above at 97–100 (para. 183–90); and the dissenting opinion of Judge Tanaka in the *South West Africa Cases (Second Phase)* (1966) *ICJ Reports* 6, 291.

[31] See, e.g., on the history of the development of the prohibition against torture, Bonin (1986); and Rodley (1987) 17–70.

[32] See, e.g., the debate on this issue that took place in the Sixth (Legal) Committee of the United Nations General Assembly in 1974: *Review of the Role of the ICJ*, GAOR, 29th Session, A/C.6/SR.1460–1521 at 38 (Mexico), 133–4 (Netherlands and Mexico) and 166–70 (various States); Weil (1983) 417; Schwebel (1986); Seidl-Hohenveldern (1986) 68; and D'Amato (1987a). For a particularly strong, recent expression of this view from a Polish author, see Wolfke (1993b) 3–4.

[33] See note 5, p. 36 above.

interests of five powerful States are protected by their power of veto and by their permanent rather than rotating membership.[34]

Ironically, as a result of the fact that five powerful States maintain an advantage in the Security Council, the positions adopted by States in respect of whether resolutions and declarations constitute State practice may be reversed when they consider the role that Security Council resolutions might play in the process of customary international law. Little scholarly attention has been devoted to this question due to the Security Council's relative inactivity during the Cold War.[35] Yet the Security Council has in recent years become quite active. It has authorised a number of enforcement actions on the part of member States and on several occasions has made what might be considered unnecessary and perhaps even illegal determinations of international law.[36] Although most States are unlikely to desire a role for Security Council resolutions in the customary process, some powerful States, and especially permanent members of the Council, may well have an interest in such a role being ascribed. It remains to be seen whether those powerful States are able to distinguish between Security Council and General Assembly resolutions in a way which enables them to argue for customary law-making effects on the part of one kind of resolution, but not on the part of the other.

More generally, it may be that a compromise position on the role of the resolutions and declarations of international organisations has been emerging, to the effect that, although they are instances of State practice, they do not carry as much weight as those instances which involve more traditional forms of State action.[37] A few writers have even sought to remove the debate, at least as it relates to human rights, from the area of customary international law altogether. Simma and Alston, for example, have attempted to relocate the debate under the rubric of general principles of law, while Koskenniemi has suggested that international human

[34] See Art. 27(3) of the UN Charter. [35] See, however, Higgins (1994) 28.

[36] For enforcement actions see, e.g., Res. 678 of 29 November 1990 (on Iraq), reproduced in (1990) 29 ILM 1565; Res. 794 of 3 December 1992 (on Somalia); Res. 787 of 16 November 1992 (on the former Yugoslavia), reproduced in (1992) 31 ILM 1481; Res. 929 of 22 June 1994 (on Rwanda); and Res. 940 of 31 July 1994 (on Haiti). Of particular concern are the Security Council's demarcation of the boundary between Iraq and Kuwait (Res. 687 of 3 April 1991, reproduced in (1991) 30 ILM 847) and its effective determination of the non-applicability of the 1971 Montreal Convention for the Suppression of Unlawful Acts against the Safety of Civil Aviation (1975) 974 UNTS 177 and the lack of a requirement for an extradition treaty in order to extradite in Res. 731 of 21 January 1992, reproduced in (1992) 31 ILM 732.

[37] This is the position adopted in this book. See pp. 156–7 below. For support, see Lacharrière (1983) 55–8; and Pellet (1992) 44. For a suggestion of support, see Jennings and Watts (1992) 31.

rights are based on shared political convictions and shared values rather than on the customary process.[38] Nonetheless, even these attempts to find compromise or alternative positions reveal that, when it comes to the question of whether resolutions and declarations constitute State practice, States and scholars are in fact arguing about the role and definition of power within the process of customary international law.[39]

## Power and the scope of international human rights

The role of power in the customary process is also an important but not explicit part of the debate concerning the extent to which international human rights can penetrate the territorial jurisdictions of non-consenting States.[40] It is generally accepted that rules and procedures set out in human rights treaties apply only to those States which have ratified those treaties. Yet many States and scholars insist that even those States which have failed to ratify international human rights treaties nonetheless do have international human rights obligations.

They base this position on two main grounds. First, they argue that by ratifying the Charter of the United Nations all member States accepted the general human rights obligations set out in Articles 55(c) and 56.[41] Subsequent human rights treaties are seen as elaborating rather than transforming those obligations.[42] Secondly, they argue that rules of customary international law have developed in respect of the content of specific human rights and the jurisdiction of international society to

[38] See Simma and Alston (1992); and Koskenniemi (1990a). For a strong critique of Simma and Alston's position, see Lillich (1995/96).

[39] For support of this conclusion, see Danilenko (1993) 86–91.

[40] The traditional position is exemplified by Art. 2(7) of the UN Charter:

> Nothing contained in the present Charter shall authorize the United Nations to intervene in matters which are essentially within the domestic jurisdiction of any State or shall require the Members to submit such matters to settlement under the present Charter . . .

See also Brownlie (1988) 21.

[41] Art. 55 states:

> With a view to the creation of conditions of stability and well-being which are necessary for peaceful and friendly relations among nations based on respect for the principle of equal rights and self-determination of peoples, the United Nations shall promote . . . (c) universal respect for, and observance of, human rights and fundamental freedoms for all without distinction as to race, sex, language, or religion.

Art. 56 states: 'All Members pledge themselves to take joint and separate action in co-operation with the Organization for the achievement of the purposes set forth in Article 55.'

[42] See, e.g., Sohn (1982) 13–17; Bonin (1986) 171–3; and Meron (1989) 81–5.

monitor, encourage respect for and even enforce the implementation of those rights within the territory of non-consenting States.[43]

Many States and some scholars disagree strongly with such arguments.[44] The objections of many non-industrialised States to the 'cultural imperialism' of the international human rights movement and continued stonewalling of outside interference in national affairs by States such as Burma, China and Indonesia stand in stark contrast to the language of instruments such as the 1948 Universal Declaration on Human Rights[45] and to the claims of most academics working in this field. In practice, most States and international organisations have settled on a compromise. This compromise accepts the development of some human rights as rules of customary international law but limits the international community to a '*droit de regard*': a right to monitor and encourage from the outside the protection of those rights within non-consenting States.[46] This compromise does not empower individual States, groups of States or international organisations to intervene directly in the internal affairs of non-consenting States.

Although the parameters of this compromise are not always clearly defined,[47] humanitarian intervention is the one significant area in which it might be breaking down. Yet recent State practice in support of a right of humanitarian intervention is scanty, especially when compared with decades of non-intervention on humanitarian grounds. Moreover, most recent humanitarian interventions have been conducted within the penumbra of Chapter VII of the Charter of the United Nations, which has meant that situations such as those in northern Iraq, Somalia, Haiti and Rwanda were classified, somewhat tenuously, as threats to 'international peace and security', and that the 'right' to intervene on humanitarian grounds did not therefore need to exist as a right under customary international law.[48]

[43] See generally Meron (1989) 79–135; Lillich (1995/96); and, for a review of various positions, Simma and Alston (1992) 84–96.

[44] See, e.g., Watson (1977) 71–7; Lane (1978) 279–86; and Weisburd (1988) 39–41. This study does not deal with the first of these arguments. However, it should be noted that the language of Arts. 55(c) and 56 is language of promotion, and not enforcement or protection.

[45] UNGA Res. 217 (III) A.

[46] See Simma and Alston (1992) 98–9.

[47] For example, many States consider the provision, by other States or international organisations, of financial support to opposition groups to constitute intervention in their internal affairs. Nevertheless, such support is sometimes openly provided.

[48] The existence of large numbers of refugees in these situations would seem to provide the strongest basis on which threats to international peace and security could have been established. However, refugee flows received little attention in the relevant debates of the Security Council. As for the status of humanitarian intervention outside the scope of Chapter VII, many recent scholarly contributions on the subject have not even considered its legality under customary international law. See, e.g., Luca (1993); Hutchinson (1993); Gordon (1994); and Kresock (1994). For exceptions, see Lillich (1993); Greenwood (1993); Ofodile (1994); and Franck (1995) 272–3.

As with the debate as to whether resolutions and declarations constitute State practice, and even though it is rarely framed in these terms, this human rights debate clearly concerns the role and definition of power in the process of customary international law. At the most basic level, it is a debate about the exclusive competence which States have traditionally had to apply power in respect of all matters within their borders which do not affect other States, and the ability of international society to challenge the exclusivity of such applications through customary rules.

## Power and critical legal scholarship

In recent years the role of non-legal power in the international legal system has been exposed to some degree by Critical Legal Studies scholars. This may partially explain the disquiet with which many international lawyers regard the work of jurists such as Kennedy and Koskenniemi.[49] The project of these scholars, like their counterparts working within national legal systems, has been to expose the myths of objectivity, of value-freedom and of determinacy in law and law creation by deconstructing legal texts, and thus demonstrating that legal systems are neither self-contained nor politically neutral. Instead, they aim to show that legal systems are based on tensions inherent in liberal ideology between, for example, the community and the individual, or positivism and naturalism.[50]

However, those Critical Legal Studies scholars working in international law have themselves only just begun to explore the non-legal factors which, from their perspective, must be responsible for the inconsistencies they criticise. Koskenniemi, for example, has suggested that customary international law in the human rights field is determined, not by formal tests of legal validity, but by 'an anterior – though at least in some respects largely shared – criterion of what is right and good for human life'.[51] According to Koskenniemi, shared values and differing

[49] The two most important works are Kennedy (1987) and Koskenniemi (1989). For a summary and critique of these books, see Carty (1991) 66–83. For what appears to be disquiet, see Bederman (1988); and Trimble (1990) 822–32. For a discussion of the reasons why legal scholars might feel disquiet concerning the role of power in international law, see pp. 46–50 below.

[50] Critical Legal Studies scholars who focused on national legal systems had a second project, which was to design alternative modes of discourse, resource distribution and conflict resolution. See, e.g., Unger (1983); Jabbari (1992); and Collins (1993). In the last chapter of his book, Koskenniemi ((1989) 458–501) offered a tentative and rather nebulous agenda for reconstructing the international legal order which he previously attempted to disassemble; an agenda based on free-ranging communication, imaginative context-transformation and deeply felt notions of justice.

[51] Koskenniemi (1990a) 1953. With regard to non-human rights rules he has reaffirmed the dominant role of politics and power. See, e.g., Koskenniemi (1990b) 7. This is why, in response to theories attempting to explain the sources of international human rights, he cautioned against 'the pull of the mainstream'.

degrees of political conviction about the value of particular norms – rather than a legal process as such – account for the existence of, and hierarchy among, various international human rights.[52] However, this consideration of non-legal factors has remained peripheral to Koskenniemi's larger project of exposing inconsistencies in international law.[53]

Kennedy, for his part, refused to consider non-legal factors at all. He stated emphatically:

> I do not analyze the relationship between international legal materials and their political and interpretive milieu. I am not concerned about the context within which arguments are made and doctrines developed.[54]

Writers from the non-industrialised world have long recognised that non-legal power plays a role in the international legal system. They have argued that the system, including its rule-creating processes, was created by industrialised States to serve their own interests, and not the interests of newer or less powerful States.[55] Their perspective on the role of power also helps to explain their position in respect of whether the resolutions and declarations of international organisations constitute State practice for the purposes of customary international law.[56]

More recently, feminist legal scholars have argued that the international legal system is dominated by male power.[57] Many academics are uneasy with this proposition.[58] It is possible that their discomfort is accentuated by the fact that some feminist legal scholars have also noted that disparities among States are incongruous with the concept of sovereign equality.[59] Yet, as with Critical Legal Studies scholars, feminist scholars and writers from the non-industrialised world have, for the most part, only exposed the importance of power; they have yet to explain how power operates within the international legal system to affect the creation of law.

## Power as a threat to international law?

There would seem to be at least two reasons why most international lawyers are reluctant to engage in detailed explorations of the role of power in the process of customary international law. First, as Stern explained:

[52] For an explanation of how Koskenniemi's suggestion might accord with the explanation of the customary process advanced in this book, see pp. 210–13 below.

[53] It should also be noted that Koskenniemi's tentative consideration of non-legal factors has followed the direction already taken by some of his national law counterparts. See, e.g., Kairys (1990).

[54] Kennedy (1987) 7.

[55] See, e.g., Lall (1974); Bedjaoui (1979); and Kwakwa (1987).

[56] See pp. 40–3 above.

[57] See, e.g., Charlesworth *et al.* (1991); Charlesworth (1992); Chinkin (1992); Wright (1992); Knop (1993); and Dallmeyer (1993).

[58] See, most notably, Téson (1993).

[59] See, e.g., Wright (1993).

> [La] coutume joue un rôle de dévoilement, de mise à nu du système juridique. Elle est si troublante car elle pose inlassablement la question de l'origine de l'obligation dans un système juridique qui évacue assez facilement la question essentielle du fondement de son caractère obligatoire, qui est impossible à résoudre sur le plan strictement juridique, au profit de la question existentielle du fondement du caractère obligatoire de ses différentes normes qui peut, elle, être résolue de façon très rassurante dans le cadre de sa structure formaliste.[60]

In short, to study the role of power in the customary process inevitably raises the broader question of the basis of obligation in international law. Although some international lawyers have considered this question,[61] the majority of them have chosen not to do so. Instead, they have restricted their analyses to the confines of the international legal system, and in doing so have also, consequently, precluded themselves from considering the very issue of power and custom that so clearly raises the question of obligation. In Kelsen's terms, they have chosen to focus on law as 'norm' rather than law as 'fact'.[62] And as we have seen, international relations scholars have a different perspective on the scope of analysis that should be adopted when considering rules of international law,[63] which explains the frustration that some of them feel about what they perceive to be the overly narrow focus of international lawyers.[64]

Yet the fact that most international lawyers have paid little attention to

[60] Stern (1981) 480. My translation reads:

> [C]ustom plays a role of unveiling, of laying bare the legal system. Custom is troubling because it continually poses the question as to the origin of obligation in a legal system which rather easily abandons the essential question of the foundation of its own, obligatory character. This latter question, which cannot be resolved on a strictly legal plane, is abandoned in favour of the existential question of the foundation of the obligatory character of the legal system's different norms, a question which can be resolved in a very reassuring fashion within the limits of the system's formalist structure.

Stern made a similar observation with regard to the study of treaties. See Stern (1981) 480, note 5.

[61] See, e.g., Brierly (1958); p. 7 above.

[62] Kelsen ((1961) 122) wrote:

> According to the dynamic concept, law is something created by a certain process, and everything created in this way is law. This dynamic concept, however, is only apparently a concept of law. It contains no answer to the question of what is the essence of law, what is the criteria by which law can be distinguished from other social norms . . . it furnishes an answer only to the question whether or not and why a certain norm belongs to a system of valid legal norms, forms a part of a certain legal order.

[63] See generally pp. 24–34 above.

[64] For example, Beck ((1996) 17) has noted with 'concern' that 'a pronounced gap exists between the predominantly explanatory aspirations of the [international relations] scholarship devoted to international rules and the predilection of most modern [international law] scholarship for prescribing doctrine' (by which he means the existence and content of rules).

the role played by power in the development, maintenance and change of customary rules should not necessarily be regarded as a failure. As Danilenko has explained with regard to applications of customary international law by the International Court of Justice:

> It is clear that the ICJ cannot apply to a specific case a continuous community practice leading to the recognition of a binding rule of conduct. It can only apply a customary legal rule established as a result of the emergence of general practice.[65]

The principal task of international lawyers is to determine the existence and content of rules as those rules apply in specific situations. When they act as judges or arbitrators, appear before courts or tribunals, or advise government and private clients, they are expected to explain *the law* and not, in most instances, how the law is developed, maintained and changed. It is therefore perhaps understandable that most academic writings in the field have had a similar focus.

Some international lawyers may even regard a consideration of the role of power in the customary process as unhelpful, perhaps even dangerous, and think that considering the role of power might lead some States and scholars to conclude that relative power positions are – or should be – relevant to the determination of individual customary rules. For example, Brownlie has written:

> The hegemonial approach to international relations may be defined as an approach to the sources which facilitates the translation of the difference in power between States into specific advantages for the more powerful actor. The hegemonial approach to the sources involves maximizing the occasions when the powerful actor will obtain 'legal approval' for its actions and minimizing the occasions when such approach may be conspicuously withheld.[66]

Higgins, for her part, has explained that many international lawyers believe that, 'if international law is regarded as more than rules . . . international law becomes confused with other phenomena, such as power or social or humanitarian factors' and that 'only by insisting on international law as rules to be impartially applied will it be possible to avoid the manifestation of international legal argument for political ends'.[67]

There is clearly a fine line between examining the role of power in the customary process and allowing that examination to influence how one determines the existence and content of individual customary rules. However, it is also true that the lack of much distance between these two activities is an aspect that all customary legal systems share.[68] It is also a

[65] Danilenko (1993) 76. [66] Brownlie (1995) 49. [67] Higgins (1994) 3.

[68] See pp. 4–5 above. On customary legal systems other than customary international law, see, e.g., Reid (1980); Comaroff and Roberts (1981); Reisman (1983); Weyrauch and Bell (1993); and Goode (1997).

reason why the role of power should consciously be considered rather than avoided by international lawyers, in order to avoid situations where the distinction between the two activities becomes unconsciously ambiguous or confused.

It would seem that a second reason why most international lawyers are reluctant to engage in detailed explorations of the role of power in the process of customary international law is that any international lawyer who examines rigorously this question risks seeing an important area of international law rendered largely redundant, strictly as a result of what States do rather than as a factor which affects how they behave. In other words, such a study might reveal that individual customary rules are subject to change as a result of short-term modifications in the power relationships among States. Sepúlveda has written:

> In the preoccupation of international jurists to preserve the purity of international law, they abjured politics, also international, since they considered these unstable or as a dangerous, disruptive and malevolent influence, capable of contaminating the law of nations with uncertainty and infiltrating it with anarchy, for which reason a kind of asepsis for the juridical process was instinctively expected.[69]

In short, there would be no point in having rules of international law if those rules were, at least potentially, in a continuous state of flux. Indeed, the essence of obligation and the purpose of law would seem to be an ability to control both present *and* future behaviour.

The risk is perhaps even larger in scope than it may at first seem, since most of the principles which provide structure to the international legal system would themselves appear to be customary in origin.[70] If this is the case, international law as a whole would be rendered inherently unstable and lacking in any sustained, determinant effect. International lawyers, in turn, would be nothing more than participants in an illusion, citing nominally objective, stable and determinable rules while ignoring the impossibility of objectivity, stability and determinacy.[71]

This book seeks to explain the role played by power in the customary process while at the same time demonstrating that, within the international political system, international law retains a degree of stability and determinacy that distinguishes it from the other, non-legal factors which operate there. It thus seeks to deconstruct without destroying, to develop a different intellectual framework both for thinking about custom and for devising meaningful generalisations about State behaviour in a manner

69 Sepúlveda (1990) 441.

70 These principles would seem to include those of reciprocity and legitimate expectation, which ground the treaty-making process. See pp. 88–105 and 106–26 below.

71 This, indeed, has been Koskenniemi's main point. See Koskenniemi (1989) 476–83. See also Allott (1971).

which recognises and accommodates the unique character of law. And it does so, first, by analysing the effects that four principles of international law have had on applications of power by States as those States have sought to develop, maintain and change a variety of different customary rules. It is to the effects of the first of these principles – the principle of jurisdiction – to which we now turn.

*Part 2*

# International law and the application of power

# 4 The principle of jurisdiction

Jurisdiction may be defined generally as the authority to engage in activities of control or regulation within a certain geographic area. In international law, jurisdiction appears always to be linked to territory in some way. It is a defining characteristic of statehood and an important point of State interaction.[1] As Huber explained in his judgment as sole arbitrator in the 1928 *Island of Palmas Case*:

> The development of the national organisation of States during the last few centuries and, as a corollary, the development of international law, have established this principle of the exclusive competence of the State in regard to its own territory in such a way as to make it the point of departure in settling most questions that concern international relations.[2]

More recently, Higgins has commented:

> There is no more important way to avoid conflict than by providing clear norms as to which state can exercise authority over whom, and in what circumstances. Without that allocation of competences, all is rancour and chaos.[3]

Initially, it might appear that jurisdiction is not so much a principle of international law which may qualify applications of power, as a principle which recognises, and is therefore dependent on, applications of power that result from the absolute control that each State has over its own territory. Yet such an analysis does not explain how jurisdiction and a lack of State control may co-exist in certain situations, such as during civil wars[4]

[1] See generally: Mann (1964); Akehurst (1972–73); Bowett (1982a); Mann (1984); and pp. 10–13 above. It should, however, be noted that traditional conceptions of 'territorial' jurisdiction are currently under some challenge, not least by developments in international environmental law. See generally: Kiss and Shelton (1991) 115–54; Raul and Hagen (1993); Schwartz (1993); and the discussion of An Act to Amend the Coastal Fisheries Protection Act (SC 1994, c. 14, reproduced in (1994) 33 ILM 1383) at pp. 97–101 below.

[2] *Island of Palmas Case* (1928) 2 *Reports of International Arbitral Awards* 829, 838.

[3] Higgins (1994) 56.

[4] See Akehurst (1992); and Nolte (1993) 621–6.

or, in the case of some less powerful States, with regard to fishing activities in their exclusive economic zones.[5] Nor does it explain the fact that boundaries are delimited and statehood itself defined by rules and principles of international law. State-like entities may have preceded the international legal system, but the power relationships which gave rise to the territorial State have subsequently been conceptualised, transformed and legitimised into rules and principles of international law.[6] It would be difficult to explain the high degree of stability which exists in the modern world in respect of territorial boundaries without at least some reference to international law. For all of these reasons, jurisdiction may be considered a principle of international law.[7]

A legal system's jurisdiction may be defined as its authority to make, apply and enforce rules within a certain geographic area. Although the jurisdictions of different legal systems occasionally overlap, each legal system has its own, specific jurisdiction. Consequently, any particular legal system will be defined in large part by its jurisdiction, which in the case of national legal systems is usually linked to State territory. The legal system of the United Kingdom, for example, is distinguishable from other legal systems in part because it has jurisdiction within the United Kingdom, and more precisely, because it has 'full jurisdiction' within that State's territory.[8]

The term 'full jurisdiction' signifies that the legal system in question has jurisdiction in three different forms, namely jurisdiction to prescribe rules, to adjudicate over disputes and to enforce rules and the decisions which result from adjudications.[9] A legal system may not have all three forms of jurisdiction in any particular situation; sometimes it will have only one or two. Jurisdiction to prescribe usually precedes jurisdiction to adjudicate, which in turn usually precedes jurisdiction to enforce. In some situations, such as those involving foreign judicial or arbitral decisions, rules may be prescribed and adjudicated by one legal system and enforced by another.[10] In other situations, such as those involving ques-

[5] See O'Connell (1982) vol. 2, 1063–5; Food and Agriculture Organisation (1985) 8 ('In areas where no effort [i.e., fishing] control measures have been introduced [most States in the Asia–Pacific region] direct intervention is either politically or socially unacceptable, too expensive or administratively impractical').

[6] See generally Crawford (1979). [7] See pp. 10–13 above.

[8] The sub-systems within the legal system of the United Kingdom (i.e., the legal systems of England/Wales and Scotland) may also be defined territorially.

[9] It should be noted that applications of the latter two forms of jurisdiction may to some degree be limited by international law and, more specifically, the customary rules of State immunity when directed at other States. See pp. 57–8 and 110–14 below.

[10] See generally Park and Cromie (1990) 459–519; and Redfern and Hunter (1991) 447–54.

tions of private international law, rules may be prescribed by one legal system and adjudicated and enforced by another.[11]

## Jurisdiction and customary international law

The principle of jurisdiction qualifies the application of power within the process of customary international law by giving each State the right to control, and therefore to limit, the legally relevant practice of other States within its own territory. In certain situations this right to territorial control may provide an important advantage to States in their efforts to manipulate the behaviour patterns which drive the customary process, thus enabling them to protect and promote their own interests more effectively than might otherwise be the case.

The ability of the principle of jurisdiction to qualify applications of power may be observed in the fact that the efficacy of a State's participation in that process frequently depends on the geographic relationship between the area or activity governed, or potentially governed, by the particular customary rule in question and the jurisdictions of the various States which are interested in supporting or opposing that rule. Rules of customary international law may be divided into three categories on the basis of the relationship between the areas or activities governed by those rules and the jurisdictions of those States which are interested in supporting or opposing them. These three categories are internal rules, boundary rules and external rules. Internal rules are rules which one State seeks to apply to another State within the first State's jurisdiction; boundary rules relate to issues arising at the intersection of a State's jurisdiction with an international or internationalised zone; and external rules involve restrictions which one State seeks to impose on the freedom of another State to act within that second State's jurisdiction.

These categories are to some degree subject to the differing perspectives of different States: what appears as an internal rule to one State may well appear as an external rule to another. In addition, it may sometimes prove difficult to categorise State practice in geographic terms. Some legal issues may give rise to instances of practice in a variety of geographic locations. For example, an act in one State may lead to acts or statements in another State in response. This book seeks to distinguish between internal, boundary and external rules in terms of the geographic location

[11] See the comments by Joseph Dellapenna and Ian Sinclair, 'Working Session of the Committee on Extraterritorial Jurisdiction', in *Report of the 66th Conference of the International Law Association, Buenos Aires* (1994) 683; and Bowett (1982a) 1. On private international law, see generally Collier (1994); and Mayer (1994).

of the *preponderance* of the State practice which is of relevance to any particular legal issue. It does so for analytical purposes only and recognises that many customary rules do not fit neatly into any of these three categories.

When considering the differences between internal, boundary and external rules, it may be useful to think of these rules as resulting from tensions among other rules or principles having relatively greater degrees of resistance to change.[12] One more resistant rule or principle, such as the principle of jurisdiction, pulls one way; another more resistant rule or principle, such as that of the freedom of the seas, pulls another way. The result, at any time when State practice allows the tensions among these competing rules or principles to stabilise, is a (less resistant) rule of customary international law, such as the rule concerning the breadth of the territorial sea.[13]

As a result of these tensions among competing rules or principles, and because the factors producing the tensions can always change, some customary rules are quite unstable, with the degree of stability varying from rule to rule.[14] The instability of some customary rules may make them easily subject to change according to changing State interests and consequently changing patterns of State behaviour. It may also make them susceptible to changes in inter-State power relationships, since the ways in which States support their interests are related to the relative abilities of those States to apply power *vis-à-vis* each other.[15] However, within those power relationships, the application of power is qualified by the principle of jurisdiction and, as has already been suggested, the qualifying effects of that principle may be observed when the development, maintenance and

[12] On relative degrees of resistance to change, see pp. 157–60 below.

[13] See pp. 114–20 below. A good expression of this tension in respect of the breadth of the territorial sea follows:

> The limit of this zone [the territorial sea] is . . . commonly recognised as extending to three miles from low-water mark . . . It may, indeed, be that the present limit, in view of modern conditions, needs to be extended; but however desirable such an extension of territorial rights may be for some purposes, it must, until ratified by common usage or international agreement, be regarded as inadmissible, and as an infringement of the principle of the freedom of the sea.

Cobbett (1922) 144 (footnotes omitted). Other rules would also seem to have resulted from the tension between the principle of jurisdiction and the freedom of the seas, the most important of these being the rule concerning the exclusive economic zone. See generally O'Connell (1982) vol. 1, 553–81; and Churchill and Lowe (1988) 133–52. Another example of a customary rule developing out of tension between competing principles may be the rule of restrictive State immunity from jurisdiction. See pp. 57–8 below.

[14] See pp. 157–60 below. In the case of boundary rules instability may render them indeterminate. See pp. 117–18 below.

[15] See pp. 5–6 above.

change of particular customary rules is considered in the light of whether those rules are internal, boundary or external rules.

### *Internal rules*

A State is most powerful within the confines of its own borders. Although States are able to project power outside their borders, the strength of that projected power will normally wane further away from the State, and will generally be weakest within the territories of other States. These differing degrees of power are the result of control over territory, itself directly dependent on power, but that control over territory is legitimised and given effect in the international legal system by the principle of jurisdiction.[16]

Internal rules may be considered as those rules which one State seeks to apply to another State within the first State's jurisdiction. In these situations, States with jurisdiction have a power advantage over States without jurisdiction. This power advantage accrues to States with jurisdiction because they are, in most cases, better able than other States to maintain or alter behaviour patterns in respect of particular legal issues arising within their own territory. Such territorially based control over behaviour patterns may have significant effects on the customary process, especially if a particular legal issue is of such a character that the State practice of greatest relevance to it occurs predominantly within the jurisdiction of those States which have a strong interest in developing, maintaining or changing an associated customary rule.

A good example of an internal rule may be the rule concerning State immunity (or 'sovereign' immunity) from the jurisdiction of foreign courts, a rule which is widely regarded as having changed from an absolute to a restrictive standard over the course of the last century.[17] The tension in this instance, between the principles of jurisdiction and legitimate expectation (in the sense that States cannot be subject to compulsory jurisdiction without their consent),[18] stabilised in favour of the principle of jurisdiction.

The rule of restrictive State immunity would appear to have developed at least partly because the large majority of disputes concerning State

[16] See pp. 53–4 above.

[17] For standard reviews of the history of the State immunity from jurisdiction rule see Sucharitkul (1979); Trooboff (1986); and Jennings and Watts (1992) 341–63. For somewhat different perspectives see Emanuelli (1984); pp. 110–14 below. This study does not consider the related issue of State immunity from execution, as to which see Crawford (1981); and Byers (1995).

[18] See generally Crawford (1981) 852 and 856; and pp. 106–26 and 201 below.

immunity arose within the jurisdiction of States which supported that rule. In short, the States which most strongly supported the rule's development were the relatively small trading States of Western Europe.[19] The relatively large amount of trade occurring in Western Europe meant that the likelihood of disputes over State immunity was greater in these States than in the rest of the world. Moreover, the issue of State immunity would rarely if ever arise in States which accorded absolute immunity to other States, for the simple reason that a State which is being granted immunity has no motive for complaint. Since national court judgments and the results of dispute resolution exercises generally constitute instances of State practice for the purposes of customary international law,[20] these Western European States and their national courts were, by applying restrictive immunity within their borders, thus able to alter the preponderance of State practice in respect of the issue of State immunity worldwide. The principle of jurisdiction thus enabled them to play a notably important role in the development of this particular, generally applicable rule of customary international law.

A second example of an internal rule may involve the attempt by non-industrialised States to change the customary rule concerning the standard of compensation required in cases of expropriation of foreign-owned property. Although their efforts were strongly resisted by more powerful Western industrialised States, the non-industrialised States managed to shift the applicable standard away from that of 'prompt, adequate and effective compensation'.[21] It seems that they were able to do this despite their relative power disadvantages *vis-à-vis* the Western industrialised States at least, in part, because they had jurisdiction in most situations where the issue of compensation for the expropriation of foreign-owned property arose. Western industrialised States have been the traditional source of foreign investment, while many non-industrialised States have experimented with nationalisation as a means of improving their own economic performances. Since the property expropriated in such cases was almost invariably within the territory of a non-industrialised State, the acts of expropriation and therefore the preponderance of State practice in respect of this issue took place within the non-industrialised world. Short of military intervention there was no way in which the Western industrialised States could recover the expropriated property directly.

[19] See pp. 110–14 below. [20] See pp. 133–6 below.

[21] See generally Lillich (1975); Dolzer (1981); Siegel (1985); and Amerasinghe (1992). For a suggestion that the 'prompt, adequate and effective compensation' standard was never a rule of customary international law, see Schachter (1984).

More recently, the collapse of the Soviet Union (a long-time supporter of nationalisation policies in the non-industrialised world and an alternative source of military and developmental assistance generally) has placed the Western industrialised States in a stronger position in terms of foreign direct investment. Increasingly, these States have sought to protect their investments through the negotiation of bilateral investment treaties with individual non-industrialised States, which provide for higher levels of compensation than that available under customary international law. It is possible that the proliferation of these treaties will operate, as State practice, to return the customary standard to 'prompt, adequate and effective compensation',[22] and one could even interpret recent efforts on the part of the Organisation for Economic Co-operation and Development to negotiate a Multilateral Agreement on Investment which contains that formula as an attempt to generate precisely that outcome.[23] However, such a shift would again seem to demonstrate the qualifying effects of the principle of jurisdiction because these treaties may in fact allow Western industrialised States to transfer a significant proportion of the State practice relevant to this rule outside the territories of the non-industrialised States. In other words, the conclusion of an investment treaty constitutes State practice of relevance to the standard of compensation which occurs between rather than within States, and indeed before many of the investments have been committed to the territories of non-industrialised States, and property acquired.

Similarly, international arbitral decisions concerning the standard of compensation for expropriation appear to have shifted the *locus* of adjudication of this issue out of the jurisdiction of non-industrialised States and into the international arena. In this sphere any influence which the non-industrialised States may have over the applicable law is diminished, as is the ability of those States to influence the implementation of the arbitral

[22] See Robinson (1984) 177–8. See also Lillich and Weston (1975) 34–43 (regarding the analogous situation of lump sum agreements). Compare Dolzer (1981) 565–8; Schachter (1984) 126–7; and Amerasinghe (1992) 30. It is also noteworthy that in the 1970 *Barcelona Traction Case (Second Phase)* (note 1, p. 3 above) the International Court of Justice was asked to recognise the existence in international law of procedural rights (for shareholders indirectly injured by damage caused to their company) on the basis of State practice in the form of arbitral decisions and lump sum agreements. The Court responded (at 40 (para. 62)):

> It should be clear that the developments in question have to be viewed as distinctive processes, arising out of circumstances peculiar to the respective situations. To seek to draw from them analogies or conclusions held to be valid in other fields is to ignore their specific character as *lex specialis* and hence to court error.

[23] For the consolidated text, see http://www.oecd.org/daf/cmis/mai/negtext.htm.

decisions. The importance of the principle of jurisdiction in this context is exemplified by the decisions of the Iran–United States Claims Tribunal, in that the tendency of those decisions to favour 'prompt, adequate and effective compensation' may be linked to the fact that the Tribunal was set up primarily to facilitate the release of frozen Iranian assets in Western industrialised States.[24] The *locus* of the implementation of the Tribunal's decisions, as well as the Tribunal's proceedings themselves, are in this sense in the industrialised rather than the non-industrialised world.

### *Boundary rules*

Boundary rules differ from internal rules in that they relate to issues arising at the intersection of a State's jurisdiction with an international or internationalised zone, namely, a part of the earth's surface not under the exclusive jurisdiction of any State. A good example of a boundary rule is the rule concerning the breadth of the territorial sea, which concerns where the territory of a State intersects with the high seas. In boundary rule situations, a State which is in geographic proximity to the area in which the rule is to be applied will usually be in a more powerful position than States which are more distant. This variation in power occurs because the ability to project power derived from some sources, especially military capabilities, is at least partly dependent on geographic proximity.[25] The 'cannon-shot rule' of the nineteenth century, which asserted that a State's territorial sea extended as far as the maximum range of artillery, was but one manifestation of this more general phenomenon.[26]

The advantage held by geographically proximate States in boundary rule situations played an important role in the extension of the territorial sea to twelve nautical miles, in the face of strong opposition from powerful maritime States, notably the United States, the United Kingdom and Japan.[27] In short, it was easier for relatively weak coastal States to enforce claims in respect of the waters directly off their coasts than it was for relatively powerful States to challenge those claims in waters which, for them, were thousands of miles away. Were it not for the effects of the principle of

[24] See Norton (1991) 482–6 and 505.

[25] Power derived from other sources, such as wealth, travels better.

[26] See generally: O'Connell (1982) 134–5 and 151–3; and p. 115 below.

[27] See pp. 114–20 below. Legitimacy, of the general variety described by Franck, pp. 9–10 above, may also have played a role here, in that a coastal State's claim to control over the harvesting of fisheries, the exploitation of seabed minerals and the prevention of pollution in the area involved would seem more legitimate than the claims of distant States.

jurisdiction, the breadth of the territorial sea would almost certainly have remained at three nautical miles.

The advantage held by geographically proximate States in boundary rule situations may also explain why relatively weak States (e.g., Iceland) have been able to play such an important role in the development of new customary rules governing coastal fisheries.[28] Geographic proximity would appear to be particularly advantageous in relation to rules based on continuing economic activity, such as fishing.

In some boundary rule situations international lawyers may actually seek constructively to extend the scope of the principle of jurisdiction, thus enabling it to be used to support legally relevant State practice within the geographic area of contention. A constructive extension of this kind was involved in the 1927 judgment of the Permanent Court of International Justice in the *Lotus Case*.[29] There, an act which occurred on board a French ship on the high seas but which had harmful effects on board a Turkish ship was held to fall within the criminal jurisdiction of a Turkish court. The Permanent Court based its decision on two grounds. First, the Turkish vessel was an extension of the territory of its flag State, which meant that the harmful effects of the act were felt on Turkish territory. The Court wrote: 'A corollary of the principle of the freedom of the seas is that a ship on the high seas is assimilated to the territory of the State the flag of which it flies.'[30] Secondly, an illegal act committed in one State's territory but causing harm in another State's territory fell within the jurisdiction of the second State's national legal system. As the Court explained:

> [T]he courts of many countries . . . interpret criminal law in the sense that offences, the authors of which at the moment of commission are in the territory of another State, are nevertheless to be regarded as having been committed in the national territory, if one of the constituent elements of the offence, and more especially its effects, have taken place there . . . the Court does not know of any cases in which governments have protested against the fact that the criminal law of some country contained a rule to this effect or that the courts of a country construed their criminal law in this sense. Consequently, once it is admitted that the effects of the offence were produced on the Turkish vessel, it becomes impossible to hold that there is a rule of international law which prohibits Turkey from

[28] See, e.g., *Fisheries Jurisdiction Case* (1974) *ICJ Reports* 3. See generally O'Connell (1982) vol. 1, 510–81; and Burke (1994) 1–24. [29] Note 1, p. 3 above.

[30] Note 1, p. 3 above, at 25. The same approach has been taken to aircraft and spacecraft. See, e.g., Art. 3(1) of the 1963 Tokyo Convention on Offences and Certain Other Acts Committed on Board Aircraft, reproduced in (1964) 58 *American Journal of International Law* 566; and Art. 8 of the 1967 Treaty on Principles Governing the Activities of States in the Exploration and Use of Outer Space, 610 UNTS 205, reproduced in (1967) 61 *American Journal of International Law* 644.

prosecuting Lieutenant Demons because of the fact that the author of the offence was on board the French ship.[31]

It is possible that such constructive extensions of the principle of jurisdiction will also qualify the application of power in the process of customary international law. For example, at the time the rule concerning the twelve-mile territorial sea was developing, the presence of merchant vessels flagged by the powerful maritime States in the various zones of contested jurisdiction may have enhanced the involvement of those States in resisting the development of that rule. This increased involvement was possible partly as a result of the first rule set out by the Permanent Court in the *Lotus Case*, namely that international law regards a merchant vessel as part of the territory of its flag State.[32] Aspects of the jurisdictions of powerful maritime States were thus extended to those distant, disputed areas, which increased the opportunities that those States had to make claims and apply countermeasures in response to arrests of their merchant vessels by coastal States.[33]

Moreover, the claims and countermeasures which were based on a constructive extension of the principle of jurisdiction might have had more of an effect on the customary process than similar claims and retaliatory actions would have had in situations where they were not supported, or at least not potentially supported, by international law. In a sense, by basing their actions on a constructive extension of an existing principle, States

[31] Note 1, p. 3 above, at 23. It should be noted that this particular customary rule has since been superseded by treaty rules, as well as a parallel customary rule, to the effect that a flag State has sole penal jurisdiction over most acts committed on board its ships on the high seas. See Art. 1 of the 1952 Brussels Convention for the Unification of Certain Rules Relating to Penal Jurisdiction, 439 UNTS 233; Art. 11(1) of the 1958 Geneva Convention on the High Seas, 450 UNTS 2; and Art. 97 of the Law of the Sea Convention, note 29, p. 41 above. The exceptions to this new rule concern acts committed by non-nationals, with the State of nationality having concurrent jurisdiction over such acts, and acts which attract universal jurisdiction. On universal jurisdiction see p. 64 below. The Court's decision may also have been influenced by the fact that the accused was, at the time of its judgment, physically present in Turkey. In international criminal law custody over the accused is frequently decisive. See, e.g., 1961–62 *Eichmann Case* (1968) 36 ILR 5 (District Court of Jerusalem), 277 (Supreme Court of Israel); *US* v. *Alvarez-Machain*, 119 L Ed 2d 441 (1992), (1992) 31 ILM 900.

[32] See p. 61 above. The concept of diplomatic protection also played an important role. See pp. 79–82 below. On the development of the twelve-mile territorial sea as a rule of customary international law, see generally pp. 114–20 below.

[33] See, e.g., Loring (1970–71); and Jónsson (1982). Countermeasures involve the legal, reciprocal imposition of detrimental effects by one State upon the interests of another State which has violated, or is violating, international law. See generally Zoller (1984). The issue of what limits exist on countermeasures has been the subject of much debate in the International Law Commission. See, e.g., Symposium (1994); Gaetano Arangio-Ruiz, *Seventh Report on State Responsibility*, 9 May 1995, UN Doc. A/CN.4/469 (with addenda: 24 and 29 May 1995).

were acting within an accepted conceptual framework of legality and thus building, by analogy, on similar specific rules of international law, rather than attempting to develop an entirely new rule.

The rule that a merchant vessel is part of the territory of its flag State may also have reinforced certain interests held by the States which were making claims or applying countermeasures, or at least assisted in the identification of such interests. The States participating in the development of this particular customary rule had, by creating such a close conceptual link between a vessel and its flag State, indicated a strong interest in the activities of their own merchant vessels – activities which in this case required unrestricted navigation in the waters between three and twelve nautical miles offshore. And though State interests will usually be indicated through behaviour which follows those interests directly, additional indications of this kind may sometimes play an important role. Among other things, State practice which is not supported by a rule is more likely to have been engaged in gratuitously, or in support of a less direct or less important interest. Moreover, it is possible that States will increasingly identify their interests with such a rule, once it comes into being, so that the existence of the rule reinforces the interests associated with it.[34] In any given situation a principle of international law may work to the benefit of more than one State or group of States, thus making it difficult to analyse effects which may, in some situations, even work to cancel each other out.

This increased ability to participate in the customary process as it concerned the breadth of the territorial sea was, as has already been suggested, particularly important to the powerful maritime States because many of the areas of contention were located a great distance away from them. However, the presence of foreign-flagged merchant vessels in those areas may have enabled coastal States to participate more effectively in the customary process as well. They could enforce their own national laws by arresting those vessels rather than just making claims to extended territorial waters.[35]

A variety of other constructive extensions of the principle of jurisdiction may be used in similar fashion to enable States to prosecute individuals who, for one reason or another, are within their custody even though the offence in question was committed outside the territory of the prosecuting State. First, the 'passive personality principle' is sometimes asserted as a ground for jurisdiction when an extraterritorial act has caused harm to a national of the State which is

[34] See, e.g., the discussion of 'sunk costs', at p. 108 below.
[35] See, e.g., Loring (1970–71); and Jónsson (1982).

exercising jurisdiction.[36] The national is, for this purpose, treated as a manifestation of that State abroad. Secondly, the 'protective principle' is sometimes used to support extraterritorial jurisdiction over activities which are prejudicial to the security interests of the State.[37] It is the State which is in some way threatened, even if the threat comes from abroad. Thirdly, the 'nationality principle' is sometimes used to support extraterritorial jurisdiction over acts committed by nationals of the State which is exercising jurisdiction.[38] The national is again, for this purpose, treated as a manifestation of that State abroad.

Although one could in each instance regard the link between the ground on which extraterritorial jurisdiction is asserted and the offence in question as a rationalisation of State interest, the point is that the interests of a State in exercising jurisdiction are usually rooted in its territorial self. This enables States, when seeking to justify specific assertions of jurisdiction through constructive extensions of that principle, to act within an accepted conceptual framework of legality and to build, by analogy, upon other similar rules of international law – rather than attempting to develop an entirely new rule.

Even the 'principle of universal jurisdiction' might be regarded as such a constructive extension.[39] Universal jurisdiction, which is sometimes said to be available in respect of piracy, war crimes, crimes against humanity, hijacking and the sabotage of aircraft, means that every State has jurisdiction, within its territory or on the high seas, in respect of these activities regardless of where they occur and the nationality of the persons involved in them.[40] In short, if States have accepted the idea of universal jurisdiction, they have done so because these activities pose a threat to each and every State, thus justifying a global extension of the principle of jurisdiction to all areas not covered by another State's jurisdiction (in the unextended, strictly territorial sense of that term).

[36] See generally Mexico's position in *Cutting's Case* (1886), as reflected in (1906) 2 Moore 228–42; *Eichmann Case*, note 31, p. 62 above, at 50–7 and 304; Bishop (1965) 324; and Akehurst (1972–73) 162–6.

[37] Such activities might include terrorism, espionage, sedition or the counterfeiting of currency. See generally *Rocha* v. *US*, 288 F. 2d 545 (9th Cir. 1961), 32 ILR 112; Sahovic and Bishop (1968) 362–5; Akehurst (1972–3) 157–9; and Bowett (1982a) 10–11.

[38] See, e.g., Art. 4(b) of the Tokyo Convention on Offences and Certain Other Acts Committed on Board Aircraft, note 30, p. 61 above. See generally: Harvard Research Project (1935) 523–35; Akehurst (1972–3) 156–7; and Bowett (1982a) 7–10. In some national legal systems the nationality principle has also been used in the context of civil actions. See the discussion of Arts. 14 and 15 of the French *Code Civil* at p. 73 below.

[39] See Bowett (1982a) 11–14; Rubin (1988); and Rubin (1997).

[40] See, e.g., Akehurst (1972–3) 160–6. Compare Bowett (1982a) 11–14, who, after an extensive review of the evidence, concluded that universal jurisdiction only exists with regard to piracy. Rubin (1988 and 1997) argued that universal jurisdiction over piracy (and slave trading) is never exercised.

*External rules*

External rules involve restrictions which some States seek to impose on the freedom of other States to act within those other States' own territories. In these situations the States seeking to impose the restrictions are at a power disadvantage because they do not have jurisdiction. International human rights provide an example of this. Motivated in part by applications of power devolved from moral authority, States have either participated or acquiesced in the creation of a multitude of rules concerning such rights. Many States have consented to the application of treaty-based review and individual petition procedures. However, apart from a few small (but nonetheless significant) developments, such as the Resolution 1503 procedure of the United Nations Human Rights Commission (which allows the Commission to consider situations involving gross violations, as revealed in communications to it)[41] and the establishment of United Nations special rapporteurs for a number of subjects,[42] mechanisms to facilitate the application of international human rights within the territories of non-consenting States have not been developed.[43] The ability of non-consenting States to control behaviour patterns within their own territories is a formidable barrier to those who seek to create rules of customary international law which provide effective protection to all human beings.

Another example of an external rule may concern attempts by United States courts, and later the United States Congress, to prescribe and enforce laws concerning restrictive business practices ('anti-trust' regulations) directed at the territories of other States.[44] These attempts, which initially relied on generous interpretations of internally directed anti-trust legislation,[45] were justified on a basis similar to the second rule identified by the Permanent Court of International Justice in the *Lotus Case*, namely that an illegal act committed in one State's territory but causing harm in another State's territory falls within the jurisdiction of the second State's national legal system.[46] For example, in *United States* v. *Aluminum Co. of America* the United States Federal Court of Appeals, Second Circuit, stated: '[A]ny state may impose liabilities, even upon persons not within

[41] See generally Steiner and Alston (1996) 374–88.
[42] There are currently United Nations special rapporteurs on disappearances, summary executions and torture, and since 1993 there has been a High Commissioner for Human Rights with a similar, albeit broader, mandate. See generally Lord (1995).
[43] See pp. 43–5 above.
[44] See generally: Jennings (1957); Sornarajah (1982); Meesen (1984); and Roth (1992).
[45] The relevant legislation included the Sherman Antitrust Act (1890) 15 USC sections 1–7; and the Wilson Tariff Act (1894) 15 USC section 8.
[46] See pp. 61–2 above; and Bowett (1982a) 7.

its allegiance, for conduct outside its borders that has consequences within its borders which the state reprehends.'[47]

These attempts to prescribe and enforce anti-trust regulations extraterritorially were strongly opposed by other States, as were associated efforts to collect evidence abroad and the frequent awarding of triple damages to plaintiffs in such cases.[48]

In response to this opposition, courts in the United States introduced various balancing tests for the determination of extraterritorial jurisdiction. These tests were based, to some degree, on concepts such as comity.[49] For example, in *Timberlane Lumber Co.* v. *Bank of America* the United States Federal Court of Appeals, Ninth Circuit applied the following three-part test:

> Does the alleged restraint affect, or was it intended to affect, the foreign commerce of the United States? Is it of such a type and magnitude so as to be cognizable as a violation of the Sherman Act? As a matter of international comity and fairness, should the extraterritorial jurisdiction of the United States be asserted to cover it?[50]

The United States Congress soon followed suit by enacting the 1982 Foreign Antitrust Improvements Act, which prescribes that United States anti-trust laws will apply only if the conduct in question has 'a direct, substantial, and reasonably foreseeable effect' on United States commerce.[51] However, even these modified approaches to extraterritorial jurisdiction were heavily criticised by other States, and by scholars from other States.[52]

A number of States responded to attempts to impose anti-trust regula-

[47] 148 F. 2d 416, 443 (1945). See also *US* v. *Timken Roller Bearing Co.*, 83 F. Supp. 284 (ND Ohio, ED 1949), affirmed 341 US 593 (1951); *US* v. *Watchmakers of Switzerland*, 133 F. Supp. 40 and 134 F. Supp. 710 (SDNY 1955), 22 ILR 168; *US* v. *General Electric Co.*, 82 F. Supp. 753 (D. New Jersey 1949) and 115 F. Supp. 835 (D. New Jersey 1953); *Hazeltine Research Inc.* v. *Zenith Radio Corp.*, 239 F. Supp. 51 (ND Illinois, ED 1965), affirmed 395 US 100 (1969).

[48] See, e.g., *Report of the 51st Conference of the International Law Association, Tokyo* (1964) 565–92; the statement of the Attorney-General of the UK in *Rio Tinto Zinc Corp.* v. *Westinghouse Electric Corp.* [1978] 2 WLR 81, 93–4.

[49] On comity as a legal concept (as developed in the US through the work of Joseph Story) and its relationship to customary international law, see Baker (1993) 492–8. For a different view, see Macalister-Smith (1992).

[50] 549 F. 2d 597, 615 (1976); 66 ILR 270, 286. See also *Mannington Mills* v. *Congoleum Corporation*, 595 F. 2d 1287, 1301–2 (3d Cir. 1979), 66 ILR 487, 500–1; letter of 27 September 1979, US Department of State to Senate Committee on the Judiciary, reproduced in (1980) 74 *American Journal of International Law* 179, excerpted in Bowett (1982a) 21; *Third Restatement of Foreign Relations Law of the United States* (1987) vol. 1, sections 403 and 415.

[51] *Public Law* 97–290, Title IV, section 402; 96 Stat. 1246; 15 USC section 6a.

[52] See, e.g., Bowett (1982a) 21–2; and Marston (1985) 479–83. For criticism from a United States scholar, see Maier (1983); and Maier (1984).

tions and gather evidence extraterritorially by introducing 'blocking statutes'. For example, under the United Kingdom's 1980 Protection of Trading Interests Act a United Kingdom national or resident may sue for the recovery of multiple damages paid under the judgment of a foreign court which has acted extraterritorially, and the Secretary of State may prohibit the production of documents or other information to the courts or authorities of a foreign State.[53] Blocking statutes, as assertions of the power advantage that is conferred by jurisdiction over territory, have in most instances discouraged United States courts from engaging in further attempts to exercise extraterritorial jurisdiction over unfair business practices without the authorisation of the territorial State. They have also led to a series of international agreements concerning the prevention of unfair business practices.[54] The history of attempts by United States courts and the United States Congress to prescribe, adjudicate and enforce anti-trust regulations extraterritorially would thus seem to provide another example of how the principle of jurisdiction plays a role in external rule situations, by qualifying the application of power in the process of customary international law. Were it not for the principle of jurisdiction, there would have been far less incentive for the United States to compromise on this effort to exercise jurisdiction abroad.

A similar situation may exist today in respect of the United States' Cuban Liberty and Democratic Solidarity (LIBERTAD) Act of 1996 (Helms–Burton Act)[55] and Iran and Libya Sanctions Act of 1996 (D'Amato Act).[56] Among other things, Title III of the Helms–Burton Act

[53] Chapter 11, reproduced in: (1982) 21 ILM 840; Lowe (1983a) 187. For commentary see Lowe (1981). See also the Foreign Antitrust Judgments (Restriction of Enforcement) Act 1979, reproduced in (1979) 18 ILM 869 (Australia); the Foreign Extraterritorial Measures Act, SC 1984, c.49, reproduced in (1985) 24 ILM 794 (Canada); the Economic Competition Act, No. 413, 28 June 1956, as Amended by Act of 16 July 1958, reproduced in Lowe (1983a) 123 (the Netherlands); the Act to Restrict Enforcement of Certain Foreign Judgments, Arbitration Awards and Letters of Request (Protection of Business Act) 1978, reproduced in (1979) 18 ILM 127 (South Africa); Loi relative à la communication de documents et renseignements d'ordre économique, commercial ou technique à des personnes physiques ou morales étrangères, No. 80–538, 16 July 1980, (1980) 1 *Gazette du Palais* 484 (France).

[54] See, e.g., Canada–United States Memorandum of Understanding on Anti-Trust Laws (1984), reproduced in (1984) 23 ILM 275; Federal Republic of Germany–United States: Agreement Relating to Mutual Cooperation Regarding Restrictive Business Practices (1976), reproduced in Lowe (1983a) 228; Australia–United States: Agreement Relating to Cooperation on Antitrust Matters (1982), reproduced in (1982) 21 ILM 702; UNGA Res. 35/63 of 5 December 1980, adopting the Set of Multilaterally Agreed Equitable Principles and Rules for the Control of Restrictive Business Practices, reproduced in Lowe (1983a) 256. However, the US Supreme Court judgment in *Hartford Fire Insurance Co.* v. *California*, 113 S. Ct 2891 (1993) may lead to violations of those agreements. See Robertson and Demetriou (1994).

[55] Public Law 104-114 of 12 March 1996, reproduced in (1996) 35 ILM 357.

[56] Public Law 104-172, 5 August 1996, reproduced in (1996) 35 ILM 1273.

enables United States nationals to institute proceedings in United States courts against foreign individuals or companies 'trafficking' in property expropriated in Cuba,[57] while the D'Amato Act allows for the imposition of sanctions on individuals or companies participating in the development of petroleum resources in either Iran or Libya. Both pieces of legislation have attracted widespread opposition from other States. For example, the European Union has issued a number of formal protests against the Helms–Burton Act,[58] while Canada has announced that it will introduce legislation under the Foreign Extraterritorial Measures Act 1985 in order to protect Canadian companies.[59] Moreover, the General Assembly of the Organisation of American States asked that organisation's Inter-American Juridical Committee to examine the Helms–Burton Act, whereupon the committee concluded:

> A prescribing state does not have the rights to exercise jurisdiction over acts of 'trafficking' abroad by aliens under circumstances where neither the alien nor the conduct in question has any connection with its territory and where no apparent connection exists between such acts and the protection of its essential interests.[60]

Although the disputes over the Helms–Burton Act and the D'Amato Act have yet to be resolved, the President of the United States has already compromised in one significant way. He has repeatedly suspended Title III of the Helms–Burton Act, thus denying United States nationals the option of suing foreign nationals and companies in United States courts for 'trafficking' in property expropriated in Cuba. This compromise, like the compromises made in respect of extraterritorial anti-trust measures, recognises the power advantage held by territorial States as a result of the principle of jurisdiction, which facilitates effective blocking or retaliatory action. These various examples thus demonstrate that in some situations, especially those involving external rules, the principle of jurisdiction renders relatively weak and ineffective those States which are, in other contexts, relatively powerful.

[57] Section 4 of the Act defines trafficking to include when a person 'knowingly and intentionally . . . Sells, transfers, distributes, dispenses, brokers, manages, or otherwise disposes of confiscated property, or purchases, leases, receives, possesses, obtains control of, manages, uses or otherwise acquires or holds an interest in confiscated property . . . [or] engages in a commercial activity using or otherwise benefiting from confiscated property'. [58] See (1996) 35 ILM 397.

[59] Ministry of Foreign Affairs and International Trade (Canada), Press Release No. 115, 17 June 1996.

[60] *Opinion of the Inter-American Juridical Committee on Resolution AG/Doc. 3375/96 'Freedom of Trade and Investment in the Hemisphere'*, CJI/SO/II/doc.67/96 rev.5, 23 August 1996, reproduced in (1996) 35 ILM 1328, 1333. The European Union, Canada and Mexico also threatened to challenge the Helms–Burton Act and the D'Amato Act in the World Trade Organisation and under the North American Free Trade Agreement.

## Jurisdiction by analogy

There is at least one other way in which the principle of jurisdiction may qualify the application of power within the customary process. The exercise of jurisdiction by national legal systems over certain issues would seem to encourage, and thus qualify, the development, maintenance or change of rules of customary international law concerning jurisdiction over related or analogous issues. This phenomenon would appear to be at least partly responsible for a territorial limitation, in the customary international law of State immunity, on the authority of national courts to assert jurisdiction over non-commercial torts (i.e., breaches of legal duties not involving contracts, which have, for example, caused personal injury or damage to or loss of tangible property) committed by foreign States. It seems that no such limitations exist in respect of actions arising out of commercial activities.

Most national legislation on the subject of State immunity places no territorial restriction on the exercise of jurisdiction over commercial activities engaged in by foreign States. For example, Article 5 of the 1982 Canadian State Immunity Act states simply: 'A foreign state is not immune from the jurisdiction of a court in any proceedings that relate to any commercial activity of the foreign state.'[61]

Similarly, the only multilateral treaty on the subject, the 1972 European Convention on State Immunity, does not contain any territorial limitation on the exercise of jurisdiction over commercial activities.[62] Article 10(1) of the International Law Commission's Draft Articles on Jurisdictional Immunities of States and their Property, which was drafted after an extensive review of State practice, reads:

> If a State engages in a commercial transaction with a foreign natural or juridical person and, by virtue of the applicable rules of private international law, differences relating to the commercial transaction fall within the jurisdiction of a court of another State, the State cannot invoke immunity from that jurisdiction in a proceeding arising out of that commercial transaction.[63]

[61] Act to Provide for State Immunity in Canadian Courts, c. 95 (1982), reproduced in (1982) 21 ILM 798. See also the State Immunity Act 1978, c. 33 (1978), reproduced in (1978) 17 ILM 1123 (UK); and the Foreign States Immunities Act 1985, No. 196 (1985), reproduced in (1986) 25 ILM 715 (Australia).

[62] (1972 II) UKTS 74; reproduced in (1972) 11 ILM 470.

[63] *Report of the ILC on the Work of its 43rd Session* (1991) 2(2) *Yearbook of the International Law Commission* 12, 33; reproduced (without the commentary found in the *Yearbook of the International Law Commission*) in (1991) 30 ILM 1565, 1568. See also Art.III.B of the ILA 'Buenos Aires Revised Draft Articles for a Convention on State Immunity', in *Report of the 66th Conference*, note 11, p. 55 above , at 488, 490.

The territorial scope of jurisdiction in this context is therefore left to be determined according to the regular jurisdictional rules of the forum State.[64]

The one possible exception to this general pattern is section 1605(a)(2) of the 1976 United States Foreign Sovereign Immunities Act (FSIA), which reads, *inter alia*:

> A foreign state shall not be immune from the jurisdiction of courts of the United States or of the States in any case in which the action is based . . . upon an act outside the territory of the United States in connection with a commercial activity of the foreign state elsewhere *and that act causes a direct effect in the United States.*[65]

However, this limitation on the exercise of jurisdiction is not a territorial limitation, strictly speaking, since it does not preclude the assertion of jurisdiction over actions occurring outside the United States *simply* because of where those actions occur. Moreover, it does not reflect customary international law. Not only is it an exception to the general trend in State practice, but all other State immunity statutes were introduced subsequent to, and following careful consideration of, the FSIA. It was introduced for reasons specific to the United States, namely to bring the unusually relaxed jurisdictional rules applied by United States courts into line with the jurisdictional rules of other national legal systems, within the specific context of actions against foreign States.

In contrast, all State immunity statutes contain territorial limitations on the exercise of jurisdiction over foreign States with regard to non-commercial torts. For example, section 1605(a)(5) of the FSIA reads:

> A foreign state shall not be immune from the jurisdiction of courts of the United States or of the States in any case . . . in which money damages are sought against a foreign state for personal injury or death, or damage to or loss of property, *occurring in the United States* . . .[66]

Similarly, Article 11 of the European Convention on State Immunity reads:

> A Contracting State cannot claim immunity from the jurisdiction of a court of another Contracting State in proceedings which relate to redress for injury to the person or damage to tangible property, *if the facts which occasioned the injury or*

[64] See generally: Crawford (1983) 90–2.

[65] 28 USC sections 1330, 1602–11 (1976); reproduced in (1976) 15 ILM 1388, 1389 (emphasis added). On the issue of direct effect in State immunity, see generally Crawford (1983) 90–2.

[66] *Ibid.* See also Art. 5 of the State Immunity Act 1978, note 61, p. 69 above (UK); Art. 13 of the Foreign States Immunities Act 1985, note 61, p. 69 above (Australia); and Art. 6 of the Act to Provide for State Immunity in Canadian Courts, note 61, p. 69 above.

*damage occurred in the territory of the State of the forum, and if the author of the injury or damage was present in that territory at the time when those facts occurred.*[67]

Article 12 of the International Law Commission's Draft Articles on Jurisdictional Immunities of States and their Property reads:

Unless otherwise agreed between the States concerned, a State cannot invoke immunity from jurisdiction before a court of another State which is otherwise competent in a proceeding which relates to pecuniary compensation for death or injury to the person, or damage to or loss of tangible property, caused by an act or omission which is alleged to be attributable to the State, if the act or omission occurred in whole or in part *in the territory of that other State and if the author of the act or omission was present in that territory at the time of the act or omission.*[68]

The only exception to this general pattern is Article III.F.2 of the International Law Association's Revised Buenos Aires Draft Articles for a Convention on State Immunity, which introduced a 'direct effect' test for jurisdiction over non-commercial torts committed by foreign States outside of the forum State.[69] Article III.F.2 was, however, rather controversial in the Working Session of the ILA's Committee on State Immunity.[70] It may therefore be that customary international law, in contrast to its treatment of commercial activities, does not allow for the exercise of jurisdiction over non-commercial torts committed by foreign States outside of the territory of the forum State.

There are at least two possible explanations for this apparent difference in what customary international law permits in terms of jurisdictional scope over foreign States with regard to commercial activities and non-commercial torts. First, commercial activities generally occur on the basis of consensual, contractual relations. This means that the definition of what constitutes a breach of a legal obligation has been spelled out, at least to some degree, by the parties in advance of any subsequent dispute. In contrast, non-commercial torts are usually non-consensual and involve some kind of injury to an individual who has not willingly assumed that risk. The definition of breach has not been the subject of prior agreement, which means that the task of defining the breach and protecting the non-consenting victim, is left to the national legal system concerned.

In the absence of any consensual basis for defining what constitutes a non-commercial tort in any particular situation, that definitional exercise is closely tied to the national legal system's particular conception of 'public policy'. This link between tort law and public policy would also

[67] Note 62, p. 69 above (emphasis added).

[68] Note 63, p. 69 above, at 44 (emphasis added).

[69] Note 63, p. 69 above, at 491.

[70] *Report of the 66th Conference*, note 11, p. 55 above, at 500.

appear to account for the close connection between recovery in tort and statutory compensation schemes.[71]

Conceptions of public policy vary greatly among States, which means that the risks of subjective, culturally specific assertions of jurisdiction are greater with regard to laws concerning non-commercial torts than they are with regard to laws concerning commercial activities. The existence of such greater risks and the fact that the assertion of jurisdiction over a foreign State in this context involves applying one State's conceptions of public policy to another State, may help to explain the general reluctance of national legislatures and courts to bring the rules on State immunity for non-commercial torts into line with those rules which apply to cases concerning commercial activities.[72]

Another possible explanation for the apparent difference in what customary international law permits in terms of jurisdictional scope over foreign States, as between commercial activities and non-commercial torts, involves the existence, or non-existence, of an accepted basis for jurisdiction in analogous situations in other areas of law.

The courts and legislatures of many States have long exercised jurisdiction over non-State commercial activities engaged in outside their territory, on the basis of limited connections between those extraterritorial activities and the forum State. In contrast, those same courts and legislatures have, for the most part, been reluctant to exercise jurisdiction over non-State torts, especially torts involving personal injury or damage to or loss of tangible property, unless the defendant is domiciled in the forum State or the tort was committed within that State's territory.[73] Exceptions to this state of affairs, such as some recent applications of the United States Alien Tort Statute and the enactment of the United States Torture

[71] See generally Harris *et al.* (1984).

[72] It may be that *some* delictual acts are considered wrong in all or most national legal systems as well as in international law, and that immunity may consequently be lifted in respect of such extraterritorial activities on the basis of an *international* public policy exception. For instance, on the basis of this approach, a foreign State which engaged in torture might not be entitled to State immunity in customary international law in respect of that activity, regardless of the territorial limitation which would otherwise have precluded the exercise of jurisdiction by a national court. See *Controller and Auditor-General* v. *Sir Ronald Davison* [1996] 2 NZLR 278, (1997) 26 ILM 721, where the New Zealand Court of Appeal supported a similar approach in respect of tax evasion. This approach might also prove useful in interpreting the otherwise unambiguous territorial limitations in State immunity statutes (see note 61, p. 69 above), although this argument was rejected by the English Court of Appeal in *Al-Adsani* v. *Government of Kuwait* [1996] *Times Law Reports* 192, (1996) 67 *British Yearbook of International Law* 535.

[73] See generally 'Report of the Committee on International Civil and Commercial Litigation', in *Report of the 66th Conference*, note 11, p. 55 above, at 600. See also *Re Union Carbide Corp. Gas Plant Disaster at Bhopal, India*, 809 F. 2d 195 (2d Cir. 1987), cert. denied 484 US 871 (1987).

Victim Protection Act of 1991, are relatively new and isolated developments.[74]

For example, under the common law, English courts have jurisdiction in any case where the defendant was served with the writ or equivalent document within England.[75] This means that it is relatively easy to sue a company if it conducts business in England, even if the activities giving rise to the action occurred abroad.[76] In contrast, defendants in tort actions which are not related to commercial activities, but which concern, for example, personal injury or damage to or loss of tangible property suffered abroad, are much less likely to be present within the jurisdiction. Similarly, the Rules of the Supreme Court (of England and Wales) allow for the possibility of service abroad in any case concerning a contract which 'is by its terms, or by implication, governed by English law'.[77] Service abroad for tort actions may only be available if 'the claim is founded on a tort and the damage was sustained, or resulted from an act committed, within the jurisdiction'.[78]

In France, the *Code Civil* grants jurisdiction to French courts in any case which concerns a contract involving a French national, regardless of whether the national in question is the plaintiff or the defendant.[79] There is no similar provision in the *Code Civil* concerning delicts (i.e., torts).

The result of this general situation is that judges and legislators in many States have become accustomed to the idea of exercising extraterritorial

[74] The Alien Tort Statute was originally enacted as the Judiciary Act of 1789, c. 20, section 9(b), 1 Stat. 73, 77. See currently 28 USC section 1350. Key cases extending the reach of the statute extraterritorially include *Filartiga* v. *Pena-Irala*, 630 F. 2d 876 (2d Cir. 1980) (see, for commentary, Burley (1989)); and *Kadic* v. *Karadzic* (1995) 34 ILM 1595 (2d Cir.). The Torture Victim Protection Act, which put the decision in *Filartiga* into legislative form, is found at *Public Law* 102–256; 106 Stat. 73; 28 USC section 1350.

[75] See, e.g., *Colt Industries* v. *Sarlie (No. 1)* [1966] 1 WLR 440; and *Maharanee of Baroda* v. *Wildenstein* [1972] 2 QB 283 (Court of Appeal). This rule has since been modified within a treaty context among the States parties to the 1968 Brussels Convention on Jurisdiction and the Enforcement of Judgments in Civil and Commercial Matters and the 1988 Lugano Convention on Jurisdiction and the Enforcement of Judgments in Civil and Commercial Matters. Reproduced in *Court of Justice of the European Communities* (1992) Annexes 1 and 2. [76] See Collier (1994) 89.

[77] Order 11, rule 1(1)(d)(iii). [78] *Ibid.*, rule 1(1)(f).

[79] *Code Civil* (Paris: Dalloz, 1995), Arts. 14 and 15. Art. 14 reads:

> L'étranger, même non résidant en France, pourra être cité devant les tribunaux français, pour l'exécution des obligations par lui contractées en France avec un Français; il pourra être traduit devant les tribunaux de France, pour les obligations par lui contractées en pays étranger envers des Français.

Art. 15 reads:

> Un Français pourra être traduit devant un tribunal de France, pour des obligations par lui contractées en pays étranger, même avec un étranger.

For criticism of Art. 14 see Delaume (1953) 57; and Mann (1964) 79–81.

jurisdiction in the context of commercial activities, but not in similar situations involving personal injury or damage to or loss of tangible property. Thus, they may find it easier to apply the rationale behind restrictive State immunity – that a State acting like a private party should be treated like a private party – to assert jurisdiction extraterritorially over commercial activities engaged in by foreign States, than to exercise jurisdiction over non-commercial torts committed by those same States abroad. Since national court judgments and legislation have been the principal forms of State practice in the area of State immunity, this factor – the encouragement of jurisdictional extension by analogy – may therefore have had some influence on the development, maintenance or change of customary rules here. In other words, the current state of the law on State immunity and non-commercial torts may not be solely the result of what States perceive, and are able to manifest, their interests to be. This suggests yet another qualifying effect of the principle of jurisdiction on applications of power in the process of customary international law.

# 5 The principle of personality

When used in a legal sense, the term 'personality' usually refers to the *capacity* of an individual or entity to hold rights and be subject to obligations within a particular legal system. But personality, like jurisdiction, may be more than just something which is objectively determinable. It may also be a *requirement* or, in some cases, an *entitlement*, and to the degree that it is either or that it subsumes more specific requirements or entitlements within the international legal system, it may be considered a principle of international law.[1]

For example, different degrees of personality may exist within any legal system, in that some individuals or entities may be able, required or entitled to hold more rights or be subject to more obligations than others. Among these, an individual or entity with full legal personality is *capable* of holding as many rights and being subject to as many obligations as any other individual or entity within the legal system. But in a legal system in which the same individuals or entities are both subjects and creators of the law, having full legal personality also means that the individual or entity in question is formally *entitled* to participate in the relevant processes of law creation to the same extent as any other individual or entity.[2] In the international legal system the principle of personality has the consequence that only those individuals or entities which have international legal personality are entitled to participate in the process of customary international law, and only those individuals or entities which have full international legal personality are entitled to participate fully in that process.

Within the international legal system, States are usually considered to be the only holders of full legal personality. In principle, all States have the same degree of legal personality, and in that sense all States are formally equal. Consequently all States, from the weakest to the most powerful, have an equal entitlement to participate in the process of customary international law.[3]

[1] For a discussion of jurisdiction as a principle of international law, see pp. 53–4 above.
[2] See pp. 35–40 above. [3] See pp. 35–40 above.

This equal entitlement may immediately act to qualify the application of power by States, because the supporting and opposing practice of less powerful States is considered together with that of more powerful States when determining the existence and content of individual customary rules. Large numbers of less powerful States might, if behaving in unison, sometimes be able to engage in enough practice to develop, maintain or change customary rules even if the more powerful States are opposed to that happening. It would seem that such a situation existed during the development of the rule concerning the twelve-mile territorial sea: the powerful maritime States were so vastly outnumbered by less powerful States that their opposition to that rule failed to prevent its development.[4] Similarly, attempts by Western industrialised States to prevent a change in the standard of compensation required for the expropriation of foreign-owned property were probably ineffective at least partly because of the large number of less powerful States which supported that change.[5]

One of the best examples of a customary rule which developed at least partly because of a numerical advantage on the part of less powerful States is the right of self-determination in the context of decolonisation. In this instance an ever-growing number of relatively less powerful States was able to expand the scope of a rule despite the fact that many of the more powerful States were initially opposed to that expansion.[6]

This particular, numerically based qualifying effect of the principle of personality may be greatest when the practice leading to the development, maintenance or change of a rule is the sort of practice in which less powerful States easily engage. In particular, rules which are developed, maintained or changed largely or entirely as a result of statements may be more open to the participation of less powerful States than rules which are largely or entirely the result of acts. It may be partly for this reason that relatively less powerful States have been able to play an influential role in the development, maintenance or change of customary rules in the field of international human rights.[7]

Another qualifying effect of the principle of personality may be found in the context of recognition. Recognition is the process whereby States formally acknowledge that other entities are States, and that they therefore have full international legal personality.[8] Unrecognised and largely

[4] See pp. 60–6 above and 114–20 below. It is noteworthy that the powerful maritime States did not themselves act *en bloc*. [5] See pp. 58–60 above.

[6] See generally Eagleton (1953); Umozurike (1972); and Gayim (1990), especially 36–9.

[7] See pp. 43–5 above.

[8] States will sometimes also recognise new governments. See generally Frowein (1987); and, on the recognition of States, Crawford (1979) 10–25. To the degree that this book considers recognition, it confines itself to the recognition of States.

unrecognised States do have some rights and are subject to some obligations – as States – under international law.[9] But though they are able to participate in the international legal system, they are usually unable to do so to the same extent as recognised States. Among other things, they are generally not admitted to international organisations, and, if they are admitted, they are usually not allowed to participate to the same degree as widely recognised States.[10] This prevents unrecognised and largely unrecognised States from contributing, or at least limits their ability to contribute, to the negotiation and adoption of resolutions and declarations within those organisations. And this in turn may reduce their ability to participate in the process of customary international law, at least if one considers resolutions and declarations of international organisations to be instances of State practice for the purposes of that process.[11]

Moreover, the fact that unrecognised and largely unrecognised States do not generally have diplomatic representation in other States means that their positions concerning the development, maintenance and change of particular customary rules may not always be made clear. In such instances their supporting and opposing practice may escape being considered alongside that of other States. The fact that the acts and statements of unrecognised and largely unrecognised States are frequently excluded from the customary process is thus one additional way in which the principle of personality qualifies applications of power within the process of customary international law.

A similar situation may exist in respect of new States. By definition, a new State has never enjoyed full international legal personality and therefore has not previously been able to participate fully, if at all, in the customary process. The question therefore arises as to whether the new State is bound by customary rules which developed before it became a participant in that process, or whether, in fact, it is bound by that process at all.[12] The best answer to this question might be that the new State, by participating in the customary process and relying on customary rules, is implicitly consenting to that process as well as to all of the customary rules which have previously been developed through it.[13] This is not as unjust as it might seem, since by becoming a participant in the customary process the new State puts itself in a position where it can work to change

[9] See generally Jennings and Watts (1992) 197–203.

[10] See, e.g., UNGA Res. 2024 (XX) (concerning the refusal to admit Rhodesia to the United Nations in 1965); UNGA Res. 3237 (XXIX) (concerning the granting of observer status in the General Assembly to the Palestine Liberation Organisation in 1974); and Higgins (1994) 43.

[11] See pp. 40–3 above and pp. 133–6 and 156–7 below.

[12] See p. 145 below. [13] See D'Amato (1971) 42; pp. 142–6 below.

those customary rules with which it does not agree.[14] Nevertheless, by contributing to a situation in which pre-existing rules apply to new States, the principle of personality might here be regarded as qualifying, yet again, the application of power in the process of customary international law. It is likely that all new States, no matter how powerful, will initially be constrained by at least some rules with which they do not agree, and that some degree of sustained effort will be required on their part if they are to change those rules to their own advantage.

Perhaps the most obvious way in which the principle of personality qualifies the application of power is by imposing limits on who can participate in the customary process. It is due to the principle of personality that States are the principal, if not the exclusive, *direct* participants in the process of customary international law.

International organisations do play an increasing role in the customary process, as is demonstrated by their contributions in the human rights field. They adopt resolutions and declarations, and in some cases engage in enforcement actions. For some purposes they are even recognised as having a degree of international legal personality.[15] However, the role of international organisations in the customary process would seem in most respects to be a collective role played by their member States. When, for example, the United Nations General Assembly adopts a resolution, it is not the United Nations which is engaging in legally relevant behaviour, but rather its individual, vote-casting member States.[16]

Other entities, and individuals, are excluded from the customary process to an even greater degree. These other entities include corporations, which are some of the most powerful of international actors. Although corporations are legal persons in national legal systems they

[14] A good expression of the double-edged nature of entry into the international legal system is found in the commentary to Art. 2 of the ILC Draft Articles on State Responsibility (Part One), in *Report of the ILC on the Work of its 25th Session* (1973) 2 *Yearbook of the International Law Commission* 177:

> States establish themselves as equal members of the international community as soon as they achieve an independent and sovereign existence. If it is the prerogative of sovereignty to be able to assert its rights, the counterpart of that prerogative is the duty to discharge its obligations.

[15] See *Reparation for Injuries Suffered in the Service of the United Nations, Advisory Opinion* (1949) *ICJ Reports* 174; Art. 8(1) of the Marrakesh Agreement Establishing the World Trade Organization (1994) 33 ILM 1125, 1147; and Art. 1(2)(b)(ii) of the Agreement for the Implementation of the Provisions of the United Nations Convention on the Law of the Sea of 10 December 1982, Relating to the Conservation and Management of Straddling Fish Stocks and Highly Migratory Fish Stocks, UN Doc. A/CONF.164/33, reproduced in (1995) 34 ILM 1542, 1549. On the latter treaty, see pp. 98–9 below.

[16] See pp. 156–7 below.

have, at best, only limited international legal personality.[17] This absence, or near absence, of international legal personality renders them largely incapable of participating in the process of customary international law, at least in terms of being able to represent themselves directly – and even though some corporations are able to exert considerable influence on States. The same is true of individuals, notwithstanding the many assertions that have been made to the effect that individuals have limited international legal personality, for example, in respect of human rights, and despite the fact that individuals can be held responsible under international law for certain crimes.[18]

Some international human rights may be regarded as entailing corresponding legal obligations of an *erga omnes* character, i.e. obligations, not only to the individuals concerned, but also between and among all States, regardless of the nationality of the individuals concerned.[19] Similarly, some forms of individual criminal responsibility under international law may be regarded as entailing responsibility *erga omnes*, i.e. responsibility to all States, regardless of the nationality of the individuals concerned.[20] However, *erga omnes* rules represent only a small portion of the rights and obligations which States have under international law in respect of individuals and other non-State entities.

## Diplomatic protection

To the degree that individuals and corporations play a role in the process of customary international law, they do so largely through the mechanism of diplomatic protection.[21] Diplomatic protection means that, for the

[17] See Kokkini-Iatridou and de Waart (1983); and Fatouros (1987).

[18] For a developed assertion of the international legal personality of individuals in the human rights context, see Lauterpacht (1950). On individual criminal responsibility in international law, see S/RES/827 (1993) (Security Council Resolution Establishing an International Tribunal for the Prosecution of Persons Responsible for Serious Violations of International Humanitarian Law Committed in the Territory of the Former Yugoslavia), reproduced in (1993) 32 ILM 1203; *Report of the Secretary-General Pursuant to Paragraph 2 of Security Council Resolution 808* (1993), UN Doc. S/25704 (1993), reproduced in (1993) 32 ILM 1163; S/RES/955 (1994) (Security Council Resolution Establishing the International Tribunal for Rwanda), reproduced in (1994) 33 ILM 1598); ILC Draft Statute for an International Criminal Court (and commentary), in *Report of the ILC on the Work of its 46th Session*, UN Doc. A/49/10 (1994) 43, reproduced in (1994) 33 ILM 253; Rome Statute of the International Criminal Court, 17 July 1998, http://www.un.org/icc; and generally, Bassiouni (1986). Some individuals, such as judges and writers, may play an *indirect* role in the customary process by identifying rules and exposing and analysing legally relevant State practice. See Art. 38(1)(d) of the Statute of the International Court of Justice; and pp. 120–4 below.

[19] On *erga omnes* rules, see pp. 195–203 below.

[20] See the discussion of universal jurisdiction on p. 64 above.

[21] See Danilenko (1993) 84.

purposes of international claims, the rights of an individual or corporation are assimilated to the rights of the State of which that individual or corporation holds nationality. As the Permanent Court of International Justice stated in the *Mavrommatis Palestine Concessions Case*:

> By taking up the case of one of its subjects and by resorting to diplomatic action or international judicial proceedings on his behalf, a State is in reality asserting its own rights – its right to ensure, in the person of its subjects, respect for the rules of international law.[22]

There is thus a close link between diplomatic protection and the principle of personality.

Although the assimilation of rights is clearly something of a legal fiction which addresses the procedural incapacity of individuals and corporations to bring claims in international law,[23] it has the consequence that States are considered to have legal obligations towards other States concerning the treatment of those other States' nationals.[24] Many of the obligations which States have in respect of individuals and corporations in international law exist, through the concept of diplomatic protection, as obligations to other States.[25]

Perhaps the most interesting qualifying effects of the principle of personality on the application of power in the customary process occur as a result of that principle's role in diplomatic protection, in that the individuals and corporations which are accorded diplomatic protection not only benefit from the international legal personality of their State, but to some degree act as extensions of it. In short, the involvement of nationals in any given area or activity may allow the State of nationality to participate in the process of customary international law in a way, or to an extent, that might otherwise be precluded. There are at least three reasons for why this may be possible.

First, the involvement of nationals will usually increase the opportuni-

[22] (Jurisdiction) (1924) PCIJ Reports, Ser. A, No. 2, 12. See also *Panevezys-Saldutiskis Railway Case* (1939) PCIJ Reports, Ser. A/B, No. 76, 16. See generally Seidl-Hohenveldern (1987) 7–12; Brownlie (1990) 480–94; and Dinh *et al.* (1994) 757–64.

[23] See Lauterpacht (1950) 27; and Higgins (1994) 71, note 68.

[24] It may be argued that nationality is not a rule of international law because it is open to any State to grant nationality as it chooses. However, although the choice of whether to grant nationality is within the State's reserved domain (see, e.g., *Nationality Decrees in Tunis and Morocco Case* (1923) PCIJ Reports, Ser. B, No. 4, 24; and *Nottebohm Case* (1955) *ICJ Reports* 4, 20), whether a grant of nationality is valid for the purposes of diplomatic protection has long been treated as a question of international law (see *Nottebohm Case, ibid.*, 20–1; and *Mergé Claim* (1955) 22 ILR 443 (Italian–US Conciliation Commission); and more recently, *Iran–United States, Case No. A/18* (1984) 5 *Iran–United States Claims Tribunal Reports* 251 (full tribunal)).

[25] For the classic expression of this distinction see *Barcelona Traction Case*, note 1, p. 3 above.

ties that the State of nationality has to make claims, thus directly increasing its ability to participate in the customary process. Since only international legal personalities are entitled to make claims, and since claims are generally regarded as an important form of State practice in the process of customary international law, the principle of personality is here again qualifying the application of power within that process.[26]

Secondly, the involvement of nationals will usually provide the State of nationality with opportunities to make specific rather than general claims in respect of certain issues. Since such claims in diplomatic protection are based on rights in international law, they may be accorded more weight in the customary process than similar claims made in the abstract.[27]

Thirdly, the involvement of nationals may in some circumstances enable the State of nationality to support its claims with countermeasures, which may contribute to the process of customary international law more effectively than similar but illegal acts carried out in the absence of nationals.[28]

One example of the qualifying effects of the principle of personality in the context of diplomatic protection occurred in respect of the customary rule concerning the standard of compensation for expropriation of foreign-owned property. For each of the three reasons set out above, the fact that most of the corporations involved were incorporated in Western industrialised States was able to enhance the involvement of those States in the customary process in respect of this rule. This opportunity for greater involvement may have been especially important given that, from the perspective of the industrialised States, this particular rule was an external rule. The industrialised States were already at a disadvantage because the preponderance of State practice relevant to this rule occurred within the jurisdictions of non-industrialised States.[29] The principle of personality, operating in the context of diplomatic protection, thus

[26] On the link between international personality and claims, see *Reparation for Injuries Suffered in the Service of the United Nations, Advisory Opinion*, (1949) *ICJ Reports* 174, 181–2. On the nationality of claims generally, see Donner (1994). There are only a few exceptional cases, involving protected persons and alien members of a State's armed forces or merchant marine, where a State may provide diplomatic protection to non-nationals. It should also be noted that there are at least two differences between claims made by a State on its own behalf and claims involving diplomatic protection. The former, with the exception of claims involving activities in the territory of foreign States and for which the State is not entitled to immunity from foreign courts, may be made without having to establish a genuine link of nationality and without having to exhaust local remedies. This is not the case with claims involving diplomatic protection.

[27] See pp. 62–3 above.

[28] For an argument that only such behaviour as supports or opposes claims to rights constitutes State practice for the purposes of customary international law, see Weisburd (1988). On countermeasures, see generally Zoller (1984); and the discussion in note 33, p. 62 above.

[29] See pp. 58–60 above.

provided a qualifying effect which at least partly counteracted the qualifying effect of the principle of jurisdiction, and did so in favour of the industrialised States. The qualifying effects of different rules and principles may often work against each other, making it more difficult to assess their significance within the international system.

Boundary rules provide another example of how the principle of personality, operating within the context of diplomatic protection, may improve the efficacy of States' involvement in the customary process.[30] As was explained in chapter 4, the activities of merchant vessels flagged by the powerful maritime States may, during the development of the twelve-mile territorial sea, have enhanced those States' ability to resist the development of that rule.[31] In effect, the principle of personality extended a notional part of those States' territory to the disputed areas, many of which were located a great distance away. However, the presence of those vessels enabled coastal States to participate more effectively in the customary process as well, by arresting foreign vessels rather than just making claims to extended territorial waters.

Thus, the principle of personality enables States to engage in practice in respect of potential, emerging or existing customary rules in situations where, without it, their ability to do so might be limited. However, this principle may do more than just enable States to participate to a greater degree in the development, maintenance or change of customary rules concerning their own nationals abroad. It may also, indirectly, enable certain States to have a greater effect on the development of human rights for persons, other than their own nationals, who live or otherwise find themselves within the jurisdictions of other States. This is because diplomatic protection enables States which support the development of general human rights to raise such issues within the specific and relatively uncontroversial context of the rights of their own nationals abroad.

## The 'international minimum standard'

The violation of the rights of a national in a foreign State allows the State of nationality to raise the issue of human rights within the context of a direct legal claim. Although that claim will be directed at the treatment of the claiming State's national, it will, nevertheless, often draw attention to how the foreign State treats its own nationals and the nationals of third States. Claims of this character have contributed to the development of an 'international minimum standard' by promoting, through example, an

[30] See pp. 60–4 above. [31] See pp. 60–3 above.

awareness and concern for human rights within even the most abusive of States, as well as within international society more generally.[32] Moreover, the direct legal claim, based on a violation of rights which are assimilated to those of the State of nationality, is likely to have a greater effect on the customary process than a statement made in the abstract.[33] But perhaps most importantly, the development of customary rules concerning the treatment of aliens may have enabled the development of international human rights to benefit from a shared conceptual universe of legality, through the analogical extrapolation of a belief in the legitimacy of existing rules, into a similar belief about similar rules concerning a group of persons whose situation differs only slightly.[34]

In the history of diplomatic protection, the relationship between the standard of treatment required for aliens and that required for nationals has frequently been unclear. However, a link with international human rights has long been apparent. For example, in the 1926 *Roberts Claim* the United States–Mexican General Claims Commission wrote, in respect of the standard of treatment required when a United States national was kept in a Mexican jail:

> Facts with respect to equality of treatment of aliens and nationals may be important in determining the merits of a complaint of mistreatment of an alien. But such equality is not the ultimate test of the propriety of the acts of authorities in the light of international law. That test is, broadly speaking, whether aliens are treated in accordance with ordinary standards of civilization.[35]

Similarly, in 1957 Garcia Amador, then the International Law Commission's Special Rapporteur on State Responsibility, proposed the following draft article in his Second Report to the Commission:

> The State is under a duty to ensure to aliens the enjoyment of the same civil rights, and to make available to them the same individual guarantees as are enjoyed by its nationals. These rights and guarantees shall not, however, in any case be less than the 'fundamental human rights' recognized and defined in contemporary international instruments.[36]

[32] On the 'international minimum standard', see Lillich and Neff (1978); Lillich (1984); and Brownlie (1990) 526–8. [33] See pp. 62–3 above.

[34] See, similarly, the discussion of jurisdiction by analogy at pp. 69–74 above.

[35] (1926) 4 *Reports of International Arbitral Awards* 77, 80.

[36] (1957) 2 *Yearbook of the International Law Commission* 104 (Art. 5(1)). However, this draft article was not adopted by the ILC due to strong opposition from a number of its members. The ILC has since concentrated on codifying the general ('secondary') principles of responsibility, rather than the specific content of this particular area of law. On State responsibility, see generally ILC Draft Articles on State Responsibility (Part One), note 14, p. 14 above; Arts. 1–5 of the ILC Draft Articles on State Responsibility (Part Two), in *Report of the ILC on the Work of its 40th Session* (1988) 2(2) *Yearbook of the International Law Commission* 107; Brownlie (1983); Dinh *et al.* (1994) 729–73; and http://www.law.cam.ac.uk/RCIL/ILCSR/statresp.htm.

The United Nations General Assembly also took a human rights approach to diplomatic protection in its 1985 Declaration on the Human Rights of Individuals Who Are Not Nationals of the Country in Which They Live.[37] This Declaration sets out the specific human rights and fundamental freedoms which aliens 'shall enjoy'. For example, Article 6 reads: 'No alien shall be subjected to torture or to cruel, inhuman or degrading treatment or punishment and, in particular, no alien shall be subjected without his or her free consent to medical or scientific experimentation.'[38] This article is similar to provisions in numerous declarations and treaties aimed at codifying the customary international law of human rights.[39]

Although it is difficult to assess the overall effect of diplomatic protection on the development of customary rules concerning general human rights, by providing an alternative means for raising issues and focusing moral authority, the principle of personality would here, once again, seem to qualify the application of power in the process of customary international law. This conclusion is confirmed by an examination of the position in international law of those individuals and groups for whom diplomatic protection is normally never available, namely, stateless persons and refugees, in terms of the relative absence of legal protections concerning their unique situation.

## Stateless persons and refugees

Stateless persons are individuals who do not have the nationality of any State. An injury to a stateless person is not an injury to any State and cannot form the basis of an inter-State legal claim in the absence of a treaty obligation to that effect, or an *erga omnes* rule.[40] Refugees are individuals who, according to traditional legal definitions, have been forced to

[37] UNGA Res. 144 (XL), GAOR, 40th Session, Supp. 53, 253. For background and commentary see Lillich and Neff (1978); and Lillich (1984) 55–6. [38] *Ibid.*

[39] See, e.g., Art. 5 of the 1948 Universal Declaration of Human Rights, note 45, p. 44 above; Art. 7 of the 1966 International Covenant on Civil and Political Rights, UNGA Res. 2200 A (XXI), reproduced in (1967) 6 ILM 368; Arts. 1–4 of the 1975 Declaration on Protection from Torture, UNGA Res. 3452 (XXX); and Arts. 1 and 2 of the 1984 Convention Against Torture and Other Cruel, Inhuman or Degrading Treatment or Punishment, UNGA Res. 39/46, reproduced in (1984) 23 ILM 1027.

[40] In the 1931 *Dickson Car Wheel Company Case* ((1931) 4 *Reports of International Arbitral Awards* 669, 678) the arbitral tribunal wrote:

> A State . . . does not commit an international delinquency in inflicting an injury upon an individual lacking nationality, and consequently, no State is empowered to intervene or complain on his behalf either before or after the injury.

On *erga omnes* rules see pp. 195–203 below.

flee their State of nationality or habitual residence because they have been persecuted, or have a legitimate fear of persecution by that State.[41] In these circumstances it is inconceivable that the State which is engaging in the persecution would choose to exercise diplomatic protection over those individuals whom it is persecuting, and, in any case, it is impossible for a State to exercise diplomatic protection against itself. In reality, refugees are no better off in terms of their access to diplomatic protection than stateless persons.[42]

Stateless persons and refugees have received relatively little protection from international law. For example, States have no legal obligation to grant nationality to stateless persons, nor to admit them to their territory. Any international law obligations concerning refugees – as refugees – apply only in respect of those individuals who are fortunate enough to make it out of the territory of the State of persecution and into the territory of another State.[43] When compared to the protections available under customary international law to foreign nationals (and to persons in closely analogous situations), it becomes clear that the difference in the

[41] Art. 1 of the 1951 Geneva Convention Relating to the Status of Refugees (189 UNTS 137), as amended by Art. 1 of the 1967 Protocol Relating to the Status of Refugees (606 UNTS 268), defines a refugee as any person who:

> owing to a well-founded fear of being persecuted for reasons of race, religion, nationality, membership of a particular social group or political opinion, is outside the country of his nationality and is unable or, owing to such fear, is unwilling to avail himself of the protection of that country; or who, not having a nationality and being outside the country of his former habitual residence is unable or, owing to such fear, is unwilling to return to it.

Many commentators and the UN High Commissioner for Refugees recognise that this definition is overly restrictive because it does not include individuals who have fled civil wars, famines or environmental disasters. See, e.g., Bodart (1995); Goodwin-Gill (1995); and UNHCR (1995) 19–55. However, in recent years many States of refuge have adopted extremely strict interpretations of the Art. 1 definition. See, e.g., Zimmermann (1993); Carlier and Vanheule (1994); Joint Position of 4 March 1996 defined by the Council [of Ministers] on the basis of Article K.3 of the Treaty on European Union on the harmonised application of the definition of the term 'refugee' in Article 1 of the Geneva Convention of 28 July 1951 relating to the status of refugees (1996) Official Journal of the European Communities No. L63/2.

[42] It is interesting, however, to note that the United Nations has assumed what amount to diplomatic protection functions for Palestinian refugees in respect of their claims (arising out of the Iraqi invasion of Kuwait) before the UN Compensation Commission. See Guidelines relating to paragraph 19 of the criteria for expedited processing of urgent claims (Decision 5 of the Governing Council of the United Nations Compensation Commission, adopted 18 October 1991), UN Doc. S/AC.26/1991/5, reproduced in (1992) 31 ILM 1031.

[43] This was graphically demonstrated by the fact that no State objected to the decision made by the United States in 1992, to return persons who claimed to be refugees from the high seas to Haiti without considering their claims. See generally: Goodwin-Gill (1994).

levels of protection available is linked to the principle of personality. The principle of personality enables States to participate effectively in the development of rules to protect nationals abroad (and, concurrently, in the development of rules to protect persons in closely analogous situations), which means that in situations where the principle is not available (or in situations which are not closely analogous to a situation where it is available), the ability of States to participate in the customary process is seriously impaired – and that any rules which do develop are relatively ineffective.

### Non-governmental organisations

The qualifying effects of the principle of personality may also be seen in the difficulties faced by non-governmental organisations when they seek to participate in and influence the process of customary international law. Non-governmental organisations have had a great deal of influence on the development of some customary rules, especially in the human rights field.[44] However, this influence has been exercised largely, if not exclusively, within the framework of the State-centric system. Non-governmental organisations do not have international legal personality and are therefore incapable of participating directly in the customary process. Instead, they mobilise public pressure on States to engage in practice supportive of, or opposed to, potential, emerging or existing customary rules. Sometimes they also succeed in persuading States directly, for example, by bringing to light information that might not otherwise be available, or public. This latter role has been enhanced by States having allowed non-governmental organisations to participate, to a limited degree, in certain bodies of some international organisations, such as the Sub-Commission of the United Nations Human Rights Commission.[45] However, such participation should not lead one to conclude that non-governmental organisations thus play any sort of direct role in the customary process,[46] for it is the behaviour of the States they seek to persuade which then develops, maintains or changes customary international law.

This chapter has demonstrated that there are at least two ways in which the principle of personality qualifies the application of power in the customary process. First, the principle limits the number of participants in that process, and the degree to which they are able to participate in it. Secondly, by operating through the concept of diplomatic protection, the

[44] See, e.g., the role played by Amnesty International in the development of the prohibition against torture, as detailed in Rodley (1987).
[45] See Lagoni (1994).
[46] For a different view, see Gunning (1991).

principle of personality sometimes enhances the ability of States to participate in the development, maintenance and change of external and boundary rules. Like other principles of international law, the principle of personality not only restricts, but sometimes promotes change.

# 6 The principle of reciprocity

One of the concepts normally considered fundamental to the rule of law is that the law of any society must in principle apply to all its members. In national legal systems this concept may be understood in at least two ways. First, it is possible to understand law as being imposed from above by the State or sovereign, and as generally applicable to all citizens.[1] Secondly, it is possible to understand law as a multitude of bilateral relationships, either between individual persons or between individuals and the State.[2]

In international society there is no overarching sovereign, and international law has frequently been understood as involving a multitude of bilateral relationships between those entities which have international legal personality, i.e. predominantly States.[3] Since there is no overarching sovereign at least some parts of this law do not necessarily need to apply to any one State, nor does this law have to apply in the same way to all States, that is, it does not need to be generalised. Instead, the application of rules of international law to a State is usually regarded as being dependent on that State's consent, which may be accorded either to specific rules, or to legal processes more generally.[4] This consent operates bilaterally, as can be seen in the requirement of consent by States parties to reservations to multilateral treaties,[5] and in the existence of special customary international law.[6]

It may appear that this bilateralist understanding of international law is incompatible with the existence of generally applicable rules, especially those principles which structure the international legal system.[7] Simma has criticised bilateralism as being 'a barrier in the way of stronger solidarity in international law' and argued that *jus cogens* and *erga omnes* rules

1 See Austin (1954) Lecture I, 9–33; and Dicey (1959) 70–6.
2 See Hohfeld (1916–17); reprinted in Hohfeld (1923) 65.
3 See, e.g., Slouvka (1968); and Lowe (1983a). 4 See p. 14 above.
5 See Art. 20 of the Vienna Convention on the Law of Treaties, note 10, p. 36 above. This requirement is also part of customary international law. See McNair (1961) 158–77.
6 On special customary international law, see the citations in note 3, p. 3 above. On this point, see Lowe (1983a), quotation, note 9, p. 89 below. 7 See pp. 10–13 above.

represent the 'antithesis' of bilateralism.[8] However, if a bilateral legal relationship in respect of any particular rule is multiplied so that similar relationships in respect of the same rule exist between all States, the rule would seem to become general in application. Furthermore, the bilateral relationships which make up any general rule appear not to exist in isolation. The customary process adds weight to, and therefore increases the resistance to change of, the legal rule which grounds the various bilateral legal relationships. The process, and the State practice which drives the process, are general in scope; the bilateral relationships which connect rights with obligations in respect of rules are not.[9] To take an extreme example, an *erga omnes* rule could be thought of as a rule which has been grounded by a series of bilateral legal relationships between all States and as a rule which, if violated, justifies a response by the rights holder at the end of any of the many bilateral ties to the violating State which relate to that particular rule.[10]

The concept of reciprocity may be fundamental to bilateralism. The concept of reciprocity involves the idea that bilateral relationships between at least formally equal parties are not unidirectional, but necessarily involve at least some element of *quid pro quo*.[11] This broad social concept of reciprocity, which States apply on the basis of either short- or long-term considerations of self-interest, may be responsible for a great deal of inter-State co-operation or exchange, outside or in addition to any international legal obligations.[12] However, this general concept also finds expression in a principle of international law: thus, in the context of general customary international law any State claiming a *right* under that law has to accord all other States the same right.[13] As such, reciprocity is a

[8] Simma (1989) 822*ff*. See also Weil (1983) 432; and pp.183–203 below.

[9] Lowe ((1983a) 209 (emphasis in original)) has described international law as a 'network of obligations' in which:

> [A] rule may only be said to be general in the *descriptive* sense that it is a rule to which states in general subscribe, but this does not imply that it is general in any *prescriptive* sense, applying in principle to all states.

See also quotation, p. 144 below.

[10] See Byers (1997a); and pp. 195–203 below.

[11] In some instances, however, such as in respect of some unequal treaties, the *quid* might be considerably smaller than the *quo*. In addition, it may frequently be the case that reciprocity does not occur in the same, discrete situation, but is provided at another time, in another 'transaction'. See the discussion of Keohane's 'specific' and 'diffuse' forms of reciprocity at pp. 28–9 above.

[12] See generally Keohane (1986).

[13] This distinction between the general, social concept and the legal principle of reciprocity is similar to that made by Virally between 'la réciprocité formelle' and 'la réciprocité réelle' (i.e., between formal and real reciprocity). See Virally (1967) 29–34. See also Simma (1984). For an explanation of the general concept of reciprocity from the perspective of general legal theory, as the source of most obligations, see Fuller (1969) 19–27.

legal consequence of the formal equality of States. Yet it is a consequence which, by allowing for the generalisation of rules in response to State practice, is of paramount importance to the process of customary international law.[14] For this reason it is treated here as a principle of international law in its own right.

By ensuring that any State claiming a right under general customary international law accords that same right to all other States, the principle of reciprocity qualifies the application of power in at least three ways: first, in respect of what States claim, and, how they go about making claims; secondly, in respect of how States respond to the claims of other States; and thirdly, in respect of how States go about persistently objecting to emerging or newly developed customary rules with which they disagree. These three ways will be dealt with here in turn.

## Reciprocity and the making of claims

If the principle of reciprocity ensures that any State claiming a right under general customary international law accords that same right to every other State, States will only claim rights which they are prepared to see generalised. This is because a generalised right subjects the State to corresponding obligations *vis-à-vis* all other States. By limiting what States are prepared to claim, the principle of reciprocity is already qualifying the application of power in the process of customary international law. However, the principle of reciprocity may do more than just limit what States are prepared to claim. It may also be a tool which individual States use to their own advantage, in some circumstances, to influence the development, maintenance or change of particular customary rules. The following two examples demonstrate different ways in which the principle of reciprocity may be used for this specific purpose, and thus indicate two rather precise, additional ways in which this principle may qualify the application of power in the customary process. A third example then demonstrates how the principle of reciprocity may have been used in a purported attempt to develop or change a customary rule, in order to apply pressure in the negotiation of a treaty concerning the same issue.

### *The Truman Proclamation*

In 1945 President Truman of the United States issued a Proclamation with Respect to the Natural Resources of the Subsoil and Sea Bed of the

[14] See pp. 147–65 below.

Continental Shelf.[15] Commonly known as the 'Truman Proclamation', it stated, *inter alia*:

[T]he Government of the United States regards the natural resources of the subsoil and sea bed of the continental shelf beneath the high seas but contiguous to the coasts of the United States as appertaining to the United States, subject to its jurisdiction and control.[16]

At the time it was made, this claim was inconsistent with pre-existing international law.[17] No State had ever made a general claim to control over all of the seabed resources of its continental shelf beyond twelve nautical miles, nor had anything approaching such a claim appeared in any treaty. Yet notwithstanding the initial inconsistency between the United States' claim and pre-existing international law, the claim rapidly acquired the status of customary international law as other States followed the lead of the United States and made similar claims to jurisdiction over their own continental shelves.[18] By 1951 the International Law Commission had included coastal State rights over the continental shelf in a set of Draft Articles,[19] and in 1958 the customary status of this rule was confirmed by its inclusion in various provisions of the Geneva Convention on the Continental Shelf.[20]

Why was the Truman Proclamation so successful in promoting the development of a rule of customary international law? One important factor was undoubtedly the position of the United States. In 1945 the United States was by far the world's most powerful State, having emerged

[15] Reproduced in (1946) 40 *American Journal of International Law Supplement* 45. He also, simultaneously, issued a Proclamation with Respect to Coastal Fisheries in Certain Areas of the High Seas. Reproduced in (1946) 40 *American Journal of International Law Supplement* 46. On the Truman Proclamation and its effects on customary international law, see generally: Slouvka (1968); and Crawford and Viles (1994).

[16] *Ibid.* [17] See Hurst (1923–4) 34; and Crawford and Viles (1994).

[18] These States included Mexico (1945), Argentina (1946), Panama (1946), Nicaragua (1947), Chile (1947), Peru (1947), Costa Rica (1948), the United Kingdom for Bahamas and Jamaica (1948), Guatemala (1949), Brazil (1950), El Salvador (1950), Honduras (1950), the United Kingdom for British Honduras and the Falkland Islands (1950), and Australia (1953). See Young (1948) 851–4; Young (1950) 27–33; and O'Connell (1982) vol. 1, 474. For contemporaneous practice of a related character in the Persian Gulf, see Young (1949). On the United Kingdom's reaction, see Marston (1996) 15–19.

[19] Draft Articles on the Continental Shelf and Related Subjects, in *Report of the ILC Covering the Work of its 3rd Session* (1951) 2 *Yearbook of the International Law Commission* 123, 141.

[20] 499 UNTS 311. The only element of the Truman Proclamation which was not adopted in the 1958 Convention was its approach to the delimitation of shared continental shelves, and it was precisely this aspect of the Convention which was held by the International Court of Justice in the 1969 *North Sea Continental Shelf Cases* (note 15, p. 38 above) *not* to accord with customary international law.

victorious and relatively unscathed from the Second World War. However, a more important factor seems to have been the character of the Proclamation's claim, which promoted general acceptance and acquiescence in three ways. First, it conceded the right of all coastal States to make similar claims. At one point it stated that 'the exercise of jurisdiction over the natural resources of the subsoil and sea bed of the continental shelf by the contiguous nation is reasonable and just'.[21] In terms of rights under international law, the United States was claiming something both for itself *and* for all other coastal States.

Secondly, the rights claimed by the Proclamation did not depend for their validity on actual occupation or prescriptive use of the areas concerned. This meant that these rights could be held by all coastal States regardless of their size, strength or level of economic and technological development.

Thirdly, many other States stood to benefit from the claimed right because virtually all coastal States have continental shelves. Had these States denied the validity of the United States' claim, they would have been denying potentially substantial benefits to themselves. The idea of coastal State jurisdiction over the continental shelf was thus, in the words of one scholar, a 'marketable concept in the marts of international law'.[22] For all of these reasons the Truman Proclamation is a classic example of a conscious, successful effort to develop a new customary rule.

### *The Arctic Waters Pollution Prevention Act*

In 1970 the Parliament of Canada approved the Arctic Waters Pollution Prevention Act.[23] The Act, which was not presented as a claim to sovereignty, gave the Canadian government wide powers to regulate shipping within 100 nautical miles of Canada's Arctic coast.[24] It prescribed offences and penalties for the pollution of Arctic waters by the deposit of waste, which was broadly defined so as to include *any* substance which would degrade the waters to an extent detrimental to their use by man or by wildlife and plants useful to man. It also provided regulatory powers in respect of, among other things, the creation of shipping safety control zones and the prescription of minimum standards for ships, and granted

[21] Note 15, p. 91 above. [22] Young (1948) 849.

[23] *Revised Statutes of Canada* 1985, vol.1, c. A12; reproduced in (1970) 9 ILM 543. See generally Bilder (1970–1); Henkin (1971); Macdonald *et al.* (1971); and Beesley (1973).

[24] The Act applied to 'Arctic waters', which were described as frozen or liquid waters 'adjacent to the mainland and islands of the Canadian Arctic within the area enclosed by the sixtieth parallel of north latitude, the one hundred and forty-first meridian of west longitude and a line measured seaward from the nearest Canadian land a distance of one hundred nautical miles'. *Ibid.*, s. 2.

enforcement powers to government officials, including the authority to seize any ship anywhere within 100 miles of the Arctic coast on reasonable suspicion of its having committed an offence under the Act.

Canada claimed that the Arctic Waters Pollution Prevention Act was a balanced response to specific concerns about the dangers of marine-based pollution in the fragile Arctic environment.[25] These concerns had been greatly heightened by the voyage of the United States oil tanker SS Manhattan through the Northwest Passage in 1969.[26] Nevertheless, the Act was clearly inconsistent with pre-existing international law, a fact which was effectively admitted by Canada when it added a reservation concerning the subject matter of the Act to its declaration of acceptance of the compulsory jurisdiction of the International Court of Justice under Article 36(2) (the 'optional clause') of that Court's Statute.[27]

The Act was subject to strong protests from the United States, which asserted:

> The United States does not recognize any exercise of coastal state jurisdiction over our vessels in the high seas and thus does not recognize the right of any state unilaterally to establish a territorial sea of more than three miles or exercise more limited jurisdiction in any area beyond 12 miles.[28]

An official note to Canada explained the reason for the United States' position:

> We are concerned that this action by Canada if not opposed by us, would be taken as precedent in other parts of the world for other unilateral infringements of the freedom of the seas. If Canada had the right to claim and exercise exclusive pollution and resources jurisdiction on the high seas, other countries could assert the right to exercise jurisdiction for other purposes, some reasonable and some not, but all equally invalid according to international law.[29]

[25] See, e.g., Trudeau (1970). [26] See (1969–70) Keesing's 23759.

[27] See (1969–70) *International Court of Justice Yearbook* 55; reproduced in (1970) 9 ILM 598. The reservation excluded from the Court's compulsory jurisdiction over Canada:

> disputes arising out of or concerning jurisdiction or rights claimed or exercised by Canada in respect of the conservation, management or exploitation of the living resources of the sea, or in respect of the prevention or control of pollution or contamination of the marine environment in marine areas adjacent to the coast of Canada.

In explaining the need for the reservation, Prime Minister Trudeau acknowledged that there was a 'very grave risk that the World Court would find itself obliged to find that coastal states cannot take steps to prevent pollution. Such a legalistic decision would set back immeasurably the development of law in this critical area' (8 April 1970, reproduced in Bilder (1970–1) 29).

[28] Statement of Robert McCloskey, Department of State, *New York Times*, 10 April 1970, 13, col. 3.

[29] Department of State statement of 15 April 1970, reproduced in (1970) 9 ILM 605 and (1971) 9 *Canadian Yearbook of International Law* 287.

The United States suggested that Canada voluntarily submit the issue to the International Court,[30] but Canada refused to do so.[31]

The United States was the only State to protest publicly against the enactment of the Arctic Waters Pollution Prevention Act. Other States appeared to acquiesce in this new assertion of jurisdictional competence. Canada's unilateral claim may thus have been an important factor in changing the pre-existing customary international law in respect of the rights of coastal States to introduce and enforce pollution prevention measures beyond the territorial sea. This change is reflected in Article 234 of the 1982 Law of the Sea Convention, which accords coastal States pollution prevention powers in 'ice-covered areas' extending to 200 nautical miles – which is in fact twice what Canada claimed.[32] Perhaps as importantly, under Article 220 of that Convention coastal States are accorded pollution prevention powers within all waters – ice-covered or otherwise – within their exclusive economic zones, although the powers available in areas not covered by ice are less extensive than those in ice-covered areas.[33] In recognition of the success of its attempt to develop customary international law, parallel to these treaty provisions, Canada later rescinded the reservation to its acceptance of the compulsory jurisdiction of the International Court *without* having ratified the Law of the Sea Convention, which in any event by that time was not yet in force.[34]

[30] *Ibid.*, 606 and 289 respectively.

[31] See Summary of Canada's Note of 16 April 1970 to the United States, reproduced in (1970) 9 ILM 607 and (1971) 9 *Canadian Yearbook of International Law* 289.

[32] (1982) 21 ILM 1261, 1315. Art. 234 reads:

> Coastal States have the right to adopt and enforce non-discriminatory laws and regulations for the prevention, reduction and control of marine pollution from vessels in ice-covered areas within the limits of the exclusive economic zone, where particularly severe climatic conditions and the presence of ice covering such areas for most of the year create obstructions or exceptional hazards to navigation, and pollution of the marine environment could cause major harm to or irreversible disturbance of the ecological balance. Such laws and regulations shall have due regard to navigation and the protection and preservation of the marine environment based on the best available scientific evidence.

[33] For example, Art. 220(3) reads:

> Where there are clear grounds for believing that a vessel navigating in the exclusive economic zone or the territorial sea of a State has, in the exclusive economic zone, committed a violation of applicable international rules and standards for the prevention, reduction and control of pollution from vessels or laws and regulations of that State conforming and giving effect to such rules and standards, that State may require the vessel to give information regarding its identity and port of registry, its last and its next port of call and other relevant information to establish whether a violation has occurred.

[34] See (1985–6) 40 *International Court of Justice Yearbook* 64. The Law of the Sea Convention came into force on 16 November 1994, still without Canada having ratified it.

As with the Truman Proclamation, one can ask why this unilateral claim was successful in changing customary international law. One possible explanation is that the claim was relatively limited and apparently reasonable. Canada did not claim pollution prevention jurisdiction along its Atlantic and Pacific coasts, only in the Arctic where climatic conditions made oil spills a particularly dangerous threat.

A similar geographically restricted development occurred in 1984, when the Federal Republic of Germany abandoned its claim to a three-mile territorial sea within the specific confines of the German Bight and created a new limit on the basis of a box defined by geographical co-ordinates. This box extended approximately sixteen miles off the German coastline.[35] The new claim, which was explicitly designed for the limited purpose of preventing oil spills in those busy waters, met with no protests from other States. This was perhaps because the balance of interests in this specific situation was different from that which existed more generally – different enough that other States were prepared to allow for the development of a prescriptive right as an exception to the general rule governing the breadth of the territorial sea. Yet the rule that developed in response to Canada's claim to pollution prevention jurisdiction up to 100 miles was – in some respects – a general rule not limited to Arctic waters.[36]

Although it may not have been Canada's intention, the development of this more general rule was perhaps an inevitable consequence of the way its claim was framed, i.e. in such a way as to extend fairly easily into a right which all coastal States could claim for themselves, and which most coastal States were probably interested in claiming. By 1970 States were becoming aware of the acute environmental threat posed by the increasing use of ships, especially supertankers, to transport oil and other dangerous products. The *Torrey Canyon* had broken up on the shores of Cornwall in 1967.[37] In 1968 an oil spill off Southern California had caused severe damage to forty miles of coastline.[38] All coastal States thus had interests identical, or at least very similar, to those of Canada when it came to the regulation of coastal shipping for the purposes of environmental protection. It may have been this factor which resulted, not only in the Canadian claim to pollution prevention jurisdiction up to 100 miles in the Arctic being accepted as a rule of customary international law, but also in that rule being double the breadth initially claimed by Canada, and in its extending, in a somewhat restricted form, to allow all coastal States to exercise similar powers within their own exclusive economic zones.

It is possible that Canada was in fact seeking to establish the somewhat

[35] See Decree of 12 November 1984, reproduced in (1986) 7 *Law of the Sea Bulletin* 9–22.
[36] See p. 94 above. [37] See generally (1967–8) Keesing's 22002; and Nanda (1967).
[38] See generally Note (1969); and Baldwin (1970).

restricted, more general rule, rather than simply the Arctic-specific rule it claimed. One of the striking things about the Arctic Waters Pollution Prevention Act was that Canada could perhaps have achieved the immediate purpose of that legislation – the protection of the Arctic environment from oil pollution resulting from tanker traffic – without adopting a position which challenged existing international law. Canada already had the legal capacity to achieve that goal because the Northwest Passage is less than six nautical miles across at its narrowest point. Even on the most restrictive understanding of the breadth of the territorial sea, Canada could have imposed and enforced reasonable environmental protection measures against any ship wishing to pass through that channel. Although States have a right of transit passage through the territorial seas of other States, the rights of coastal States to enforce reasonable regulations within that zone have long been recognised.[39]

Canada's ability to impose and enforce such measures was strengthened by legislation, enacted simultaneously with the Arctic Waters Pollution Prevention Act, which extended its territorial sea to twelve nautical miles and thus extended the section of Northwest Passage falling within Canadian territory.[40] This move was not nearly as contentious as the making of the more geographically extensive 100-mile claim to pollution prevention jurisdiction, as similar twelve-mile claims had already been made by nearly sixty other States.[41]

Moreover, the decision to introduce the Arctic Waters Pollution Prevention Act would seem to reflect Canada's disillusionment with the failure of international law-making conferences to address the *general* issue of coastal State rights to prevent pollution, and in particular the failure of Canada's proposals at the 1958 and 1960 Geneva Law of the Sea Conferences, as well as at the 1969 Marine Pollution Conference in Brussels.[42]

This example suggests that a State wishing to develop or change a customary rule may, in some circumstances, restrict its claims to something which most States would find unobjectionable, but from which those

[39] See Art. 17 of the 1958 Geneva Convention on the Territorial Sea and the Contiguous Zone, 516 UNTS 205; Art. 21 of the Law of the Sea Convention, note 29, p. 41 above; and Churchill and Lowe (1988) 77–84. Note, as well, the differences between Art. 220(2) and Art. 220(3), (5), (6) of the Law of the Sea Convention, note 29, p. 41 above.

[40] *An Act to Amend the Territorial Sea and Fishing Zones*, 18–19 Eliz. 2, c. 68 (1970); reproduced in (1970) 9 ILM 553.

[41] Trudeau (1970) 600. On the development of the twelve-mile territorial sea as a rule of customary international law, see pp. 114–20 below.

[42] See Bilder (1970–1) 23–4. It is also noteworthy that Canada's reservation to the compulsory jurisdiction of the International Court of Justice was *not* limited to measures taken solely in respect of Arctic waters, but was instead framed in more general terms. See note 27, p. 93 above.

States are themselves unable to benefit. A State taking such an approach then waits for the principle of reciprocity to transform its claims, and the responses of other States, into something from which most States could benefit, but to which they might not have agreed had it been made the direct subject of the initial claim. Such a strategic approach to law-making may not only facilitate the establishment of a customary rule, but also ensure that the rule has greater effect, or at least greater scope of application, than might otherwise be the case. And as the following example demonstrates, the principle of reciprocity may be applied in a similar, strategic manner, by extending it beyond the process of customary international law in order to exert pressure on other States in the negotiation of treaties.

### *An Act to Amend the Coastal Fisheries Protection Act*

On 10 May 1994 the Parliament of Canada approved An Act to Amend the Coastal Fisheries Protection Act.[43] This legislation allowed Canadian fisheries officers to arrest foreign vessels in international waters off Canada's east coast if they believed those vessels to be violating conservation measures agreed by the member States of the North Atlantic Fisheries Organisation (NAFO), or established by Canada.[44] It was introduced in what Canada claimed was an attempt to create a rule of customary international law allowing coastal States to engage in such extraterritorial enforcement measures, and as such it was based explicitly on a number of precedents. The most important of these precedents were the Truman Proclamation and the Arctic Waters Pollution Prevention Act.[45] As it had done shortly before the enactment of the Arctic Waters Pollution Prevention Act, Canada again amended its declaration accepting the compulsory jurisdiction of the International Court of Justice so as to exclude any challenges before that Court to its new legislation.[46]

43 See note 1, p. 53. For background and commentary, see Davies (1995); and Davies and Redgwell (1996).

44 *Ibid.*, s. 2. NAFO was founded in 1978 and currently manages the harvest of ten species. See Convention on Future Multilateral Cooperation in the Northwest Atlantic Fisheries, CTS 1979, No. 11. Its member 'States' are Bulgaria, Canada, Cuba, Denmark, Estonia, the European Union, Iceland, Japan, Latvia, Lithuania, Norway, Poland, Romania, Russia, and the United States. Denmark, although an EU member, is an independent NAFO member because Greenland, although Danish territory, is not part of the EU.

45 See 'Tobin Moves on Fish "Pirates" ', *Globe and Mail* (Toronto), 11 May 1994, A1/A2; and pp. 90-2 and 92-7 above, respectively.

46 See (1993–4) 48 *International Court of Justice Yearbook* 88; and p. 93 above. The revised declaration excluded 'disputes arising out of or concerning conservation and management measures taken by Canada with respect to vessels fishing in the NAFO Regulatory Area . . . and the enforcement of such measures'.

Canada's actions were met by strong protests from other States. The French Foreign Minister condemned the legislation in the French National Assembly and European Union fisheries ministers agreed to inform Canada that the Act was illegal under international law.[47]

In August 1994 the United Nations Conference on Straddling Fish Stocks and Highly Migratory Fish Stocks began in New York. At that conference the United States ambassador and the chair of the conference both decried Canada's unilateral actions, while European Union representatives said that they were 'extremely worried'.[48] Canada responded by pushing hard for a multilateral treaty which would allow coastal States to manage, to the outer edge of their continental shelves, fish stocks that straddle the 200-mile limit of the exclusive economic zone.[49] On the opening day of the conference Canada and Norway announced that they were working towards a bilateral treaty which would allow each State to police the other State's fishing vessels outside the 200-mile limit. They expressed the hope that the treaty would serve as a model to regulate fishing and conserve stocks on the high seas.[50]

On 9 March 1995 Canada arrested a Spanish fishing vessel 245 miles off the Canadian coast and towed it to St John's, Newfoundland.[51] The European Union described the arrest as 'an act of organised piracy',[52] while the Spanish government filed proceedings against Canada in the International Court of Justice.[53]

Notwithstanding the widespread condemnation of its unilateral actions in apparent violation of customary international law, Canada's principal

[47] 'Putting Pirate Fishing Boats on the Spot', *Globe and Mail* (Toronto), 2 June 1994, A8; 'EU Protests Fisheries Law', *Financial Post* (Toronto), 11 June 1994, 16. Yet the protesting States were reportedly less concerned about Canadian intentions to seize and prosecute vessels fishing in violation of NAFO conservation measures than they were about how Canada might use its new powers more broadly in the future to protect its other interests in international waters. They were also concerned that Canada's actions might set a precedent for other States to protect similar, or perhaps not so similar, national interests. See 'All at Sea if Canada Takes the Law into its Own Hands', *Globe and Mail* (Toronto), 12 May 1994, A24.

[48] 'Norway Sides with Canada on Fishing Deal', *Calgary Herald* (Calgary), 16 August 1994, A7.

[49] 'Tobin to Speak at UN on Overfishing', *Globe and Mail* (Toronto), 15 August 1994, A3; and 'Showdown Nears on High-Seas Fishing', *Financial Post* (Toronto), 13 August 1994, 8.

[50] 'Norway Sides with Canada on Fishing Deal', *Calgary Herald* (Calgary), 16 August 1994, A7.

[51] 'EU Brands Seizure of Spanish Trawler an Act of Piracy', *Times* (London), 11 March 1995, 15; and Keesing's (March 1995) 40447–8.

[52] 'EU Brands Seizure of Spanish Trawler an Act of Piracy', *Times* (London), 11 March 1995, 15; and Keesing's (March 1995) 40448.

[53] ICJ Communiqué No. 95/8, 29 March 1995. Hearings on the issue of the Court's jurisdiction concluded on 17 June 1998.

goal of providing effective protection in international law for straddling stocks was soon achieved. On 4 August 1995 the United Nations Conference adopted an Agreement for the Implementation of the Provisions of the United Nations Convention on the Law of the Sea of 10 December 1982, Relating to the Conservation and Management of Straddling Fish Stocks and Highly Migratory Fish Stocks.[54] Canada and the European Union also entered into a bilateral treaty concerning satellite tracking and the placing of fisheries inspectors on each other's vessels.[55] Although these instruments do not go as far as the 1994 Canadian legislation, they have much the same effect in terms of fisheries conservation. For instance, Article 21(1) of the Agreement allows any State party to board and inspect, in 'any high seas area covered by a subregional or regional fisheries management organization or arrangement', fishing vessels flagged by other States parties 'for the purpose of ensuring compliance with conservation and management measures for straddling fish stocks and highly migratory fish stocks established by that organization or arrangement'.[56] Article 21(5) allows the inspecting State to secure evidence where 'there are clear grounds for believing that a vessel has engaged in any activity contrary to' those measures, and, if a flag State fails to respond or take action once being notified of an apparent violation, Article 21(8) allows the inspecting State, 'where appropriate', to bring the offending vessel to port.[57]

This third example of An Act to Amend the Coastal Fisheries Protection Act thus demonstrates another use for the principle of reciprocity in international law, namely, to apply pressure in treaty negotiations through purported attempts to develop, maintain or change customary rules. Although Canada claimed to be seeking to establish a new customary rule in this instance, this does not appear to be the real motive for its actions. It may be observed that, in its representations to the Second Tuna Panel established under the General Agreement on Tariffs and Trade and concurrent with its unilateral assertion of enforcement jurisdiction beyond 200 miles, Canada opposed unilateral trade measures on the part of the United States to protect dolphins outside the United States' exclusive economic zone.[58]

It may be possible to differentiate among these three attempts to use the principle of reciprocity in the context of claims. First, there are instances, such as the case of the Truman Proclamation, where the claim which is made offers an obvious advantage to every State, or at least most

[54] Note 15, p. 78 above. See generally Barston (1995).
[55] Agreed Minute on the Conservation and Management of Fish Stocks (20 April 1995), reproduced in (1995) 34 ILM 1260. [56] Note 15, p. 78 above.
[57] Note 15, p. 78 above. [58] See (August–September 1994) 110 *GATT Focus* 6.

States, and where there is little or no associated disadvantage. In this type of situation the benefits offered to other States as a result of the principle of reciprocity ensure that they will acquiesce in the unilateral claim, thus permitting the relatively rapid development or change of a rule of customary international law.

Secondly, there are situations, such as that involving the Arctic Waters Pollution Prevention Act, where the claim which is made offers an advantage to every State, or most States, but where that advantage may not immediately be clear. In 1970 not all States would have seen the development of a customary right to exercise pollution prevention jurisdiction as far as 100 miles from the coast as an immediate necessity, whereas the United States was more concerned with preserving, as much as possible, the freedom of the seas. Canada's response was to claim a new, geographically limited and apparently reasonable right, while at the same time adopting a fairly non-contentious means – a twelve-mile territorial sea – to strengthen its existing legal capacity to deny the United States full freedom of transit through the Northwest Passage. Its claim to a pollution prevention jurisdiction that was restricted to Arctic waters effectively denied other States the right to benefit reciprocally from that claim, since most other States do not have Arctic coastlines. Yet other States were not prepared to be denied their reciprocal benefit and, on seeing the need for a similar rule in respect of their own coasts, soon generalised Canada's claim into the generally available, if somewhat more substantively restricted, right to exercise pollution prevention jurisdiction which is reflected in the Law of the Sea Convention. This, in the end, probably gave Canada what it wanted from the beginning, i.e. the right to exercise an extended pollution prevention jurisdiction along all of its three coasts, and did so in a way which reduced the risk of international incidents by opening the way for United States participation in the development of that more general pollution prevention rule.

Thirdly, there are situations, such as that involving An Act to Amend the Coastal Fisheries Protection Act, where the claim in question fails to offer any benefit, in itself or by extension, to more than a few States. Apart from Canada, only a few States have continental shelves that extend beyond 200 miles. This meant that Canada was unlikely to achieve what it said it was seeking through its unilateral claim, namely, the development of a customary rule allowing coastal States to exercise fisheries conservation jurisdiction on the continental shelf beyond 200 miles regardless of whether those States are acting in co-operation with other States and regional fishing organisations. Yet enough States have an interest in co-operating in the preservation and management of high seas fisheries for a majority of States to be prepared, when pushed, to agree to a treaty rule allowing coastal States to exercise fisheries conservation jurisdiction when, and only when, such measures are consistent with guidelines established through international or regional organisations such as NAFO. And from Canada's perspective, such a treaty may be sufficient to achieve its primary goal of conserving the North Atlantic fisheries, and does so in accordance with international law. Moreover, it is possible that this treaty rule might, in the future, develop into a generally applicable rule of customary international law.[59]

In some ways, the process of customary international law is like a negotiating process in which States seek to maximise their interests by offering the same rights to others that they seek for themselves.[60] And it is a negotiating process that may be manipulated, first, by denying other States reciprocity, and then by allowing the 'pull' of that principle to take other States to positions they might not have been willing to consider, had the proposition been made to them directly. Understanding the role of the principle of reciprocity in the process of customary international law may thus offer distinct benefits, in terms of strategic planning, to States which wish to develop, maintain or change customary rules, or use the customary process to further their positions in the negotiation of treaties.

### Reciprocity and negative responses to claims

If there is no potential for reciprocal benefit, States may be unwilling to support a unilateral initiative which is directed at developing or changing a rule of customary international law. Rather, they may perceive that initiative as being disadvantageous to their interests. This is because the principle of reciprocity will promote the generalisation of the putative rule, making it applicable to all States which have not objected to or opposed it in some way. In such situations States may respond to the unilateral initiative either by engaging in practice in support of the *status quo* (which in many cases will be an existing customary rule), or by engaging in practice in support of an alternative, new rule which is more attuned to their own interests. And this responsive behaviour, if it supports an existing rule, may actually add greater weight or precision to it.

One example of such a situation may be the attempts by United States courts and the United States Congress to exercise jurisdiction extraterritorially in the context of anti-trust regulation and, more precisely, their reliance on legal concepts such as comity to justify their actions.[61] This

[59] See pp. 166–80 above. [60] See Danilenko (1993) 75, quoted at p. 37 above.
[61] See pp. 65–7 above. On comity as a legal concept (as developed in the US through the work of Joseph Story) see Baker (1993) 492–8. For a different view, see Macalister-Smith (1992).

initiative caused other States to behave in such a way as to create relatively more weighty and precise rules of customary international law in response, or, perhaps more accurately, to define in more detail the existing prohibition against intervention so as to deny legitimacy to subsequent, similar attempts to exercise jurisdiction extraterritorially.[62] Had the courts and Congress not justified their actions in legal terms, as falling within an exception to the general prohibition against intervention, the content of that prohibition might not have been elaborated, through the customary process, to the degree that it is now. This would have left a degree of ambiguity in that general rule, which the United States and other powerful States might have been able to exploit in subsequent situations.

Similar developments may occur after judicial pronouncements on questions of international law, such as, for example, the Permanent Court of International Justice's application of the constructive approach to jurisdiction in the 1927 *Lotus Case*.[63] As with the justifications provided by the United States courts and Congress for the exercise of extraterritorial jurisdiction in the context of anti-trust regulation, the judgment in the *Lotus Case* prompted responsive behaviour on the part of a substantial number of States. As a result, there are now treaty rules, as well as a parallel customary rule, to the contrary effect – in this instance that a flag State has sole penal jurisdiction over most acts committed on board its ships on the high seas.[64]

In both these situations States were apparently aware that the particular putative rule or interpretation of an existing rule, if relied on by one or most States, could, as a result of the principle of reciprocity, have led to the development, reinforcement or change of a rule of customary international law applicable to all States. They consequently responded to these initiatives or pronouncements by engaging in practice which either added weight to or clarified the existing rule, or led to the development of a new rule which was different from that asserted initially. By providing the impetus for States to engage in this strengthening, clarification or development, the principle of reciprocity was here, once again, qualifying the application of power in the process of customary international law.

## Reciprocity and persistent objection

The principle of reciprocity would also seem to qualify the application of power as a result of its effects on persistent objection. Persistent objection is the term used to describe the option each State may have, not only to oppose the development of a new rule of customary international law, but

[62] See pp. 65–7 above. [63] See pp. 61–4 above. [64] See note 31, p. 62 above.

to continue opposing that rule once it comes into existence. It is widely considered that this continuing objection, which may be expressed either through actions or through statements, enables the objecting State to avoid being bound by the newly developed rule.[65]

The principle of reciprocity appears to affect persistent objection in the following way. As a result of its persistent objection, the objecting State remains governed by the old rule (or absence of a rule) in its relations with all other States. But as a result of the principle of reciprocity and despite the existence of the new, generalised rule, other States may also claim the same rights *vis-à-vis* the objecting State as they were previously able to claim. However, these other States are governed by the new rule as among themselves. They are thus able to benefit from the existence of the new rule without having to share any of those benefits with the objecting State. There is, in effect, no 'free rider' problem. This places the objecting State at a disadvantage, since it can neither freeze the state of general customary international law so as to benefit itself, nor take advantage of any benefits the new rule may offer.

The effects of the principle of reciprocity in this context may be exacerbated by the fact that many States appear reluctant to recognise the rights of persistent objectors. State agencies and national courts are frequently unaware of or even ignore such positions of objection. In fact, national courts may be fully entitled to ignore persistent objection. National courts do not deal in diplomatic relations; they are merely required, authorised, or have taken it upon themselves, to apply the general standards of international law. When a national court applies customary international law, it may therefore choose to apply that law as general law – thus precluding the possibility of persistent objection – and not as a series of bilateral legal relationships between States. If the court fails to take into account an exception to the generality of that law, it is not the court but the State of which the court is but an internal agency which is responsible *vis-à-vis* the other, exempted State. The situation is thus similar to that of the international legal responsibility of federal States for the actions of their constituent units.[66]

[65] See generally: Akehurst (1974–75a) 23–7; Stein (1985); and Colson (1986). Compare Charney (1985).

[66] See Art. 7(1) of the ILC Draft Articles on State Responsibility (Part One), note 14, p.14 above. The reasons for which a national court may ignore persistent objection may be many and varied, although the most important of these may well be a lack of expertise with regard to international law. In some instances national courts may be prevented from looking at customary international law and acknowledging persistent objection as a result of statutory action on the part of national legislatures, as has been the case under the US Foreign Sovereign Immunities Act, note 65, p.70 above. See, e.g., *United Euram Corp.* v. *USSR*, 461 F. Supp. 609 (SDNY 1978); *Jackson* v. *People's Republic of China*, 550 F. Supp. 869 (ND Alaska 1982), dismissed on other grounds, 596 F. Supp. 386 (ND Alaska 1984) (dismissed due to the non-retrospective character of the FSIA).

There may be little that a persistent objector can do about such treatment if the rule is being applied within or in close proximity to the jurisdiction of another State.[67] If the objecting State is serious about its objection, the principle of reciprocity requires that it continue to deal with other States on the basis of the old rule (or absence thereof) even if those other States are not doing the same in respect of it. If it does not, it may effectively have abandoned its position of persistent objection.

The pressure created in this type of situation may be substantial. For example, it would seem that the United States, the United Kingdom and Japan eventually abandoned their persistent objection to the development of a twelve-mile territorial sea at least partly as a result of coastal fishing and security concerns.[68] Although foreign fishing vessels and spy ships were able to operate just outside the three-mile limits of the persistently objecting States, the objecting States' vessels were excluded from waters within twelve miles of other States' coastlines. Similarly, the fact that the Soviet Union and other socialist States eventually accepted, at least in practice, the restrictive doctrine of State immunity, would seem to be at least partly due to the fact that they were according immunity to other States which were not doing the same in return.[69]

Finally, by persistently objecting, the State may eventually exclude itself from the customary process in the area governed by the new rule. The new rule may become the focus of new interests and correspondingly new patterns of supporting, ambivalent and opposing State practice, while the objecting State remains locked in the past, governed by the old rule, without any opportunity to influence the continuing development of the new one.

[67] See discussions of external and boundary rules on pp. 57–64 above.

[68] On the development of the twelve-mile territorial sea, see pp. 114–20 below. For examples of statements (these from the UK) attempting to uphold the three-mile limit see E. Lauterpacht (1958) 537–42; and E. Lauterpacht (1960) 278–9. Japan adopted a twelve-mile limit in 1977, although it retained a three-mile limit in those areas adjacent to international straits. See Yanai and Asomura (1977) 92. The Japanese Prime Minister, in introducing the bill in the Diet, cited increased foreign fishing in the waters around Japan as one of the reasons for the change in policy. See Oda and Owada (1985) 94. The US abandoned its position, in respect of the claims of other States, in 1983. See Proclamation 5030, reproduced in (1983) 22 ILM 461, 462. It adopted a twelve-mile limit of its own in 1988, with a Presidential Proclamation which made explicit reference to national security interests. See Proclamation 5928, reproduced in (1989) 28 ILM 284. The UK abandoned its stance of persistent objection with the approval of the Territorial Sea Act 1987 (c. 49). The debates on the Bill made reference to fishing interests, security concerns and the problem of 'pirate broadcasting' between three and twelve miles offshore. See (1987) Hansard, HL, vol. 484, cols. 381–401.

[69] See generally: Crawford (1981) 824–31; Crawford (1983) 78–80; Sgro (1983) 124–31; Emanuelli (1984) 37 and 68; and pp. 110–14 below. The situation may have been exacerbated by the fact that, from the perspective of the socialist States, restrictive immunity was an external rule. See pp. 57–8 above.

The principle of reciprocity thus operates to discourage persistent objection. Some States may oppose a potential or emerging rule in an effort to prevent it from coming into force. A few may continue to oppose the new rule even after it comes into force, perhaps hoping to reverse matters in the early stages before the rule gathers weight, or to buy themselves time before conceding to a rule which affects their interests in some detrimental way. And it may be that some States, in some situations, will be more effective at persistently objecting than others. Danilenko has suggested that specially affected States and groups of States may stand a better chance of protecting their interests in this way.[70] But no State, not even the most powerful, persistently objects for an indefinite period of time. In this way, and the other ways discussed earlier in this chapter, the principle of reciprocity clearly qualifies applications of power in the process of customary international law.

[70] See Danilenko (1993) 112.

# 7 The principle of legitimate expectation

## Legitimate expectation, acquiescence and customary international law

It is a widely held view that States are only bound by rules of international law to which they have consented.[1] For this reason consent might itself be considered a fundamental principle of international law. But though States consent explicitly to treaty rules through the act of signature or ratification, they usually do not consent explicitly to rules of customary international law. Instead, they are held to have consented to those customary rules to which they have acquiesced.[2]

The word consent is not a particularly accurate description of the role of acquiescence in the customary process. Acquiescence often signifies ambivalence or even apathy to the rule in question rather than a conscious support for the rule on the part of the acquiescing State. Furthermore, the development of new rights or obligations based on acquiescence necessarily involves other States in addition to the acquiescing State. Rights and obligations in international law are never entirely the creation of a single State's will because they exist between and among States.[3] Instead, it seems that all States consider that one State's acquiescence to a customary rule may give rise to rights or obligations having the potential to affect all States in some way, either as subjects of corresponding obligations, or as holders of corresponding rights. And this shared understanding would seem to be based not so much on consent as on legitimate – i.e., legally justifiable – expectations concerning the legal relevance and effect of a certain type of behaviour.[4] Consequently, acquiescence in this context may more accurately be described as being based on a principle of legitimate expectation, even though the principle of legitimate expectation may itself be based on some earlier, general acceptance of the process of customary international law.[5]

[1] See pp. 7–8 above and pp. 142–6 below. [2] See pp. 7–8 above.
[3] See pp. 7–8 above.
[4] See discussion of the role of shared understandings in the customary process at pp. 147–51 below. [5] See pp. 7–8 above and pp. 142–6 below.

It may be that all rules of international law involve legitimate expectations. Apart from the role played by acquiesence, rules of customary international law involve legitimate expectations because any change from a voluntary pattern of behaviour to a customary rule involves the transformation and legitimisation of patterns of behaviour, around which expectations of a legal character necessarily develop.[6] Treaty rules involve legitimate expectations because they are based on the general customary rule of *pacta sunt servanda*, which requires that treaty obligations be upheld in good faith.[7] In short, States expect other States to abide by their treaty obligations. This expectation may be considered as legitimate – i.e., legally justifiable – because States usually behave accordingly *and* regard their behaviour as having legal relevance.

Certain, more specific rules of international law, such as the rules concerning estoppel and unilateral declaration, may be subsumed within the broader principle of legitimate expectation. 'Estoppel' means that when one party relies on a misleading assurance or statement of intent from another party, and does so to its detriment, then that assurance or statement constitutes a legal wrong which gives rise to a legal obligation of specific performance or compensation.[8] 'Unilateral declaration' operates in a similar manner, but without the requirement of detrimental reliance.[9] Under both rules States expect each other to behave in certain ways as a result of their earlier behaviour, and failures to do so are treated as violations of international law.

In summary, the principle of legitimate expectation means that States are legally justified in relying on each other to behave consistently with previous assurances or patterns of behaviour – if those assurances or that behaviour is of a type, and takes place within a context, such that it is considered legally relevant by most if not all States.

## Legitimate expectation and international institutions

If the principle of legitimate expectation is of such importance to international law, it should also be relevant to international regimes and

[6] See pp. 8–10 above.

[7] See generally McNair (1961) 493–505; and Art. 26 of the Vienna Convention on the Law of Treaties, note 10, p. 36 above.

[8] On estoppel in international law, see *Temple of Preah Vihear Case* (1962) *ICJ Reports* 6; Bowett (1957); and Dominicé (1968). 'Specific performance' involves the fulfilment of the obligation in question, whereas 'compensation' provides redress for the fact that the obligation was not fulfilled, and usually does so through monetary payment. See generally: Gray (1987) 11–21.

[9] See *Eastern Greenland Case* (1933) PCIJ Reports, Ser. A/B, No. 53, 22, 71; *Nuclear Tests Cases* (1974) *ICJ Reports* 252, 267 (para. 43) (*Australia* v. *France*) and 457, 472 (para. 46) (*New Zealand* v. *France*). Compare: *Nicaragua Case (Merits)*, note 16, p. 8 above, at 132.

institutions more generally, and in particular to how those regimes and institutions are developed, maintained and changed. Chapter 2 reviewed how regime theorists and institutionalists have tried to explain the growth and persistence of regimes and other international institutions. Keohane, for example, has demonstrated that the international trading regime, the General Agreement on Tariffs and Trade, was largely the result of a preponderance of United States power and influence in the years immediately following the Second World War.[10] That conclusion, in itself, was hardly surprising. However, Keohane also demonstrated that the international trading regime survived far longer than an analysis of United States hegemony would suggest it should have survived. He accounted for this finding by arguing that States sometimes maintain regimes longer than is necessary to fulfil the initial purpose for their creation – generally the advancement of a hegemonic State's power – if those regimes have come to serve other purposes. Such other purposes could include improving efficiency by removing the need to deal with situations on a case-by-case basis, and facilitating communication, negotiation and the resolution of disputes, not necessarily for the hegemonic State alone but for other States as well.[11]

The persistence of regimes and other institutions is accentuated by something which Keohane referred to as 'sunk costs', namely the irretrievable investment of an actor's time and power in creating a regime or institution.[12] Faced with the loss of this investment, actors will sometimes choose to maintain the regime or institution even if purely utilitarian calculations, which do not take into account that past investment, do not justify their so doing.

In international society, the various factors which contribute to the persistence of regimes and institutions may well be exaggerated due to the multitude of independent actors, with the result that sustainable regimes and institutions cannot normally be imposed by a single, powerful State but instead require extensive negotiation and compromise. Agreement on any given issue may be difficult to achieve once, let alone several times. Cognisant of the risk of failure associated with inter-State negotiation, States may sometimes choose to retain an existing regime or institution rather than take the risks inherent in trying to create a new one.[13] All of these factors help to explain the remarkable persistence of regimes and

[10] Keohane (1984). [11] Keohane (1984) 243–59.

[12] Keohane (1984) 102. See also Stinchcombe (1968) 120–1.

[13] See generally: Young (1989) 65–7. Young wrote that '[t]he image of a dominant state or a hegemon playing the role of lawgiver is severely distorted' (Young (1989) 65) and that 'the difficulties of putting together a winning coalition, much less achieving general consensus, in support of specific alternatives to prevailing institutional arrangements are notorious' (Young (1989) 203–4).

institutions in international society. However, it would seem necessary to consider whether legal obligation also plays a role.

The principle of legitimate expectation, in particular, may be as important as the non-legal factors put forward by Keohane and others, in terms of its ability to explain the persistence of international regimes and institutions. Moreover, it would seem that an explanation for the persistence of regimes and institutions that was based on the principle of legitimate expectation could be compatible with an understanding of the international system as largely responsive to applications of power in the furtherance of State interests. In short, the principle of legitimate expectation, unlike other, non-legal factors, is largely external to short-term interest calculations and applications of power precisely because it is a principle of international law.

## Legitimate expectation and relative resistance to change

Earlier in this chapter it was suggested that, within the customary process, it is the principle of legitimate expectation which gives legal effect to acquiescence, and that the principle of legitimate expectation is, in a sense, at the heart of all customary and treaty rules.[14] Even more generally, in chapter 1 it was suggested that the customary process legitimises patterns of State behaviour, and thus State expectations, by transforming those patterns into law.[15] However, the principle of legitimate expectation may have its most interesting effects on the customary process in terms of how it relates to the relative degrees of resistance to change exhibited by different customary rules.

It has already been suggested that different customary rules attract differing degrees of supporting, ambivalent and opposing State practice and that, as a result, some rules are more resistant to change than others.[16] It may well be that the degree of legitimate expectation which is held by States in respect of whether a rule will continue in force is related to the degree of resistance which that rule has to being changed. If so, were the rule's resistance to alter as a result of changes in the relative amounts of supporting, ambivalent and opposing State practice it attracts, one would expect a corresponding change in the degree of legitimate expectation held in respect of that particular rule's continuing in force.

This conclusion might seem tautological. Indeed, it would be if legitimate expectation concerning the continuing in force of customary rules were in all cases firmly linked to the relative amounts of supporting,

[14] See pp. 106–7 above. [15] See pp. 6–10 above.
[16] See pp. 19–20 above. For a more detailed discussion, see pp. 157–60 below.

ambivalent and opposing State practice, i.e. to resistance to change *objectively* defined. However, legitimate expectation concerning whether a rule will continue in force might sometimes become detached from that rule's 'resistance to change', making it necessary to distinguish between the two. In this context, legitimate expectation is the measure of what States consider the weight of a particular rule to be, rather than what the weight of that rule actually is. And since State practice in respect of rules depends, not on what those rules are, but on what States consider those rules to be, it is legitimate expectation rather than an objectively defined resistance to change which accounts for how States behave when they attempt to contribute to, or impede, the development, maintenance or change of rules of customary international law.

## Legitimate expectation and mistaken beliefs in pre-existing rules

Sometimes what most States consider to be rules of customary international law may not in fact be rules at all. In such situations their mistaken belief in the existence of a customary rule may have the same effect on applications of power in respect of a new rule that the resistance to change of an existing rule would normally have had. In order, therefore, for State practice to create a new customary rule it may first have to overcome any widely held mistaken belief in an existing one. Since a widely held belief in the existence of a rule constitutes legitimate expectation, even when that expectation is misguided, the principle of legitimate expectation would thus be operating to qualify the application of power in the process of customary international law. In short, by according a degree of *subjective* resistance to rules which do not exist, it may act to prevent or retard the development of new rules, as is suggested by the examples below.

### *State immunity from jurisdiction*

One example of this qualifying effect at work concerns State immunity from jurisdiction. It is generally assumed that when the doctrine of restrictive State immunity from the jurisdiction of foreign courts became a rule of customary international law in the middle of the twentieth century, it did so by changing a previously existing rule that States were absolutely immune from jurisdiction.[17] However, an examination of the history of State immunity, which is primarily a history of national court judgments and national legislation, indicates that absolute immunity was

[17] See, e.g., Sucharitkul (1979); Trooboff (1986); Carter and Trimble (1991) 550; Jennings and Watts (1992) 355–63; and Shaw (1997) 491–9. For a more cautious approach see Emanuelli (1984).

not an established rule. Rather, history suggests that there was no general rule regulating State immunity from jurisdiction prior to restrictive immunity becoming a rule of customary international law, and that a mistaken belief in such a pre-existing rule served to retard that later development.

Belgian courts were applying restrictive immunity as early as 1857,[18] while Italian courts were doing so in 1886,[19] Swiss courts in 1918[20] and Austrian courts in 1919.[21] Argentine[22] and French[23] courts distinguished between acts *jure imperii* (of government) and acts *jure gestionis* (of a commercial character) from 1924, Egyptian courts from 1926,[24] Greek courts from 1928,[25] Irish courts from 1941[26] and German courts from 1949.[27]

During this period, courts in common law States were applying absolute immunity and continued to do so until legislative changes were introduced during the 1970s and 1980s. In the United Kingdom, for example, it was not until 1977 that Lord Denning and Justice Shaw controversially applied restrictive immunity in direct contradiction to clear precedents in English common law.[28] This application of restrictive

[18] *l'Etat du Pérou* v. *Kreglinger* (1857 II) *Pasicrisie Belge* 348.

[19] *Guttières* v. *Elmilik* (1886) 38(1)(1) *Giurisprudenza Italiana* 486 (Court of Cassation of Florence).

[20] *K.k. Österreich. Finanzministerium* v. *Dreyfus* (1918 I) 44 *Entscheidungen des schweizerischen Bundesgerichts* 49.

[21] *Österreichische-ungarische Bank* v. *Ungarische Regierung* (1920) 28 *Niemeyers Zeitschrift für internationales Recht* 506.

[22] *Cia Introductora de Buenos Aires* v. *Capitan del Vapor Cokato* 14 *Jurisprudencia Argentina* 705 (1924), trans. in (1923–4) *Annual Digest* 136 (Federal Court of Appeal of the Capital). Compare *The Ibai* (1937) 178 *Fallos* 173, trans. in (1938–40) *Annual Digest* 293 (Supreme Court).

[23] *Etat roumain* v. *Société A. Pascalet* (1924) *Recueil hebdomadaire de jurisprudence* 260.

[24] *Borg* v. *Caisse Nationale d'Epargne Française* (1925–6) 16 *Gazette Tribunal Mixte d'Egypte* 123 (Case 154) (Tribunal civil d'Alexandria). See also *Monopole des Tabacs de Turquie* v. *Régie co-intéressée des Tabacs de Turquie* (1929–30) 20 *Gazette Tribunal Mixte d'Egypte* 145 (Case 133) (Cour d'Appel).

[25] *Soviet Republic Case* (1927–8) 4 *Annual Digest* 172 (Court of Athens). See also *Consular Premises Case* (1931–2) 6 *Annual Digest* 338 (Court of Athens).

[26] *The Ramava* (1941–2) 10 *Annual Digest* 91 (High Court).

[27] *Das sowjetische Ministerium für Aussenhandel* (1949) 3 *Juristische Rundschau* 118 (Berlin Court of Appeal (Kammergericht)).

[28] See *Trendtex Trading Corp.* v. *Central Bank of Nigeria* [1977] 2 WLR 356, (1977) 16 ILM 471 (Court of Appeal). Precedents included: *The Prins Frederik* (1820) 2 *Dodson's Admiralty Reports* 451; *De Haber* v. *Queen of Portugal* (1851) 17 QB 171; *The Porto Alexandre* (1920) *Law Reports – Probate Division* 30; *Compania Naviera Vascongada* v. *SS Cristina* [1938] AC 485, 490 (judgment of Lord Atkin). It should be noted, however, that before 1977 numerous English judges had criticised, or at least been hesitant in applying, the doctrine of absolute immunity. See, most famously, *The Charkieh* (1873) 3 *British International Law Cases* 275, 299 (opinion of Sir Robert Phillimore). Denning and Shaw were also faced by the somewhat dubious distinction made by the Privy Council in *The Philippine Admiral* v. *Wallen Shipping Ltd* [1976] 2 WLR 214, (1976) 15 ILM 133, where the Privy Council applied the doctrine of restrictive immunity, but only in respect of an action *in rem*.

immunity was largely followed by other English judges and was almost certainly responsible for changing the English common law on this issue.[29] Before this change was firmly established, Parliament passed the State Immunity Act 1978,[30] which confirmed and solidified the judiciary's changing position.[31]

In the United States, absolute immunity was firmly entrenched in the common law.[32] However, a practice had developed, and had been accepted as law, whereby 'suggestions' from the Department of State as to the lack of immunity in specific cases were followed by the courts.[33] Then, in 1952, the Department of State announced in the so-called 'Tate letter' that, as a matter of policy, it would no longer favour claims of immunity for foreign governments in respect of commercial transactions.[34] This statement guided the courts in subsequent cases

[29] See *I Congreso del Partido* [1977] 3 WLR 778, (1983) 64 ILR 154 (QB, opinion of Goff J), [1980] 1 *Lloyd's Law Reports* 23, (1983) 64 ILR 227 (Court of Appeal), [1981] 3 WLR 328, (1983) 64 ILR 307 (House of Lords); *Planmount Ltd* v. *Republic of Zaire* [1981] 1 All ER 1110, (1983) 64 ILR 268 (QB, opinion of Lloyd J). See generally Lewis (1990) 14–29 (summarising the English common law of State immunity).

[30] Note 61, p. 69 above.

[31] See, e.g., *Alcom Ltd* v. *Colombia* [1984] 2 WLR 750, (1983) 22 ILM 1307 (QB).

[32] Chief Justice Marshall's famous words in *Schooner Exchange* v. *McFaddon* established a precedent which held for over 150 years:

> One sovereign being in no respect amenable to another; and being bound by obligations of the highest character not to degrade the dignity of his nation, by placing himself or its sovereign rights within the jurisdiction of another, can be supposed to enter a foreign territory only under an express license, or in the confidence that the immunities belonging to his independent sovereign station, though not expressly stipulated, are reserved by implication, and will be extended to him.

11 US (7 Cranch) 116, 137 (1812). Although, as Sinclair has noted, this 'judgment is in no way inconsistent with the theory that immunity may extend only so far as to secure the protection of the "sovereign rights" exercisable by a foreign sovereign' (Sinclair (1980) 122), the United States Supreme Court chose to apply this precedent in an absolutist manner. In 1926 the Court wrote that the principles set out in the *Schooner Exchange* were 'applicable alike to all ships held and used by a government for a public purpose' including, in this instance, a government-owned merchant vessel used to transport olive oil for commercial sale. *Berizzi Bros* v. *SS Pesaro*, 271 US 562, 574 (1926).

[33] See, e.g., *Ex Parte Republic of Peru*, 318 US 578 (1943); and *Republic of Mexico* v. *Hoffman*, 324 US 30 (1945).

[34] (1968) 6 Whiteman 569–71. See Bishop (1953); and Drachsler (1960). However, the executive did not always adhere strictly to its policy as expressed in the 'Tate letter'. For example, in the 1970 case of *Isbrandtsen Tankers* v. *President of India*, 446 F. 2d 1198 (2d Cir. 1970), cert. denied, 404 US 985 (1971), the United States Court of Appeals stated that it would have applied the doctrine of restrictive immunity had it not been for the provision, by the State Department, of a written 'suggestion' of immunity. Similarly, the United States continued throughout the 1950s to claim immunity whenever it was sued in foreign courts. In the 1960s the United States restricted its claims of absolute immunity to those situations in which it was sued in the courts of States adhering to that doctrine. Only in the 1970s did it stop claiming absolute immunity altogether. See Trooboff (1986) 270.

where the Department of State refused to make 'suggestions'. In these situations, the courts predictably held that foreign States were not entitled to immunity when engaged in activities of an essentially commercial character.[35]

Executive action as expressed in the Tate letter was followed twenty-four years later by legislative action in the form of the Foreign Sovereign Immunities Act of 1976.[36] After passage of the FSIA, the Department of State largely discontinued its practice of making 'suggestions' of immunity, thus leaving this question for the courts to decide on the basis of the new legislation.[37]

Developments similar to those in the United Kingdom and the United States took place in other common law States from Singapore,[38] Pakistan,[39] South Africa,[40] Canada[41] to Australia.[42]

[35] See, e.g., *National City Bank of New York* v. *Republic of China*, 348 US 356 (1955); *Victory Transport, Inc.* v. *Comisaría General de Abastecimientos y Transportes*, 336 F. 2d 354 (2d Cir. 1964); and *Ocean Transport* v. *Government of the Republic of the Ivory Coast*, 269 F. Supp. 703 (ED La. 1967).

[36] Note 65, p. 70 above. For a review of the key provisions of the FSIA, as well as a brief outline of the history of State immunity in the United States, see Leigh (1978). See also von Mehren (1978); and Brower *et al.* (1979).

[37] But see, e.g., *United States* v. *Arlington*, 669 F. 2d 925 (4th Cir. 1982). In this case the Department of State had taken the view that section 1610(a)(4)(B) of the FSIA applied and that the property of the foreign State in question was therefore immune from execution. The court noted that although the views of the Department of State were not conclusive, they carried great weight and could only be rejected if deemed to be unreasonable. *Ibid.*, 934.

[38] State Immunity Act 1979, reproduced in: *Materials on Jurisdictional Immunities of States and their Property*, UN Doc. ST/LEG/SER.B/20 (1982) 28.

[39] State Immunity Ordinance, 1981, reproduced in *ibid.*, 20.

[40] Foreign Sovereign Immunity Act (1981), reproduced in *ibid.*, 34. For comment, see Bray and Beukes (1981); and Erasmus (1982).

[41] Act to Provide for State Immunity in Canadian Courts (1982), note 61, p. 69 above. The doctrine of absolute immunity had been established as common law by the Supreme Court of Canada in *Dessaules* v. *Poland* (1944) 4 DLR 1. However, in *Flota Maritima Browning de Cuba SA* v. *SS Canadian Conqueror* (1962) SCR 598 that same court left the matter open, while leaning towards a restrictive approach. The decision in *Congo* v. *Venne* (1971) SCR 997 was similarly inconclusive. In more recent years the doctrine of restrictive immunity was applied by several lower courts. See *Zodiak International Products* v. *Polish People's Republic* (1977) 81 DLR (3d) 656 (Quebec Court of Appeal); and *Smith* v. *Canadian Javelin* (1976) 68 DLR (3d) 428 (Ontario High Court). For comment on the Act, see Molot and Jewett (1982). It is also interesting to note that section 43(7)(c) of the Federal Court Act, c. 1, 1970–1, SC, stated that: 'No action *in rem* may be commenced in Canada against any ship owned or operated by a sovereign power other than Canada, or any cargo laden thereon, with respect to any claim where, at the time the claim arose or the action is commenced, such ship was being used exclusively for non-commercial governmental purposes.' Thus, in 1970, the Federal Court had implicitly been granted jurisdiction over foreign State-owned ships used for non-governmental, commercial activities.

[42] Foreign States Immunities Act 1985, note 61, p. 69 above. See also Australian Law Reform Commission (1984) (providing background to the development of the Australian Act and a comprehensive survey of the international law of State immunity).

The difference between common law and civil law jurisdictions in terms of their willingness to incorporate the doctrine of restrictive State immunity into national law can be explained on at least three grounds. First, common law courts remained bound by the doctrine of crown immunity ('sovereign immunity' in the United States) long after civil law courts began to distinguish between immune and non-immune acts of their own sovereigns. Secondly, courts in common law systems felt bound by the doctrine of *stare decisis* not to abandon their earlier applications of absolute immunity.[43] Thirdly, common law States had a less acute interest in the development of the doctrine of restrictive immunity than most civil law States. The common law States were either large, such as the United States, or part of the former British Empire – with its internal cohesion and historic, political and commercial ties. By contrast, the smaller civil law trading States of continental Europe, such as the Netherlands and Belgium, were dependent to a far greater extent on trade between fully sovereign States.

However, it seems that the principle of legitimate expectation also played a role. In every common law jurisdiction, absolute immunity was viewed as the previously applicable rule of customary international law. Consequently, the changes in national laws were regarded as responses to a change in the existing customary rule rather than as responses to the development of a new rule, even though it is apparent, from the earlier developments in civil law jurisdictions, that a customary rule of absolute State immunity could not have existed at any date after the very early twentieth century.[44] This widely held mistaken belief would seem to have been at least partly responsible for retarding the acceptance of the doctrine of restrictive immunity in common law States and, therefore, the development of restrictive immunity as a new rule of customary international law.

### *The breadth of the territorial sea*

The development of a rule of customary international law establishing the breadth of the territorial sea at twelve nautical miles provides another example of the principle of legitimate expectation at work through a mistaken belief in a pre-existing rule. It would seem that, until the early 1980s, State practice was sufficiently inconsistent to prevent any particular breadth from becoming a rule of customary international law. However, faced with a variety of claims in excess of three nautical miles, as well as improvements in ordnance which extended the breadth covered

[43] On *stare decisis*, see pp. 120–4 below. [44] See generally notes 18–27 above.

by the 'cannon-shot rule', maritime States and writers from maritime States succeeded in convincing themselves, and others, that a customary rule already existed, to the effect that the breadth of the territorial sea was in fact three miles. This mistaken belief, in turn, imposed a serious restraint on the development of a new, more extensive rule.

Disagreement as to the breadth of the territorial sea had existed for centuries. Thus, although in 1782 Galiani asserted that the three-mile limit was part of international law,[45] Norway, Sweden and Finland had been claiming a four-mile limit since earlier in the eighteenth century.[46] In 1794, the United States Congress felt it necessary to enact the Neutrality Act to grant jurisdiction to the district courts to hear cases arising out of the capture of foreign ships 'within the waters of the United States, *or* within a marine league [three miles] of the coasts or shores thereof'.[47] Although the nineteenth and very early twentieth centuries saw a number of States claim three-mile limits,[48] some Mediterranean States claimed six-mile limits,[49] while most continental European States continued to regard the breadth of the territorial sea as being determined solely on the basis of the 'cannon-shot rule'.[50] Then, in 1921, the Soviet Union became the first State to assert a twelve-mile limit, although it did so only in respect of fishing rights along its Arctic coast and in the White Sea.[51]

Faced with this variety of claims and improvements in ordnance,

45 See Galiani (1782).

46 Sweden did so in 1779; Norway did so before that date. See Bardonnet (1962) 67, note 121.

47 Neutrality Act of 1794, 1 Stat. 369 (1794), 18 USC sections 960–2 (1982) (emphasis added).

48 These States included the United Kingdom (1800–5), Austria (1846), Chile (1855), Brazil (1859), Japan (1870), Argentina (1871), Ecuador (1889), the Netherlands (1889), Liberia (1902) and Mexico (1902). See O'Connell (1982) 131–2; and Brownlie (1990) 188, note 47.

49 See McDougal and Burke (1962) 69.

50 See generally: O'Connell (1982) 134–5 and 151–3. In the years immediately preceding World War I, France, Italy, Russia, Spain and the Ottoman Empire all claimed the right to exercise jurisdiction up to any distance from shore within the actual range of artillery, as long as the exercise of that jurisdiction was reasonable for the control of specific activities such as fishing or smuggling. See Churchill and Lowe (1988) 66. The confusion as to the breadth of the territorial sea was reflected in the writing of legal scholars. O'Connell ((1982) 153–4) noted that:

> [D]uring the critical period from 1876 to 1914, thirty-three jurists believed that the territorial sea expanded with the evolving range of artillery; twenty-six believed that State practice had established it at three miles; five proposed other fixed limits; five argued for different limits for different purposes; eight ambiguously referred to both the three-mile limit and the cannon-shot; and seven thought that there was no consensus on the matter.

51 O'Connell (1982) 155. Legislation implementing a twelve-mile limit along all parts of the Soviet Union's coastline did not follow until 1960. O'Connell (1982) 155.

maritime States and writers from maritime States argued that a rule of customary international law, to the effect that the breadth of the territorial sea was three miles, already regulated the issue. For example, in 1928 Baty wrote that

> during the nineteenth century it [the three-mile limit] has been virtually unchallenged in practice, and it has been asserted as law by the most eminent statesmen and in the most formal documents. Few if any countries have ever formally contradicted it during that period, and none has ever successfully enforced a different rule on unwilling contemporaries.[52]

Many other scholars, and groups of scholars, expressed similar views during the inter-war period.[53]

In 1930, State representatives met at The Hague to codify three areas of customary law, including the breadth of the territorial sea.[54] They grouped themselves in three different camps. Some advocated a three-mile limit without a contiguous zone; others wanted a three-mile limit with a contiguous zone; and a third group sought a territorial sea, either with or without a contiguous zone, with a breadth in excess of three miles. In the end a narrow majority supported the three-mile limit, but the two-thirds majority needed to carry the proposal forward was lacking.[55]

Following the 1930 Hague Conference, jurists 'defected *en masse* from

[52] Baty (1928) 503.

[53] See, e.g., Fenwick (1924) 250–2; Conboy (1924) 18; Colombos (1924) 96; de Staël-Holstein (1924) 630 (asserting that the Scandinavian four-mile limit was an exception to an otherwise general rule); and Jessup (1927) 62–6. For contemporaneous criticism of the three-mile limit see Brown (1923). In 1926 the International Law Association accepted the three-mile limit (*Report of the 34th Conference, Vienna*, 101, Art. 5), as did the American Institute of International Law ((1926) 20 *American Journal of International Law Supplement* 141, Art. 2) and the Deutsche Gesellschaft für Völkerrecht (Küstenmeerentwurf, Res. of 15 October 1926, (1927) 8 *Mitteilung der deutsche Gesellschaft für Völkerrecht* 116). The Institut de droit international, which in 1894 had adopted a resolution in favour of a six-mile limit ((1894–5) 13 *Annuaire de l'institut de droit international* 329, Art. 2), accepted the three-mile limit in 1928 ((1928) 35 *Annuaire de l'institut de droit international* 755, Art. 2). The Harvard Research Project, for its part, adopted the three-mile limit in 1929 ((1929) 23 *American Journal of International Law Supplement* 243, Art. 2).

[54] The other two areas were nationality and State responsibility. The conference produced the Convention on Certain Questions Relating to the Conflict of Nationality Laws, 179 LNTS 89. For a brief discussion of this convention see Brownlie (1990) 386. The area of State responsibility remains uncodified. See generally the citations in note 36, p. 83 above.

[55] Of the nineteen States which supported the three-mile limit, seven asserted that a contiguous zone should extend outward from it. In the end, the Conference considered 'that the discussions had made apparent divergences of opinion in respect of certain fundamental questions which, for the moment, do not permit the conclusion of a convention relative to the territorial sea' (my translation). See 'Extrait du compte rendu provisoire de la treizième séance tenue le jeudi 3 avril 1930', and 'Résolution concernant la continuation des travaux sur les questions afférentes aux eaux territoriales', in Guerrero (1930) Annex 5, 204 and 208.

the three-mile principle, while being increasingly unable to agree on an alternative'.[56] Many authors, including Kelsen, Rousseau, Verdross, Reuter and Alvárez, asserted that no rule of international law existed to regulate the breadth of the territorial sea.[57] Dahm suggested that the situation constituted a '*vollständige Anarchie*'.[58] Only a few writers continued to insist on the applicability of the three-mile rule.[59]

The fact that many of these writers assumed that a rule had existed,[60] and that that rule had been three miles, was due above all 'to the influence exerted by Great Britain and the United States'.[61] Only when it became clear to these writers that their best efforts could not arrest the development of a customary rule establishing the breadth in excess of three miles did they abandon their support for the supposed three-mile rule.

As this brief review of the history of the breadth of the territorial sea demonstrates, 'it is meaningless to speak of a single limit for territorial sea claims existing at any one time'.[62] Nevertheless, Jennings argued in 1967 that the three-mile limit, while having become a minority position was nonetheless a minimum limit, and therefore the only standard available against the world. This meant that any claim exceeding three miles was valid in respect of other States only on an individual basis through their acquiescence or express consent.[63]

Jennings' position may, however, be questioned in the light of the fact that the breadth of the territorial sea is a boundary rule.[64] As was explained in chapter 4, any rule of customary international law concerning the breadth of the territorial sea is the result of a stabilising of the tension between the principle of jurisdiction and the freedom of the seas. The rule thus creates simultaneous rights and legal obligations in both directions, namely, towards the coastal State in the use of its coastal waters, and towards all other States in their use of the high seas.[65] Consequently, the breadth of the territorial sea could not be a minimum standard in only one direction. Although each State will have minimum

[56] O'Connell (1982) 159.
[57] See Kelsen (1952) 220; Rousseau (1953) 437; Verdross (1955) 215; Reuter (1958) 217; and Alvárez (1959) 533.
[58] A 'complete anarchy'. See Dahm (1958) 655.
[59] See, e.g., Colombos (1967) 110.
[60] A notable exception was de Visscher, who asserted that the three-mile limit had never acquired universal authority. See de Visscher (1957) 211–12.
[61] O'Connell (1982) 165. This influence, it should be noted, had never been strong enough to alter the claims and policies of the 'dissenting' States.
[62] Churchill and Lowe (1988) 66.
[63] Jennings (1967) 383. Jennings, in advancing this argument, relied partly on Waldock (1956) 185.
[64] See pp. 60–4 above.
[65] This would not appear to be the case with non-boundary rules which, in any given situation, create rights in only one direction and obligations in another, with reciprocity occurring in another, discrete situation.

obligations, there could be no such thing as a minimum 'rule'. In a boundary situation, it would seem that indeterminacy does not result in the rule shifting to one side or the other; it remains indeterminate. Only in situations involving non-boundary rules will the rule settle, in effect, to the bottom, below any confusion of dissenting and disparate State practice. By not distinguishing between these two types of situations, Jennings may, like many other scholars, have sought to provide a rule where one never existed. The development of the twelve-mile rule should probably be regarded as just that – a development – and not a change of customary international law.[66]

This territorial sea example and the State immunity example which preceded it may have implications for our understanding of the process of customary international law. Suppose that a three-mile rule had existed, by virtue of the fact that a sufficient degree of supporting State practice and a sufficient absence of opposing State practice had given rise to a customary rule. In that case, actions contrary to that rule would have been violations of customary international law. Thus, a State wanting to oppose the rule would be forced to choose between violating international law or using the less effective means of statements to support a change to the rule. In addition, actions or statements contrary to the old rule would probably have to be regarded as contributions to its 'desuetude', before they could be considered as contributions to a new rule. The threshold for the creation of a new rule would therefore appear to be higher in cases where an old rule exists than in cases where there is no such pre-existing rule.[67]

This requirement may have consequences for those States which oppose the development or change of a customary rule. If the threshold for change is higher than it is for development, objections to change will have a greater effect in terms of arresting or retarding that change than will objections to development. In other words, the degree of uniformity of State practice which is sufficient to result in the development of a rule may not be sufficient to change an existing rule. Objectors to the change of a rule will therefore be more likely to prevent that change than objectors to a development, who may instead end up as persistent objectors to the new rule.[68]

Consequently, by believing or causing others to believe in the pre-

[66] This is not to say that States which excluded others from the waters less than three miles off their coasts were violating international law. Although there may have been no rule as to breadth, coastal States could legally exercise jurisdiction over that area because no State had ever claimed that the breadth of the territorial sea was less than three miles. Nevertheless, this would not have been a minimum rule, but rather a right to exercise jurisdiction in an area where the right to do so had never been disputed.

[67] See generally Danilenko (1993) 123–8.

[68] See the discussions of persistent objection at pp. 102–5 above and pp. 180–3 below.

existence of a three-mile rule and a rule of absolute State immunity, States and scholars may have been making it more difficult for new rules to develop in these areas. In this respect, the belief in pre-existing 'rules' that never existed is an example of the principle of legitimate expectation qualifying the application of power in the process of customary international law.

There are, of course, other possible motives for wanting to believe in the existence of a rule. Like most people, international actors prefer stability and determinacy to instability and indeterminacy, and it would seem that many States and authors preferred to think that rules existed in respect of the breadth of the territorial sea and State immunity, even when rules did not exist. Although international law has traditionally included a presumption in favour of State freedom to act, States and authors appear uncomfortable with an absence of rules because such an absence implies that there are no constraints on other States' behaviour.[69]

In some situations, where the threshold created by a fictional rule is relatively low, a mistaken belief in a pre-existing rule might actually promote change, despite the principle of legitimate expectation. It may be psychologically easier to change or modify an existing rule than it is to create a rule in an area where none exists. Lawyers, certainly, are more comfortable modifying laws than they are creating them. By believing in fictional rules, international lawyers may enable those rules to be 'changed' by State practice, 'progressive development' through 'codification' (which implies that there is something to codify), the contributions of writers, the arguments of lawyers and the determinations of courts. Law creation, on the other hand, is something lawyers may prefer to leave to diplomats and statesmen, who may not be as aware as lawyers of the need for new or 'modified' rules.

An example of this phenomenon might be the recent expansion of the 'right' to humanitarian intervention. Article 2(7) of the Charter of the United Nations prohibits intervention except in situations where, in terms of Chapter VII, there is a threat to or breach of international peace and security. The situations in northern Iraq, Somalia, Haiti and Rwanda, with the possible exception of the problem of refugees, do not seem to fall within this context as it has traditionally been understood. However, instead of changing the rule, or creating a new rule to allow intervention for humanitarian purposes in situations not threatening to international peace and security, international society has chosen to view these as unique situations justifying *ad hoc* enlargements of the international peace and security concept. In short, international society's interpretation of

[69] In respect of the presumption in favour of State freedom to act, see, most famously, *The Lotus Case*, quotation, p. 142 below.

Chapter VII has arguably been modified without the text of the Charter having been changed.[70] However, with regard to pre-existing rules having a higher threshold, as a result of having attracted relatively more supporting State practice, the pre-existence of the rule would appear to have more of an effect in deterring change than it would have in promoting it.

It is striking that, in respect of the breadth of the territorial sea, the strongest and most widespread assertions as to the existence of a three-mile rule were made only once it had become apparent that a more expansive limit might become law. One possible explanation is that States see little need to articulate and defend the assumptions they hold and the practices they engage in when there is no threat of a new rule arising. Only once those assumptions and practices are challenged, when a potential rule appears which may threaten State interests, do previously unarticulated beliefs rise to the surface. The principle of legitimate expectation, in this sense, might be used not so much to oppose new rules as to give legal value to understandings and practices which previously have not been seen as requiring the protection of legal status.

## Legitimate expectation and judgments of the International Court of Justice

In addition to instances of mistaken belief in pre-existing rules, the principle of legitimate expectation may have qualifying effects on the application of power in the customary process in terms of the probative value it accords those judgments of the International Court of Justice which deal with questions of customary international law. As with instances of mistaken belief, the effects of the principle of legitimate expectation here may, to some degree, be detached from resistance to change, as that is objectively defined.

The courts of some national legal systems rely heavily on the doctrine of *stare decisis*, which holds that decisions already made should be followed, and that like cases should therefore be decided alike. The doctrine of *stare decisis* would thus appear to be an example of the principle of legitimate expectation at work, albeit in the context of national law. And in some areas, such as that of State immunity from jurisdiction, this reliance by national courts on the doctrine of *stare decisis* has affected the development of rules of customary international law.[71] Moreover, States may rely on a similar concept in international law in respect of decisions of the International Court of Justice, and this reliance may also serve to qualify applications of power in the customary process.

[70] See similarly Franck (1995) 224–42, especially 233.

[71] See pp. 110–14 above.

According to Article 38(1)(d) of the Statute of the International Court of Justice, judicial decisions are only a 'subsidiary means for the determination of rules of law'. Article 38(1)(d) also states that it is 'subject to the provisions of Article 59', which reads: 'The decision of the Court has no binding force except between the parties and in respect of that particular case.' These two provisions, read together, might seem to suggest that judgments are 'one-off' decisions in respect of specific disputes brought before the Court, and thus preclude the possibility that the decisions of the Court could play a larger role in the international legal system. This interpretation of the two provisions has, in fact, proven inaccurate. Instead, the Court's decisions, including those involving questions of customary international law, are accorded great significance by the Court and by States in subsequent disputes. States rely heavily on prior decisions of the Court in their pleadings before it, as does the Court itself in rendering its judgments.[72] In the *Gulf of Maine Case*, the Chamber of the Court stated that the Court's judgment in the *North Sea Continental Shelf Cases* was 'the judicial decision which has made the greatest contribution to the formation of customary law in this field'.[73]

One may regard this situation in at least two ways. First, one may read Article 38(1)(d) as precluding the consideration of prior Court judgments except in the absence of any of the 'primary' means for the determination of rules of law, namely treaties, State practice providing evidence of customary international law, or proof of the existence of general principles of law. Similarly, one may read Article 59 in such a way as to exclude previous decisions of the Court from having *any* value in respect of subsequent cases, either as determinations of specific rights and obligations or as determinations of the existence and content of rules more generally.[74] On the basis of these readings, the current practice of

[72] See generally Danilenko (1993) 253–61; Higgins (1994) 202–4; and Shahabuddeen (1996). The Court, it should be noted, is a creation of States and only has jurisdiction to resolve a dispute if both disputing States consent to its so doing. Consequently, any role the Court's judgments may play in developing international law and constraining power *outside* specific disputes brought before it will not differ fundamentally from the other ways, described in this book, in which rules and principles of international law (which are all based on State consent, at least initially) themselves qualify applications of power.

[73] Note 15, p. 38 above, at 293.

[74] It is interesting to note that there is an inherent contradiction between these 'strict' readings of Article 38(1)(d) and Article 59. Shahabuddeen ((1996) 100) noted that Article 38(1)(d) refers to 'judicial decisions' in general and unqualified terms, whereas the application of Article 59 is clearly restricted to the International Court of Justice. He observed that, were the purpose of Article 59 'to prevent decisions of the Court from exerting precedential effect with binding force', it would follow that 'the decisions of other courts and tribunals presumably stand on higher ground, not being caught by the Article 59 limitation. The consequence is so improbable as to suggest that the interpretation on which it rests cannot be correct.'

States and of the Court would appear to be in violation, or has perhaps caused a modification, of Article 38(1)(d) and Article 59.[75]

Secondly, it may be possible to argue that the Court is playing an important, more general law-determining function and that its decisions, although in no way legally binding in and of themselves in subsequent disputes, provide valuable assessments as to the existence and content of specific rules of law. These assessments, because they are not legally binding in and of themselves, are only subsidiary and reliance on them is therefore not in violation of Article 38(1)(d). They are, in other words, highly persuasive – but only persuasive – authority.[76] And, as Jennings has suggested, the degree of persuasiveness accorded to such assessments varies from case to case depending on a number of factors, including the way in which these assessments are treated by subsequent State practice.[77] They might be considered particularly valuable if it is clear that there had been insufficient time, or insufficient State practice, for a rule of customary international law to have changed in the period between the previous judgment and the dispute at hand.

An example of the Court seeming to take this second approach involves the 1993 *Jan Mayen Case*.[78] In this case the Court, relying solely on the decision of its Chamber in the *Gulf of Maine Case*[79] and its own decision on an analogous but somewhat different question of law in the *Libya/Malta Case*,[80] made a determination about the existence and content of a rule of customary international law.[81] The Court did not examine State practice. However, the rule in question – that for the delimitation of fisheries zones, it is proper to begin the process of delimitation with a median line provisionally drawn, and that the line can then be adjusted or shifted following an investigation of 'relevant circumstances' – was not a rule in respect of which much State practice takes place. More precisely, it was a rule which almost certainly had not changed in the intervening nine years. The Court, in making no independent examina-

[75] On the possibility of customary law modifications to treaty rules, see pp. 166–80 below.

[76] Rubin ((1997) 25–6) (see also at 140, note 10) wrote:

> In theory today, even with parts of the Anglo-American legal orders that are overwhelmingly left to the common law, such as torts (civil wrongs), the pronouncement of a judge binds only the parties before him or her, and only with respect to the particular case presented. Generalities about the law on which a decision is argued to rest might be persuasive to other judges in other cases, but cannot bind them unless the legal order makes the pronouncement of a particular tribunal the equivalent of legislation for all others.

[77] See Jennings (1996) 8.

[78] *Maritime Delimitation in the Area between Greenland and Jan Mayen* (1993) *ICJ Reports* 38.

[79] Note 29, p. 10 above.

[80] *Case Concerning the Continental Shelf* (1985) *ICJ Reports* 13.

[81] See note 78, p. 122 above, at 61–2 (paras. 52–4).

tion of State practice, may have been justifiably satisfied as to the continuing accuracy of its previous determination.

Such reliance on previous judgments would not appear to violate Article 59 of the Court's Statute. 'Decisions' of the Court, as the assignment of specific rights and legal obligations between the two parties in respect of the problem before the Court, are not binding in subsequent cases. Nevertheless, Article 59 does not prohibit determinations within those judgments as to the existence and content of rules of international law generally from being regarded, in some circumstances, as accurate and indeed conclusive in respect of the state of the law at that time. As Shahabuddeen has written:

> Article 59 is concerned to ensure that a decision, *qua* decision, binds only the parties to the particular case; but this does not prevent the decision from being treated in a later case as 'a statement of what the Court regarded as the correct legal position'.[82]

A review of the drafting history of the Court's Statute suggests, however, that most States did not intend to give the Court's judgments the prominent place in international law which they have today, and that, while States intended judicial decisions to be considered in subsequent cases, many of them at the same time wished to confine those decisions to playing an 'auxiliary function' of 'elucidation'.[83] What we have, therefore, seems to be a modification of the meaning and scope which international society ascribes to Article 38(1)(d) and Article 59.[84]

This modification of meaning and scope would seem to be, at least partly, a result of the principle of legitimate expectation in a context where that principle has become detached from the objectively defined

[82] Shahabuddeen (1996) 63, quoting from the judgment of the International Court of Justice in the *Temple of Preah Vihear Case (Preliminary Objections)* (1961) *ICJ Reports* 16, 27. See also Shahabuddeen (1996) 99–100, 107–9 and 238–9.

[83] See Permanent Court of International Justice (1920) 294, 307–8, 317, 334, 336–8, 584, 605 and 655; Danilenko (1993) 254–5; and Shahabuddeen (1996) 48–66. As Judge Jennings suggested in his dissenting opinion in the *Libya/Malta Case*, note 80, p. 122 above, at 159–60, there may be something of a contradiction between this understanding of the drafters' intent and the presence in the Statute of Article 62 (on intervention). The same would appear to be true in respect of Article 63. See also, on this point, Danilenko (1993) 256; and Jennings (1996) 7.

[84] On the possibility of customary modifications to treaty obligations, see pp. 166–80 below. It is noteworthy that the wording of Article 38(1)(d) did not change from that found in the statute of the ICJ's predecessor, the Permanent Court of International Justice (PCIJ). That Court, like the ICJ, relied heavily on its previous judgments. The fact that Article 38(1)(d) was not changed to prevent this practice from continuing might therefore be regarded as State practice supportive of the continuing validity of the Court's practice of relying on its previous determinations, especially since at the 1920 drafting conference which drew up the PCIJ's Statute those same States had sought to impose limits on such reliance. See Permanent Court of International Justice (1920) 294, 307–8, 317, 334, 336–8, 584, 605 and 655.

resistance to change of customary rules. In short, States, out of a desire to find stability and determinacy in what may otherwise seem to be a highly fluid and largely indeterminate international legal system, may be basing legitimate expectations in respect of rules of customary international law on what the Court has to say about those rules. However, because the Court is not a State, its judgments contribute nothing to the resistance to change, as such, of customary rules.[85] By relying on past judgments, rather than on their own assessments as to the existence and content of customary rules, States are therefore relying on legitimate expectation and not on resistance to change. This reliance may then act to retard or prevent the development or change of customary rules because determinations of the Court are snapshots in time, while customary law is always changing or subject to change as a result of changing interests, changing power relationships and consequent changing patterns of State practice. Although the Court itself may be careful not to rely heavily on past judgments in areas where customary law is evolving quickly, States and authors may not be so cautious.[86] Consequently, the principle of legitimate expectation in this particular context would, again, seem to have qualifying effects on the application of power in the process of customary international law.

### Legitimate expectation and treaties

The principle of legitimate expectation may also qualify the application of power in the customary process in areas already covered by treaty, as opposed to customary rules. As rules of international law, treaty provisions would appear to give rise to legitimate expectations in and of themselves.[87] Moreover, the negotiation of treaties and their signature or ratification would all appear to be forms of State practice which may, in certain circumstances, contribute to the development, maintenance and change of rules of customary international law. For example, it seems clear that the negotiation and ratification of treaties containing provisions prohibiting torture has contributed to the development of an identical rule in customary international law.[88] The twelve-mile territorial sea was probably not definitively established as a rule of customary international law until its inclusion in the 1982 Law of the Sea Convention.[89] And it is

[85] See pp. 75–9 above; and Shahabuddeen (1996) 69–72.
[86] As the Court itself stated in the *Barcelona Traction Case*, note 1, p. 3 above, at 33 (para. 37), 'the Court has to bear in mind the continuous evolution of international law'. For a discussion of the judicial awareness of this issue, see Shahabuddeen (1996) 114–17.
[87] See p. 107 above. [88] See Bonin (1986); and Rodley (1987).
[89] Note 29, p.41 above. See Churchill and Lowe (1988) 67; and pp. 114–20 above.

sometimes argued that large numbers of bilateral investment treaties have changed the customary standard of compensation for expropriation back to the 'prompt, adequate and effective' standard.[90] In any event, the negotiation, signature and ratification of treaties seems to be relevant to the customary process, and this appears to be the case at least partly because of the legitimate expectations which are created – to the effect that States will subsequently behave in a manner which is consistent with those treaties' provisions.[91]

The effects of treaties in encouraging the development or change of customary rules, as well as the fact that many treaties actually codify existing customary rules, suggest that similar treaty and customary rules often co-exist, thus providing parallel sets of legitimate expectations.[92] The legitimate expectations associated with one type of rule may then have an effect on how susceptible the other type of rule is to change, either as a result of confusion between the parallel sets of legitimate expectations, or as a result of an implicit weighing of the two sets of legitimate expectations against each other, should their content at some point diverge. For example, customary rules might become more resistant to change as a result of parallel treaty rules, whereas treaty rules might actually be modified, without formal renegotiation, as a result of changes to parallel customary rules.[93]

Customary rules may become more resistant to change as a result of parallel treaty rules because those treaty rules are sometimes more difficult to change. Treaty rules require formal negotiation, signature and, in many cases, ratification, all of which can sometimes be exceedingly difficult to achieve, either because of the problems involved in negotiating formal agreements among what are often large numbers of States, or because of constraints arising from within national political systems. Customary rules, on the other hand, are changed through what are often gradual, and frequently less than consistent, shifts in State practice. Such changes may go relatively unnoticed, and do not require explicit consent on the part of every State which is to be bound by the new or modified rule.[94]

When treaty and customary rules exist in parallel, the State practice necessary to change the customary rule may involve violations of the treaty rule. This means that, even though the customary rule is open to informal and gradual change, the existence of a more rigid, parallel treaty rule will increase the legal and political constraints on the application of power in the customary process. Even when the State practice supportive

[90] See pp. 58–60 above. [91] See pp. 106–10 above.
[92] See *Nicaragua Case (Merits)*, quotation, p. 171 below. [93] See pp. 166–80 below.
[94] See pp. 7–8 above.

of a change to the customary rule does not actually violate the treaty rule, such as, for example, when that practice is comprised of statements and not acts, that practice may still be interpreted as a rejection or at least a calling into question of the treaty rule, and States may thus be discouraged from engaging in it.

One example of the qualifying effects of parallel treaty rules may involve Article 2(7) of the Charter of the United Nations and the development of human rights in customary international law. Many States have relied on Article 2(7) in resisting efforts to develop rules of customary international law concerning the content, monitoring and enforcement of human rights within the jurisdictions of non-consenting States.[95] Although significant progress has been made in this area, enforcement actions in favour of human rights are, in most situations, still considered violations of both customary international law and, perhaps more importantly, of Article 2(7). It would seem that the existence and relatively unambiguous language of the Article 2(7) treaty rule have contributed to the lack of more extensive customary law developments in this area.

In addition, States may be wary about becoming bound to more than one rule of international law in respect of any particular issue. Multiple legal obligations in respect of single issues are not only confusing in terms of how States should behave, but they may pose difficult problems of State responsibility when one, but not all, of the relevant rules has been violated.[96]

For all of these reasons, the principle of legitimate expectation may be seen to qualify the application of power in the customary process, both as that process operates at the interface between customary and treaty rules, as well as more broadly. Having thus established that the principles of jurisdiction, personality, reciprocity and legitimate expectation all affect how States are able to participate in the customary process, and their efficacy in so doing, it is time to turn to that process itself. More specifically, it is time to consider the fundamental problems of customary international law.

[95] See pp. 43–5 above.
[96] On State responsibility, see the citations in note 36, p. 83 above.

*Part 3*

# The process of customary international law

# 8 Fundamental problems of customary international law

Numerous attempts have been made to provide compelling answers to the many theoretical problems associated with customary international law. The number and diversity of these attempts and growing interest in the subject are indications of how the discipline of international law requires a more convincing rationalisation of the customary process as a whole.

Earlier in this book it was suggested that the process of customary international law involves the transformation of power into obligation in the form of customary rules. Power, by definition, is relational in character, and at least two aspects of this relational character are involved in the customary process. First, there are the relative abilities of different States to control or influence directly how other States behave, and, secondly, there are the relative abilities of power and legal obligation to affect each other.

It will become clear during the next three chapters of this book that many of the theoretical problems associated with the customary process are linked to the relational character of power. It is therefore somewhat surprising that so few international lawyers have considered *directly* the role played by power in the process of customary international law. As has already been explained, most of them have skirted the issue, sometimes acknowledging the importance of power but rarely examining how power affects the development, maintenance and change of different customary rules.[1]

The discipline of international relations is an obvious source of ideas and insights for a study of power in the process of customary international law. International relations scholars are accustomed to questions of power, even if most of them have yet to appreciate fully the crucial difference between non-legal factors, such as power, and normative structures based on legal obligation, such as the process of customary

[1] See pp. 15–18 and 46–50 above.

international law. Recent work on regime theory and institutionalism seems particularly relevant to a study of power in the development, maintenance and change of customary rules.[2] This book draws on this recent work in the discipline of international relations to suggest, not only that the customary process transforms applications of power into obligation in the form of customary rules, but also that it is obligation which gives customary rules their ability to qualify subsequent applications of power both within, and outside, the process of customary international law.

Most international lawyers agree that customary international law results from the co-existence of two elements: first, the presence of a consistent and general practice among States; and, secondly, a consideration on the part of those States that their practice is in accordance with law.[3] The second, subjective element is usually referred to as *opinio juris sive necessitatis*, or simply *opinio juris*. It is clear that something in addition to State practice should be necessary for customary international law, for it is essential that one be able to distinguish between legally binding rules and patterns of behaviour which are not legally required.[4] Yet there are many problems associated with *opinio juris* and the traditional bipartite conception of customary international law. This chapter reviews some of those problems, as well as a number of solutions to them which have been proposed by international lawyers in recent years. It examines the problems from the perspective that the customary process involves an interaction of power and obligation, and it is on this basis that chapter 9 then suggests a new explanation of *opinio juris* and also, therefore, of the process of customary international law more generally.

## The chronological paradox

One problem with the traditional bipartite conception of customary international law is that it involves the apparent chronological paradox

[2] See pp. 24–31 above.

[3] See generally: Art. 38(1)(b) of the Statute of the International Court of Justice; *North Sea Continental Shelf Cases*, note 15, p. 38 above, at 44 (para. 77); Brownlie (1990) 4–11; Jennings and Watts (1992) 25–31; Bernhardt (1992); Danilenko (1993) 81–109; and Dinh *et al.* (1994) 317–24. For different views, see, e.g., Kopelmanas (1937) (customary international law is composed only of State practice); and Cheng (1965) 36 ('International customary law has in reality only one constitutive element, the *opinio juris*').

[4] The International Court has affirmed repeatedly that State practice, by itself, is insufficient to constitute a rule of customary international law. See, e.g., *Lotus Case*, note 16, p. 8 above, at 28; *Asylum Case*, (1950) *ICJ Reports* 265, 276–7; *Right of Passage Case*, (1960) *ICJ Reports* 6, 42–43; and *North Sea Continental Shelf Cases*, note 15, p. 38 above, at 44 (para. 77).

that States creating new customary rules must believe that those rules already exist, and that their practice, therefore, *is* in accordance with law. As was explained by the International Court of Justice in its judgment in the 1969 *North Sea Continental Shelf Cases*:

Not only must the acts concerned amount to a settled practice, but they must also be such, or be carried out in such a way, as to be evidence of a belief that this practice is rendered obligatory by the existence of a rule of law requiring it . . . The States concerned must therefore feel that they are conforming to what amounts to a legal obligation.[5]

Similarly, in its judgment in the 1927 *Lotus Case*, the Permanent Court of International Justice wrote:

Even if the rarity of the judicial decisions to be found . . . were sufficient to prove . . . the circumstance alleged . . . it would merely show that States had often, in practice, abstained from instituting criminal proceedings, and not that they recognized themselves as being obliged to do so; for only if such abstention were based on their being conscious of having a duty to abstain would it be possible to speak of an international custom.[6]

This requirement would seem to make it impossible for new customary rules to develop, since *opinio juris* would only exist in respect of those rules which were *already* in force.[7] This paradox led Kelsen and Guggenheim to conclude that *opinio juris* is nothing but a pseudo-element which allows judges to exercise wide discretion in their analyses of State practice.[8]

One possible response to the chronological paradox was proposed by Geny, who argued that for a new rule of customary law to develop, the relevant actors must *erroneously* believe that they are already bound by that rule.[9] This approach is unsatisfactory because it is inconceivable that an entire legal process – and, since the customary process provides the basis for the law of treaties, an entire legal system – could be based on a persistent misconception.

Another possible response to the chronological paradox was proposed by Stern. She asked:

Pourquoi la croyance en l'existence d'une norme de la part de l'Etat, qui est à la fois sujet et créateur du droit international, ne pourrait-elle être à l'origine de l'émergence d'une telle norme? Les objections de Kelsen tombent peut-être si

[5] Note 15, p. 38 above, at 44 (para. 77). [6] Note 16, p. 8 above, at 28.
[7] See Geny (1919) 367; and Kunz (1953) 667.
[8] See Kelsen (1939) 265–6; Guggenheim (1950) 278; and Guggenheim (1953) tome 1, 46–8. Both authors later abandoned this position. See Kelsen (1966) 440; and Guggenheim (1967) tome 1, 101–7.
[9] See Geny (1919) 367–71; and Benson (1982) 276–7. Benson ((1982) 269) noted that, although Geny's work focused on national legal systems, his ideas have had an important influence on thinking about international law.

l'on comprend l'*opinio juris* comme le sentiment d'être lié par une norme à laquelle on consent, lui donnant existence par ce consentement.[10]

For Stern, *opinio juris* constitutes State will, and the meeting of such wills, as manifested through State practice, is the immediate cause of legal obligations. However, she also explained that the *content* of each 'will' – and therefore *opinio juris* – depends on the power situation which exists at any particular time within the international order. Those States which, through their actions, are the first to contribute to the birth of a customary rule manifest a free will, a '*volonté libre*'.[11] Other States, the silent majority, manifest wills which are conditioned by the irresistible wills of the first States.[12] The result is the adoption of a rule by 'consensus', that is to say, without express manifestation of either positive or negative will, but rather by a simple, tacit manifestation.[13] In such cases consent occasionally becomes a strained concept, as consensus, 'en dépit de l'*apparente unanimité* qui le consacre . . . constitue un instrument de coalition contre les isolés'.[14]

D'Amato also circumvented the chronological paradox by considering *opinio juris* to be the 'articulation' of rules of customary international law. 'Articulation', for D'Amato, means the prior or concurrent and public characterisation, by a State, organisation or individual, of an act or failure to act as legal under international law.[15] Articulation is the qualitative element which gives other States notice that the State's actions 'will have legal implications'.[16] When States have implicit knowledge of an articulated rule, acts or failures to act which are consistent with that rule create legal precedents for similar actions or non-actions by the acting or omitting State, or by other States. For D'Amato, these articulated actions or non-actions are what constitute State practice for the purposes of customary international law.[17]

The International Court of Justice, in its judgment in the 1986 *Nicaragua Case (Merits)*, adopted a similar stance by preferring the idea

[10] Stern (1981) 487–8. My translation reads:

> Why could not the belief in the existence of a norm on the part of the State, which is at the same time both subject and creator of international law, be at the origin of the emergence of that norm? The objections of Kelsen may fall aside if *opinio juris* is understood as the feeling of being bound by a norm to which one consents, with that consent giving existence to the norm.

[11] Stern (1981) 498. [12] Stern (1981) 498. [13] Stern (1981) 497.

[14] Stern (1981) 497, quoting from and adding emphasis to Reuter (1976) 26. My translation reads: 'in spite of the *apparent unanimity* to which it is devoted . . . constitutes an instrument of coalition against isolated States'. This latter point may shed considerable light on the concept of persistent objection, as discussed at pp. 102–5 above and pp. 180–3 below. [15] See D'Amato (1971) 74. [16] D'Amato (1971) 75.

[17] It should be noted that D'Amato does not consider statements to be capable of constituting State practice for the purposes of customary international law. See p. 134 below.

of *opinio juris* as a type of legal claim to its position in the 1969 *North Sea Continental Shelf Cases*.[18] Faced with a history of State practice contrary to a possible customary rule of non-intervention, the Court referred to the requirement of *opinio juris* but wrote:

The significance for the Court of cases of State conduct *prima facie* inconsistent with the principle of non-intervention lies in the nature of the ground *offered as justification*. Reliance by a State on a novel right or an unprecedented exception to the principle might, if shared in principle by other States, tend towards a modification of customary international law.[19]

In this way, the Court seems to have accepted, to some extent, the idea of 'articulation', to use D'Amato's term, although it does not seem to have contemplated that the 'articulation' of one State's practice could be provided by another State, or non-State actor.[20] However, the idea of 'articulation' may not be sufficient to explain some situations, such as where customary rules arise without any explicit assertions of legality having been made.[21]

Finnis, in a similar attempt to escape the chronological paradox, suggested that *opinio juris* is a forward-looking, widespread consideration on the part of States that it is desirable and appropriate to adopt a particular rule of customary international law.[22] However, this approach would seem to undermine the relative meaning of *opinio juris*, because any change in any law will almost invariably result from the will of law-makers to see that change occur. Moreover, if one understands this forward-looking *opinio juris* as a required constitutive element of any customary rule – an element which must, in certain situations, be proved – it begins to resemble D'Amato's 'articulation'. However, it would seem to restrict the capacity to articulate to a narrower range of international actors, along the lines of the Court's judgment in the *Nicaragua Case*.

## The character of State practice

A related problem concerns what forms of behaviour constitute State practice, the first element in the traditional bipartite conception of

[18] For the Court's position in the *North Sea Continental Shelf Cases*, see p. 131 above.

[19] Note 16, p. 8 above, at 109 (para. 207) (emphasis added).

[20] This does not mean that the Court adopted anything close to D'Amato's general theory of customary international law. For instance, in the same case the Court appeared to accept that United Nations General Assembly resolutions may constitute State practice for the purposes of customary international law. See *Nicaragua Case (Merits)*, note 16, p. 8 above, at 97–100 (paras. 183–90). D'Amato was highly critical of this latter aspect of the Court's judgment, without noting the adoption of a position on *opinio juris* which in some ways is very similar to his own. See D'Amato (1987a).

[21] See p. 149 below.

[22] Finnis (1980) 238–45. See also Thirlway (1972) 55; Dupuy (1974) 84; and Crawford and Viles (1994).

customary international law. Some writers, such as D'Amato and Wolfke, have insisted that only acts and not statements count as State practice, which means that any State wishing to support or oppose the development, maintenance or change of a customary rule must engage in some sort of act, and that statements or claims alone do not suffice.[23] To illustrate this point D'Amato used the example of the launching of the first Sputnik satellite and the corresponding development of the customary right of satellite overflight. D'Amato claimed that if any State had wished to oppose the development of that right, it would have had to have taken concrete action, either by interfering with the satellite's flight, or, if unable to interfere, by retaliating against the Soviet Union in some other way.[24]

Numerous writers have opposed the position adopted by D'Amato and Wolfke on this issue.[25] One reason for their opposition is that, in so far as this approach concerns the change of customary rules, it would seem to require violations of customary international law. In short, acts in opposition to existing rules constitute violations of those rules, whereas statements in opposition do not. Consequently, this approach is, in Akehurst's words, 'hardly one to be recommended by anyone who wishes to strengthen the rule of law in international relations'.[26] It leaves little room for diplomacy and peaceful persuasion, and, perhaps most importantly, marginalises less powerful States in the process of customary international law.[27]

Some writers have adopted the reverse of the D'Amato and Wolfke position and argued that any instance of State behaviour – including acts, omissions, statements, treaty ratifications, negotiating positions (as reflected in *travaux préparatoires*) and votes for or against resolutions and declarations – may constitute State practice for the purposes of customary international law. Akehurst, for example, argued that State practice 'covers any act or statement by a State from which views can be inferred about international law', including omissions and silence.[28]

This more inclusive approach has been implicitly endorsed by the International Court of Justice. For example, the Court has relied on 'official views' and treaty ratifications in determining that a 'constant

[23] See D'Amato (1971) 88; D'Amato (1987a); Wolfke (1993a) 42 and 84; and Wolfke (1993b) 3–4. See also the individual opinion of Judge Read in the *Anglo-Norwegian Fisheries Case* (1951) *ICJ Reports* 3, 191; and Thirlway (1972) 68.

[24] D'Amato (1971) 89.

[25] See, e.g., Akehurst (1974–75a) 7–8; Brownlie (1986) 156; and Onuf (1994).

[26] Akehurst (1974–75a) 8.

[27] These two objections led Brownlie to refer to D'Amato's theory of customary international law as ' "Rambo" superpositivism', Rambo being a film character of the 1980s who only knew one way in which to relate to other people – through the use of force. Brownlie (1986) 156.

[28] Akehurst (1974–75a) 10. See also Villiger (1985) 4–12; and Sur (1990) 1er cahier, 18.

and uniform usage' did not exist in the 1950 *Asylum Case*.[29] It also reviewed diplomatic correspondence to determine that a right to exercise consular jurisdiction 'founded upon custom or usage' had not been established in the 1952 *Rights of Nationals of the United States of America in Morocco Case*.[30] Similarly, in 1950 the International Law Commission included treaties, the decisions of international and national courts, national legislation, diplomatic correspondence and the opinions of national legal advisers as examples of the various possible forms of State practice.[31]

The polarisation between those writers who think that only acts constitute State practice and those who support a broader conception is perhaps most evident in the debate about whether, and how, resolutions and declarations of international organisations contribute to the process of customary international law. As was explained in chapter 3, international lawyers have traditionally considered that resolutions and declarations are only able to contribute to the customary process in so far as they are evidence of *opinio juris*. Some writers have gone so far as to suggest that resolutions and declarations cannot even constitute reliable evidence of *opinio juris* because State representatives frequently do not believe what they themselves say.[32]

More recently, many non-industrialised States and a significant number of writers have asserted that resolutions and declarations are important forms of State practice which are potentially creative, or at least indicative, of rules of customary international law. The International Court of Justice appears to have reinforced this view by accepting, in its judgment in the 1986 *Nicaragua Case (Merits)*, that a series of United Nations General Assembly resolutions played a major role in the development of rules of customary international law prohibiting intervention and aggression. However, these assertions have, in turn, been resisted by many powerful States and some writers.[33]

The related problem of States saying things which are very different from what they do, should also be noted here. There are some customary rules, such as the prohibition against torture, which have received widespread support from almost all States, e.g. in the fora of international organisations, but which are nevertheless consistently violated by many of those same States. Yet as both D'Amato and Rodley have pointed out, these violations do not necessarily contribute to the process of customary international law.[34] Nearly all States which violate the prohibition against

[29] Note 4, p. 130 above, at 277. [30] (1952) *ICJ Reports* 176, 200.
[31] (1950) 2 *Yearbook of the International Law Commission* 368–72.
[32] See p. 40 above. [33] See p. 41 above.
[34] D'Amato (1988) 466–9 (see quotation, pp. 168–9 below); and Rodley (1987) 63–4.

torture deny and attempt to conceal their violations.[35] In such cases the denials and attempts to conceal – or, to use the terminology adopted by the International Court in the *Nicaragua Case*, the lack of an attempt to offer justification – would appear to be more relevant to the customary process than the use of torture itself. As Weber wrote, albeit in a different context:

> The probability that the order be to some extent valid (as an obligatory norm) can also occur where its meaning is 'evaded' or 'violated' . . . The thief orients his conduct toward the validity of the criminal law, viz., by trying to conceal it . . . This case is, of course, marginal. Very frequently the order is violated only in one or another partial respect, or its violation is sought to be passed off as legitimate, with a varying measure of good faith.[36]

## The epistemological circle

If, as some scholars suggest, both acts and statements constitute State practice,[37] it may prove difficult to determine whether *opinio juris* exists in any given situation. From such a perspective the only evidence of *opinio juris* available will also be State practice, notwithstanding that a separate element of *opinio juris*, or something akin to *opinio juris*, is still needed to distinguish legally relevant from irrelevant State practice and to transform that practice into customary rules. The result would seem to be an epistemological circle which renders one or the other element of customary international law redundant.[38]

D'Amato and Wolfke's approach avoids the epistemological circle by dividing State behaviour into two distinct categories, namely acts (which constitute State practice) and statements (which provide evidence of *opinio juris*, or 'articulations' of rules). However, this approach is unacceptable for reasons which were explained in the previous section of this chapter. In short, it leaves little room for diplomacy and peaceful persuasion, and marginalises less powerful States in the process of customary international law.[39]

'Sliding scale' explanations of the relationship between *opinio juris* and State practice, such as that proposed by Kirgis, are similarly flawed.

[35] Burma (Myanmar) is one possible exception. On acceding to the 1989 Convention on the Rights of the Child (UN Doc. A/RES/44/25) in 1991 it entered a reservation to Art. 37 (the prohibition against torture, cruel, inhuman or degrading treatment or punishment) preserving its unfettered 'powers of arrest, detention, imprisonment, exclusion, interrogation, enquiry and investigation'. This reservation was withdrawn in 1993. See *Multilateral Treaties Deposited with the Secretary General: Status as at 31 December 1994* (New York: UN, 1995) 202. [36] Weber (1954) 4. [37] See pp. 134–5 above.

[38] See Sörensen (1946) especially 105–11; Haggenmacher (1986) 114; and Danilenko (1993) 81–2. [39] See p. 134 above.

Kirgis, who adopted D'Amato and Wolfke's position that only acts and not statements constitute State practice for the purposes of customary international law, and that *opinio juris* is a belief or claim expressed separately through statements, resolutions and declarations, argued:

> [V]ery frequent, consistent state practice establishes a customary rule without much (or any) affirmative showing of an *opinio juris*, so long as it is not negated by evidence of non-normative intent. As the frequency and consistency of the practice decline in any series of cases, a stronger showing of *opinio juris* is required. At the other end of the scale, a clearly demonstrated *opinio juris* establishes a customary rule without much (or any) affirmative showing that governments are consistently behaving in accordance with the asserted rule.[40]

Yet the epistemological circle would clearly not be broken if one were to apply such a 'sliding scale' within a conception that regarded *both* acts and statements as potential instances of State practice. In that case one would still end up looking to State practice for evidence of *opinio juris*. The sliding scale approach only works if one is prepared to accept the problems entailed by D'Amato and Wolfke's approach.[41]

MacGibbon argued that *opinio juris* might not be required in respect of some customary rules. He explained that when a customary rule develops as the result of a 'course of conduct', that is, the repetition of identical or similar acts, acquiescence constitutes inferred consent to that conduct, which consequently forms the basis of a new rule. This, he admitted, is not the case with customary rules which are prohibitions on action, because, here, engaging in supporting practice involves doing nothing. In such situations one State's doing nothing in response to another State's doing nothing cannot reasonably be inferred as consent, unless the second State was legally required to act in some way. Thus *opinio juris*, or something like *opinio juris*, is still required in these latter situations.[42] MacGibbon's argument, however, seems flawed because, even in the former situations concerning courses of conduct, *some* element of belief or shared understanding would still appear to be necessary to distinguish

[40] Kirgis (1987) 149.

[41] Kirgis developed his approach in an attempt to explain the International Court of Justice's judgment in the 1986 *Nicaragua Case (Merits)* where, from his perspective, the Court relied solely on evidence of *opinio juris*, without reference to State practice. It is noteworthy that Meron ((1989) 36) came to a different conclusion. According to him, the Court, when dealing with certain issues of humanitarian law in its judgment, paid regard neither to State practice nor to *opinio juris*. Haggenmacher (1986), after examining a number of previous judgments (not including the *Nicaragua Case*) concluded that, although the Court relies on State practice, it generally does not look to *opinio juris*, at least not *opinio juris* as it is traditionally defined. See also MacGibbon (1957) 128–9 (in respect of the judgments of the Permanent Court of International Justice). These divergent analyses confirm that the traditional bipartite conception of customary international law is seriously flawed.

[42] MacGibbon (1957) 130–1.

legally required courses of conduct from those which are not legally required.

Koskenniemi has exploited these differences of scholarly opinion, the epistemological circle and the chronological paradox to argue that the traditional bipartite conception of customary international law is nothing more than camouflage for the imposition of subjective, political preferences. He wrote:

Because both elements [State practice and *opinio juris*] seek to delimit each other's distorting impact, the theory of custom needs to hold them independent from each other. But this it cannot do. Attempting to identify the presence of the psychological element, it draws inferences (presumptions) on the basis of material practice. To ascertain which acts of material practice are relevant for custom-formation, it makes reference to the psychological element (i.e. 'those acts count which express the *opinio juris*'). The psychological element is defined by the material and *vice versa*. This circularity prevents doctrine from developing a determinate method of custom-ascertainment. It has led to determining custom in terms of an equity which it can itself only regard as arbitrary.[43]

At face value, Koskenniemi's criticism is a highly effective one. However, it may be possible to develop an explanation of *opinio juris*, along the lines suggested by MacGibbon, which avoids the bipartite conception and thus the focus of Koskenniemi's deconstructionist attack. Sur, for one, has argued that *opinio juris* constitutes the reasoning element in the customary process, and not an identifiable element of individual rules.[44] In making this argument he relied heavily on the following passage from the judgment of the Chamber of the International Court of Justice in the 1984 *Gulf of Maine Case*:

A body of detailed rules is not to be looked for in customary international law which in fact comprises a limited set of norms for ensuring the co-existence and vital co-operation of the members of the international community, together with a set of customary rules whose presence in the *opinio juris* of States can be tested by induction based on the analysis of a sufficiently extensive and convincing practice, and not by deduction from preconceived ideas.[45]

On the basis of this passage Sur claimed that there are two different categories of customary rules. Rules within the first category may be determined deductively and include those rules 'qui seraient en quelque sorte nécessaires, dictées par les exigences de la coexistence entre Etats, et con-

[43] Koskenniemi (1989) 363 (footnotes omitted); see also 388–9.

[44] Sur (1990) 2e cahier, 1–2.

[45] Note 29, p. 10 above, at 299 (para. 111). Sur also referred to the use of deductive reasoning in the *Reparation for Injuries Suffered in the Service of the United Nations Advisory Opinion*, note 26, p. 81 above. See Sur (1990) 2e cahier, 2.

stitueraient un irréductible noyau dur du droit coutumier'.[46] Rules within the second category are determined inductively through the examination of 'des propositions de droit, implicitement ou explicitement émis par certains Etats, à l'intention des autres Etats, afin qu'ils acceptent et reconnaissent la pratique correspondante'.[47] In both cases *opinio juris* constitutes 'la surdetérmination qu'impose le processus coutumier aux actes étatiques'.[48] In short, in some instances the jurist may bypass an analysis of State practice through deductive reasoning as to which rules are required in international society, whereas in other instances he must analyse the process of reasoning which States *themselves* display as they make, and respond to, statements and acts.

One problem with Sur's explanation may be that he was merely describing how international lawyers determine the existence and content of customary rules, rather than identifying what *opinio juris* actually is. The identification of reasoning as an aspect of that determination merely demonstrates that in some instances jurists may take short cuts,[49] and that the State practice which contributes to the development, maintenance and change of customary rules is usually engaged in only after careful consideration of its potential effect on the process of customary international law.[50]

In contrast to Sur, Carty has traced the origin of the concept of customary international law, and the idea of *opinio juris*, to the German historical school of Savigny and Ranke. According to this approach *opinio juris* is the common will, or legal consciousness of a *Volk*, or people.[51] Although Carty has attempted to revitalise this approach, he has also continued to restrict it to individual nations, in the context of work which focuses on nationalism. Yet customary international law is an international phenomenon. Moreover, it would seem that any shared consciousness which exists in international society is of a lesser degree than those shared consciousnesses which may be present within individual nations. It is difficult, therefore, to see how shared consciousnesses could exist in

[46] Sur (1990) 2e cahier, 1. My translation reads: '[Rules] which will be in some way necessary, dictated by the exigencies of co-existence between States, and which will constitute an irreducible hard core of customary law.'

[47] Sur (1990) 2e cahier, 1. My translation reads: 'propositions of law, implicitly or explicitly emitted by certain States, towards other States, in order that those other States accept and recognise the corresponding practice.'

[48] Sur (1990) 2e cahier, 2. My translation reads: 'the overarching determination which the customary practice imposes on State acts.'

[49] See discussion of conspicuous common interests at pp. 162–5 below.

[50] See pp. 151–6 below.

[51] Carty (1986) 30–9. See similarly Cotterrell (1992) 22–3. For the original works, see Savigny (1949); and Ranke (1973).

respect of the substantive content of each and every rule of customary international law, especially those rules of a highly technical character. In addition, from a 'traditional' international law perspective such shared consciousnesses would necessarily exist among States, as opposed to people or peoples.

Haggenmacher has argued that there is, in reality, only one element of customary international law, namely State practice, and that *opinio juris* merely concerns the interpretation of that practice at the international level.[52] Thus, for Haggenmacher, *opinio juris* involves the way in which perceptions of State practice are determined; why judges (for example) assign legal relevance to some instances of State practice, but not to others.[53] Like Sur, Haggenmacher asserted that the assignment of legal relevance is a rational conceptual exercise, and not an arbitrary one. Unlike Sur, he explained that legal relevance is assigned on the basis of perceptions of State practice, which are formed *within* the larger structure provided by a number of 'principles' of international law. These principles, such as the freedom of the seas and the exclusivity of sovereign territory, exist on an autonomous basis, independent of the practice invoked in any given case. In Haggenmacher's words:

> L'attestation d'une pratique constante, de nature à impliquer une norme sous-jacente, n'y manque certes jamais; mais, loin de surgir seule, elle s'entoure régulièrement d'une armature conceptuelle censée lui conférer sa véritable signification normative aux yeux de l'interprète. Loin de se réduire à des 'spéculations' abstraites, ces 'principes' sont directement liés aux structures mêmes de l'ordre juridique international et aux représentations communes qui s'en dégagent. C'est cet univers conceptuel partagé – par delà les divergences dues à la perspective partisane – qui rend possible un langage commun des plaideurs. A défaut d'être insérée dans cette texture de 'principes', la pratique internationale ne serait guère plus cohérente aux yeux de l'interprète qu'un paysage lunaire.[54]

[52] Haggenmacher (1986) 116–25. See also Jennings (1981) 69.

[53] Haggenmacher confined his study to a number of judgments of the International Court of Justice, while recognising that the process of customary international law is a phenomenon of much broader scope. See Haggenmacher (1986) 117.

[54] Haggenmacher (1986) 119. My translation reads:

> The attestation of a constant practice which can imply an underlying norm is never lacking; but, far from implying an underlying rule on its own, that practice usually occurs within some sort of conceptual framework. That framework serves to give the practice a normative significance in the eyes of those who interpret it. Far from being reduced to abstract 'speculations', the 'principles' which constitute this conceptual framework are linked directly to the rules and practices which result from them. This shared conceptual universe, which exists above divergences which result from partisan perspectives, enables parties to a dispute to speak a common language. If State practice did not occur within such a conceptual framework, it would be no more comprehensible to those who interpret it than a lunar landscape.

Haggenmacher's views find a parallel in recent developments within international relations theory, in the work of what might be called the 'sociological institutionalists'.[55] Sociological institutionalists focus on the 'intersubjective meanings' which are involved in, and constitute, international institutions.[56] Keohane has explained that, from this perspective, 'understanding how people think about institutional norms and rules, and the discourse they engage in, is as important in evaluating the significance of these norms as measuring the behaviour that changes in response to their invocation'.[57]

Some sociological institutionalists have focused on what they refer to as 'epistemic communities'.[58] These communities are relatively small, specialised, belief-motivated groups of individuals. As Haas has explained, their members have:

> (1) a shared set of normative and principled beliefs, which provide a value-based rationale for the social action of community members; (2) shared causal beliefs, which are derived from their analysis of practices leading or contributing to a central set of problems in their domain and which then serve as the basis for elucidating the multiple linkages between possible policy actions and desired outcomes; (3) shared notions of validity – that is, intersubjective, internally defined criteria for weighing and validating knowledge in the domain of their expertise; and (4) a common policy enterprise – that is, a set of common practices associated with a set of problems to which their professional competence is directed, presumably out of the conviction that human welfare will be enhanced as a consequence.[59]

International relations scholars who study epistemic communities argue that 'the form of specific policy choices is influenced by transnational knowledge-based networks', even though that influence 'remains strongly conditioned by the distribution of power internationally'.[60]

The perceptions of relevance to which Haggenmacher refers are held, for example, by judges, who also constitute a small, specialised and, arguably, belief-motivated group of individuals. Even if one considers – as Haggenmacher apparently does – that these perceptions of relevance are likely to be shared by all those who interpret and apply international law, and therefore by a larger community of international lawyers, policy analysts and governmental decision-makers, the parallel between these developments in international legal theory and international relations theory is striking. A later section of this chapter relies on these parallel theoretical developments in order to advance a new explanation of *opinio juris*, and thus of the process of customary international law.

[55] This term is borrowed from Beck *et al.* (1996) 166. [56] Keohane (1989e) 160.
[57] Keohane (1989e) 160. [58] See, e.g., Haas (1992a); Haas (1992b); and Haas (1993).
[59] Haas (1992b) 3. [60] Haas (1992b) 7.

### Inferred consent

International lawyers have generally assumed that rules of international law do not bind States against their will.[61] This consensual position was perhaps most famously expressed by the Permanent Court of International Justice in the 1927 *Lotus Case*:

> International law governs relations between independent States. The rules of law binding upon States therefore emanate from their own free will as expressed in conventions or by usages generally accepted as expressing principles of law and established in order to regulate the relations between those co-existing independent communities or with a view to the achievement of common aims. Restrictions upon the freedom of States cannot therefore be presumed.[62]

Consent to treaties is usually given in an explicit and precise manner, through signature and, in many cases, ratification or accession.[63] Consent to rules of customary international law, on the other hand, is rarely given explicitly. Customary international law is seldom created as the result of a single act of will, but is usually the result of a series of actions and statements over time. Furthermore, many such actions are engaged in, or statements made, without any acknowledgement that they are voluntary or in fulfilment of legal obligations. It is therefore frequently unclear where a voluntary practice ends and a rule of customary international law begins.[64]

Since customary international law usually does not depend on explicit consent, but rather on some kind of 'non-objection rules',[65] it may seem that customary rules are capable of binding States which have neither participated in their development or change nor acknowledged their prescriptive force. Most international lawyers have relied on inferred

[61] See, e.g., Corbett (1925); van Hoof (1983); and Wolfke (1993a).

[62] Note 16, p. 8 above, at 18. See also, the *Nicaragua Case (Merits)*, note 16, p. 8 above, at 135: '[I]n international law there are no rules, other than such rules as may be accepted by the State concerned, by treaty or otherwise.'

[63] See generally Arts. 11–15 of the Vienna Convention on the Law of Treaties, note 10, p. 36 above; McNair (1961); and Reuter (1995). See also *Maritime Delimitation and Territorial Questions between Qatar and Bahrain (Jurisdiction and Admissibility)* (1994) *ICJ Reports* 112, 120–2.

[64] It will be noted that this latter problem and the problem upon which the previous section of this chapter focused, namely the epistemological circle between State practice and *opinio juris*, are closely related. The following passage written by Corbett ((1925) 26) demonstrates the difficulty associated with State consent in identifying when customary legal obligations begin:

> A particular usage may be the source of a customary rule of international law . . . but custom is the generalized practice which proves the existence of the rule. . . Custom is important to the international lawyer only as demonstrating the general assent of states; it is that assent which makes the law.

[65] Charney and Danilenko (1995) 27.

consent, in the form of acquiescence, to explain the consensual basis of such obligations.[66] If a State is aware that a customary rule is developing or changing, and chooses not to object to nor actively oppose that development or change, then the failure to object or oppose is regarded as demonstrating support for the new rule. This consent is 'inferred' rather than 'implied' because its existence is determined partly on the basis of State practice, and not in the absence of any evidence of consent.[67] Inferred consent is the principal characteristic which distinguishes rules of customary international law from treaty rules.

It is, however, seldom clear that a State is acquiescing to any particular development or change of a customary rule out of a sense of legal obligation. By requiring States to make statements or to take action to prevent themselves from being bound by developing or changing rules, the doctrine of inferred consent seems to fly in the face of the traditional position that restrictions on States are not to be presumed.[68] It changes free-willing States into actors who have to remain alert lest they be caught up in legal obligations which are not to their liking. It also leads to presumptions of *opinio juris* which, as has already been explained, may create theoretical problems of their own.[69]

Some writers have responded to such concerns by arguing that States have consented to rules about the development and change of customary rules, thus binding themselves to accept new or modified rules as they arise, unless they persistently object to them.[70] D'Amato, for example, drew on the work of Hart to argue that States have universally accepted various 'secondary', procedural rules of international law by 'consensus'.[71] These secondary rules govern how States determine and debate the existence and content of 'primary', substantive rules. According to D'Amato, consensus in respect of the secondary 'rule' of customary international law has been achieved as a result of all States having relied on primary rules of customary international law in legal argumentation, or at least having claimed the benefit of such rules.[72]

[66] See generally MacGibbon (1954) 150–1; MacGibbon (1957); Akehurst (1974–75a) 38–42; Villiger (1985) 18–22; and pp. 106–7 above.

[67] See de Vattel (1758) 8, who wrote that customary international law 'is founded upon a tacit consent, *or rather upon a tacit agreement of the Nations which observe it*. Hence it evidently binds only those Nations which have adopted it' (emphasis added).

[68] See *Lotus Case*, quotation, p. 142 above.

[69] See pp. 130–41 above.

[70] On persistent objection, see pp. 102–5 above and pp. 180–3 below.

[71] D'Amato (1971) 41–4. See Hart (1961) 77–96.

[72] D'Amato (1971) 191. In this sense consensus, as a means of measuring general agreement, might be regarded as D'Amato's ultimate secondary rule. For another, less developed suggestion as to the potential for secondary rules in a theory of customary international law see Walden (1977) 356–7; developed further in Walden (1978). See also Pellet (1992) 39–40.

Similar positions have been adopted by Lowe, Sur, Raz and Allott, to the effect that all States, by accepting some rules of customary international law, are necessarily accepting rules about how those rules are developed, maintained or changed.[73] Consent to customary rules may therefore come in the form of a diffuse consensus, or general consent to the process of customary international law, rather than as an explicit and specific consent to individual rules. Acquiescence, therefore, does not necessarily represent consent (because consent regarding the process has already been given), and is but one of the ways in which States may participate in the development, maintenance or change of rules of customary international law. States retain the option of objecting to or opposing individual rules, and thus – perhaps – of retracting their consent to be bound.[74]

Lowe suggested that there are two ways of conceptualising consent to the *process* of customary international law, and the creation of exceptions to general rules:

> First, we could say that all states consent to a secondary rule of law-creation which deems all states which have not persistently objected to an emerging primary (i.e. substantive) rule of law to be bound by it, without being at all concerned with the question whether or not such states consent to the primary rule, whenever that primary rule is 'generally accepted' by states. The problem of persistent objection . . . can be explained by distinguishing between the abstract question of the nature of the rule, which is general, and its opposability to particular states by a court, which is excluded in the case of persistent objectors. Local customs may be accommodated by describing them as a sub-species of custom, prevailing over general rules by virtue of the traditional principle of interpretation that special rules prevail over general ones.
>
> A second way of interpreting customary international law is to say that all states consent to a secondary rule of law-creation according to which a general practice among states creates a presumption that all states have consented to the primary rule embodied in the practice, subject to the possibility of that presumption being rebutted in the case of any state which can show that it has persistently objected to the emergent rule. Unlike the previous interpretation, this one attaches a central importance to each state's consent to the primary rule, the presumption goes only to the question of the manner in which that consent is proved.[75]

Koskenniemi has responded that such explanations of customary law are merely camouflage and that it 'is not really – despite appearances – a consensual argument at all'. Rather, he argued that a conception of justice is at the root of all customary rules, most frequently in the sense of the principle that 'legitimate expectations should not be ignored'.[76]

However, Koskenniemi may be using an unjustifiably strict definition

[73] Lowe (1983a); Sur (1990) 2e cahier, 5 and 10; Raz (1990) 123–9; and Allott (1990) 145–77. [74] See Sur (1990) 2e cahier, 10; and pp. 102–5 above and pp. 180–3 below.
[75] Lowe (1983a) 208–9, footnotes omitted. [76] Koskenniemi (1990a) 1951.

of consent here, one which does not accord with the social construction of that concept as adopted by States. In that context, States might base 'legitimate expectations' on acquiescence because of a general understanding that a State which acquiesces in the development, maintenance or change of a particular customary rule is not objecting – and is in that sense consenting – to that particular potential, emerging or existing rule. If this is the case, then Koskenniemi's criticism does not hold. Whether States acquiesce because of larger shared conceptions of justice or morality, is another question.[77]

Other writers have ignored the possibility of 'system consent' and have thus become embroiled in disputes over the existence of specific consent in respect of each customary rule. Such disputes usually revolve around the question whether *opinio juris* constitutes consent to the specific rule in question and whether, as a result, that consent must be proved in every instance, or whether States may be bound by customary rules to which they have not specifically consented but towards which they have nevertheless developed a sense of legal obligation.[78]

Another problem associated with consent concerns new States. It is widely accepted that a new State is bound by all rules of general customary international law which existed at the time that State came into being.[79] Yet new States do not have the opportunity to participate or acquiesce in, nor to oppose, the development of pre-existing rules. However, explaining the basis for the applicability of pre-existing customary rules to new States might not be a serious problem, as there would appear to be an important difference between the act of joining the 'club' of law creators and subsequent participation in the processes of law creation. New States do both. They base arguments or otherwise rely on at least some rules of customary international law and thus indicate an acceptance of the process through which those rules have arisen, and, therefore, by extension, of existing generally applicable customary rules. Yet new States also acquire a place in the customary process and thus an opportunity to seek to change those rules which do not correspond to their interests.[80]

Two further problems arise. First, may a State which did not know that

[77] See pp. 162–5 below.

[78] See, e.g., Elias (1995); and Lobo de Souza (1995). See also Thirlway (1972) 74–5; and the discussion of Stern's approach at pp. 131–2 above.

[79] See, e.g., Waldock (1962) 51–3; O'Connell (1965) 12; Kelsen (1966) 445; Franck (1995) 44, especially note 70; and the Commentary to Art. 2 of the ILC Draft Articles on State Responsibility (Part One), note 14, p. 14 above, quoted at note 14, p. 78 above. Compare Tunkin (1958) 19; van Hoof (1983) 77–8; Villiger (1985) 16; and, to some degree, Sur (1990) 2e cahier, 11–12.

[80] See Lowe (1983a); Sur (1990) 2e cahier, 5 and 10; Raz (1990) 123–9; Allott (1990) 145–77; and pp. 77–8 above. For a useful discussion of the position of new States, see Danilenko (1993) 113–18.

a rule was being developed or changed be held to have acquiesced in that development or change?[81] Secondly, is a State which had no reason to be interested in a particular development or change, but which subsequently developed an interest in it as the result of a change of circumstances, bound to the new rule as a result of its earlier indifference? An example of the latter problem might involve a landlocked State which subsequently acquires a coastline.[82]

[81] See D'Amato (1971) 86; and Villiger (1985) 19–20. Charney and Danilenko ((1995) 37) have noted that it may be difficult for many less powerful States, given their limited resources and the increasing complexity of the international legal system, to know about all new rules.

[82] It should, however, be noted that landlocked States played an important role in the negotiation of the 1982 Law of the Sea Convention, note 29, p. 41 above, and not just in respect of the position of landlocked States. See Caflisch (1989). This may be an example of multi-subject trading among States as they collectively develop, maintain and change rules of international law.

# 9 International relations and the process of customary international law

In thinking about the chronological paradox, the problem of State practice, the epistemological circle and the problem of inferred consent, it may help to consider the customary process from the perspective of international relations theory. Before doing so, it bears repeating that this book does not set out a new *normative* theory of customary international law.[1] Instead, it seeks to cast light on traditional, theoretical problems of customary international law by considering factors which are not strictly legal in character.

On the basis of the definitions provided by Keohane and Young, the process of customary international law is clearly an institution. In Keohane's terms, it is a persistent and connected set of informal rules which prescribe behavioural roles, constrain activity and shape expectations.[2] In Young's terms, it is an identifiable social convention which results from the convergence of patterned behaviour and actor expectations, and to which States conform without making elaborate calculations on a case-by-case basis.[3] The similarities between Young's definition of institutions and traditional definitions of customary international law, namely the convergence of State practice and *opinio juris*, are striking.[4]

The process of customary international law would also seem to fit within the scope of the well-known definition of international regimes provided by Krasner *et al.*, namely, 'sets of implicit or explicit principles, norms, rules and decision-making procedures around which actors' expectations converge in a given area of international relations'.[5] Perhaps most importantly, it seems to fit comfortably within that strand of institutionalist writing which has explored the concept of epistemic communities.[6] As Wendt has explained:

[1] See pp. 15–18 above. [2] See pp. 27–9 above. [3] See pp. 29–30 above.

[4] See p. 130 above. Yet Young has been somewhat inconsistent in his definition of institutions. He has also defined them as 'behaviorally recognizable practices consisting of roles linked together by clusters of rules or conventions governing relations among the occupants of these roles' (Young (1989) 196). Actor expectations are not a part of this latter definition. [5] Krasner (1983) 2. See p. 24 above. [6] See p. 141 above.

An institution is a relatively stable set or 'structure' of identities and interests. Such structures are often codified in formal rules and norms, but these have motivational force only in virtue of actors' socialization to and participation in collective knowledge. Institutions are fundamentally cognitive entities that do not exist apart from actors' ideas about how the world works. This does not mean that institutions are not real or objective, that they are 'nothing but' beliefs. As collective knowledge, they are experienced as having an existence 'over and above the individuals who happen to embody them at the moment.' In this way, institutions come to confront individuals as more or less coercive social facts, but they are still a function of what actors collectively 'know.'[7]

An interdisciplinary approach to the process of customary international law may thus have implications for our understanding of *opinio juris*. Although traditional theories rely on *opinio juris* to distinguish State practice which is relevant to the customary process from State practice which is not, writers advocating those theories have had difficulty explaining the character of *opinio juris* and in identifying this second element of customary international law.[8] However, if the customary process is understood as involving a 'collective knowledge' or set of shared understandings, *opinio juris* may then be understood as being those shared understandings which enable States to distinguish between legally relevant and legally irrelevant State practice.[9]

What States, or more precisely the human beings who govern and represent them, believe to be legally relevant will only be apparent from their behaviour, and the assignation of legal relevance to that behaviour will often be recognised and passed over in silence. Yet customary international law is not, in Hart's terms, behaviour at the point of a gun,[10] nor is the assignation of legal relevance, as Sur has argued, a strictly rational exercise.[11] Customary international law instead reflects deeper understandings which are akin to Wittgenstein's 'forms of life';[12] it is based on a deeper social consciousness, or in Haggenmacher's terms a 'shared con-

[7] Wendt (1992) 399, footnotes omitted, quoting from Berger and Luckmann (1966).

[8] See pp. 129–46 above.

[9] These shared understandings of legal relevance will normally, but not necessarily, precede the State practice which is subjected to them. In this sense *opinio juris* usually comes before the State practice which gives rise to any specific rule. This might be seen as being consistent with the order expressed in Art. 38(1)(b) of the Statute of the International Court of Justice, i.e., 'international custom, as evidence of a general practice accepted as law'. See Jennings and Watts (1992) 26, note 5. Compare Villiger (1985) 3; and Danilenko (1993) 76–7. However, this study does not assume that States are always aware of the potential law-creating effects of their behaviour, nor that they invariably know the legal outcomes they are seeking. It is possible that these understandings could develop *ex post facto*. See, e.g., *Nuclear Tests Cases*, note 9, p. 107 above.

[10] See Hart (1961) 18–20; and Hart (1982) 243–68.

[11] See pp. 138–9 above.

[12] See Wittgenstein (1963) 226e, who wrote: 'What has to be accepted, the given, is – so one could say – *forms of life*' (emphasis in original).

ceptual universe', which accords certain instances of behaviour a normative significance in the eyes of those who interpret them.[13]

For example, there would appear to be a shared understanding among States that such actions which States deny or attempt to conceal do not constitute State practice capable of contributing to the development, maintenance or change of customary rules. As D'Amato has explained, the 'hiding, cover-up, minimization, and non-justification . . . betoken a violation of law' and therefore constitute legally relevant State practice *in support* of a rule prohibiting the actions in question.[14]

Shared understandings of legal relevance would appear to be highly sensitive to context.[15] To use a standard example, States do not consider the use of white paper for diplomatic correspondence to be State practice relevant to a legal or potentially legal issue.[16] However, the use of a sealed bag for diplomatic correspondence and the respect of that seal is considered to be legally relevant State practice. The decisive factor distinguishing this legally relevant from legally irrelevant State practice is the context in which the practice takes place.[17]

Perhaps the most important shared understandings about the legal relevance of State practice concern acquiescence. It seems that States, having accepted the process of customary international law, acquiesce in the development, maintenance or change of a customary rule knowing that their behaviour will contribute to that development, maintenance or change. Similarly, States know that, if they consistently oppose the development or change of any customary rule which is not of a *jus cogens* character but are nevertheless unsuccessful in preventing that development or change, they will find themselves in the position of persistent objectors with all of their rights – under international law – preserved.[18]

Shared understandings of legal relevance may also be important in enabling States to distinguish between inaction which is in support of a potential or emerging customary rule prohibiting a certain kind of

[13] See p. 140 above.

[14] See D'Amato (1988) 469; and pp. 135–6 above and pp. 168–9 below. Although the most obvious example of such actions involves violations of the prohibition against torture, pleadings before and decisions of international arbitral tribunals which the parties wish to keep confidential, but which are leaked, might for similar reasons be regarded as being of no relevance to the process of customary international law.

[15] Simmonds ((1991) 318), for one, has stressed the importance of context to shared understandings within national legal systems.

[16] This example is drawn from Akehurst (1974–75a) 33. See also Danilenko (1993) 120.

[17] Danilenko ((1993) 120) commented that 'in practice the problem of distinguishing between customary law and other social rules does not arise if custom-generating practice occurs in areas of relations which may be considered legally relevant'.

[18] However, the rights of persistent objectors may not generally be recognised by other States. See pp. 103–4 above.

behaviour (inaction which therefore constitutes acquiescence) and inaction which is not in support of that rule (and which therefore does not constitute acquiescence).[19] These shared understandings would also appear to be sensitive to context. Among other things, they would seem to take into account past practice, not only of the State in question, but of all other States. Such practice may include previous acts, omissions, claims, denials, concealments, the submission of disputes to courts or tribunals, and statements concerning a State's view as to the legality or illegality of its practice. All of these things may indicate that in general States consider a particular issue, or practice linked to that issue, to be legally relevant.

The importance of shared understandings to the customary process would seem to be confirmed by reference to D'Amato's approach to the issue of *opinio juris*. As was explained in chapter 8, D'Amato suggested that a rule must be 'articulated' before or in conjunction with State practice in order for that practice to be relevant to the process of customary international law.[20] Yet D'Amato's suggestion does not provide a solution for situations such as that of the sealed diplomatic bag where no explicit 'articulation' may have been made, unless one treats the *context* of the behaviour – diplomatic documents in a sealed bag – as some sort of implicit articulation. This, in turn, would appear to return to the concept of shared understandings of legal relevance.

*Opinio juris*, when defined in terms of a belief on the part of States that they are acting in accordance with pre-existing or simultaneously developing legal rules, does not seem particularly helpful, either as a practical tool for determining the existence of customary rules, or as an explanation of how those rules arise. In contrast, shared understandings appear to be most significant in the domain of the *process* of law creation rather than at the level of individual rules.[21] It is the process of customary international law which best represents 'the conjunction of behavioral regular-

[19] See MacGibbon (1957) 130–1; pp. 137–8 above. Compare Danilenko (1993) 86, note 35. [20] See D'Amato (1971) 74–87; pp. 132–3 above.

[21] Simmonds ((1991) 319) has made similar reference to the importance of shared understandings as structuring legal processes, rather than just individual rules, within national legal systems:

> But suppose that we think of the law as developing relatively clear and settled rules that reflect, but stabilise, pre-existing informal rules and convergent patterns of behaviour. Might not the 'rule of recognition' (for example) then be thought of as a further level of reflection and stabilisation? This time it would not be informal rules of conduct amongst the general populace that would be reflected and stabilised, but the convergent practices and expectations of lawyers and others in looking to certain texts (such as judgments, decrees, scholarly writings, etc.) and employing certain forms of argument in the decision of disputes and the interpretation of rules.

ities and convergent expectations'.[22] In respect of a particular customary rule – that, for example, a diplomatic bag is inviolable – the convergent expectations which would seem to be of greatest importance during the period in which the rule is developing or changing relate to the process through which that rule develops or changes, rather than to the content of the rule in question. Only after the rule has come into being will there be a shared belief in its existence; before that time any shared 'belief' will be in respect of how the rule could arise, of the legal relevance of different instances of behaviour, and perhaps of the desirability of the rule arising.[23]

As has already been explained, analyses of the judgments of the International Court of Justice support this conclusion, since the Court, while supporting the traditional conception of *opinio juris* in principle, has repeatedly ignored it in practice.[24] Instead, the Court examines what States have openly done or admitted to doing, what in some cases they have not done, what State representatives have or in some cases have not said, and the contexts in which these various kinds of State practice have taken place.

## The determination of 'common interests'

An interdisciplinary approach to the study of customary international law thus leads one to regard the customary process as a set of shared beliefs, expectations or understandings held by the individual human beings who govern and represent States.[25] Like all institutions and the international system itself, the process of customary international law is nothing but a set of ideas, no matter how tangible the consequences of those ideas may be.[26]

The most significant result of the ideas or shared understandings which constitute this process may be that State practice in respect of a legal or

[22] Young (1989) 81.
[23] See the observations on Finnis' approach to *opinio juris* on p. 133 above. Danilenko ((1993) 14) has written: 'Consensus on the procedural aspects of the global decision-making process . . . provides the most fundamental level of understanding, one which is indispensable for promotion of any common policy.'
[24] See pp. 120–4 above; Haggenmacher (1986); Meron (1989) 36 (in respect of questions of humanitarian law in the *Nicaragua Case*); and MacGibbon (1957) 128–9 (in respect of the judgments of the Permanent Court of International Justice).
[25] For a discussion of the importance of shared understandings to legal systems generally, see Simmonds (1991). For a more general discussion of the importance of shared understandings to social interaction and 'distributive justice', see Walzer (1983).
[26] For similar views from international lawyers, see, e.g., Carty (1986), especially 20–1; Koskenniemi (1989); Allott (1990); Knop (1993); Crawford (1995).

potentially legal issue generally provides an indication of the degree to which States are interested in a particular legal outcome. In other words, all States agree that practice consistent with a potential, emerging or existing rule indicates support for that rule, that practice inconsistent with the rule indicates opposition to it, and that an absence of practice in the area governed or potentially governed by the rule indicates ambivalence to the rule, and may, as a result, constitute acquiescence. The existence of such a shared understanding would be consistent with the 'realist' assumption that States behave in accordance with their own interests.[27] However, these interests are interests as States perceive them to be. They could, therefore, involve much more than simply maximising a State's power in relation to other States. Much would depend on the internal political system of the State concerned, its relative affluence and the existence or perception of external threats, be they of a military, economic, environmental or other character.

It would also seem that State practice is determined, not only by the interests which States perceive themselves as having, but also by the ability of States to manifest those interests. The ability to manifest an interest may in this way be related to the 'cost' of that manifestation. Different kinds of practice entail different costs for States, where cost is calculated in military, economic, political or human terms. Some acts, such as protecting fishing vessels in distant waters or imposing trade sanctions against other States, may be very costly. Diplomatic communications or statements in international organisations will usually entail far lower costs. The range of possible actions and statements is very broad, as is the corresponding range of costs. Moreover, costs may in many cases be offset, to some degree, by the benefits which accrue from the development or change of the customary rule in question.

Different States have differing abilities to meet the costs associated with different kinds of practice, so the costs of some forms of practice may be prohibitive for some States, but not for others. Some States may not have the capacity to engage in, nor the resources to support, certain types of action. The process of customary international law would seem to take such disparities into some account, which may help to explain why the United States, the United Kingdom and Japan found themselves together as persistent objectors to the customary rule establishing a twelve-mile territorial sea despite being the world's predominant maritime powers.[28] Greater weight may be accorded to a statement made by a State represen-

[27] See p. 14 above. The interests of States may not necessarily be identical, or even similar to the interests of those individuals who live within States. However, see the discussion of the statist assumption at pp. 13–14 above.

[28] See p. 104 and pp. 114–20 above.

tative in a situation in which that State could not act, than may be accorded to a similar statement in a situation in which it could act. Similarly, trade sanctions imposed by a small, economically vulnerable State against its main trading partner may be accorded more legal significance than if the State imposing the sanctions were larger, wealthier, or if it had only limited trading links with the other State.

This assessment may itself be skewed by other factors. For example, a powerful State may be able to allocate more resources to publicising its legally relevant practice, and will likely be paid more attention as a result.[29] Only the more affluent States publish digests of their own practice of relevance to international law.[30]

A State, when contemplating whether to engage in practice in support of, or in opposition to, a potential, emerging or existing customary rule may weigh the costs associated with that practice against its interest in any particular legal outcome, its ability to meet those costs, and the importance of that particular interest as compared to its other interests. Since all States would seem to engage in similar calculations, the customary process, by according more weight to practice involving relatively higher costs, and less weight to practice involving relatively lower costs, is able to measure the collective interests of States with a relatively high degree of accuracy.

A similar analysis has been presented by Raman:

> Where the parties are in disagreement as to the significance of past events to the determination of the requirements for present decision, the extent to which base values were expended by them may create a modest presumption that there were shared expectations about such requirements for decision. It is therefore appropriate in examining the authoritativeness of a practice to take into account the extent of commitment made by the parties through the base values at their disposal, which in this connection includes not only power and wealth but all other values.[31]

This relationship between interest and relative cost may also explain why acts are generally considered to carry more weight than statements in the process of customary international law.[32] However, in some situations

[29] See Sur (1990) 1er cahier, 20.

[30] Australia (*Australian Yearbook of International Law*), Belgium (*Revue belge de droit international*), Canada (*Canadian Yearbook of International Law*), France (*Annuaire français de droit international*), Germany (*Zeitschrift für ausländisches öffentliches Recht und Völkerrecht*), Italy (*Rivista di Diritto Internazionale*), Japan (*Japanese Annual of International Law*), South Africa (*South African Yearbook of International Law*), Switzerland (*Schweizerisches Jahrbuch für internationales Recht*) and the United Kingdom (*British Yearbook of International Law*) publish (or provide financial or logistical support for the publication of) digests of their State practice in international law. China, Russia and India do not. In 1994 the United States decided to cease publication of the *Digest of United States Practice in International Law*.

[31] Raman (1967) 466.

[32] See, e.g., Akehurst (1974–75a) 2, note 1; Danilenko (1993) 86; and pp. 133–6 above.

statements may involve significant costs, as relatively weak States may occasionally find when deciding to oppose powerful States on important issues in international organisations.[33]

The measurement of State interests through State practice is facilitated by the fact that States are usually aware when any behaviour on their part has the potential to affect the development, maintenance or change of customary rules, and realise that the resulting rules may themselves impose 'costs'. States know that by behaving in a particular way, they increase the chances that similar behaviour will subsequently be required by law.[34] States are therefore more careful than they might otherwise be to ensure that their practice is consistent with both their short- *and* long-term interests – as they perceive those short- and long-term interests to be.

Although in many situations not all States will agree as to which legal outcome is most desirable, the customary process resolves many of these disagreements by developing, maintaining or changing customary rules when State practice indicates that most States would find this either desirable or acceptable, and only a few, or none at all, would not. In this sense the customary process would seem to act as a 'universalising public interest phenomenon' which determines, and then protects and promotes with rules, the common interests of most and sometimes all States.[35]

The customary process thus fulfils the main purpose of Keohane's institutions, namely that of facilitating co-operation between States in a manner which takes into account variations in their 'mutual interest'. In other words, variations in the 'mutual interest', acting through the institution, have substantial effects on State behaviour, in this case through the development, maintenance or change of customary rules.[36]

[33] See Franck (1995) 481. [34] See Danilenko (1993) 79.

[35] This may be a particularly important insight for international relations scholars. Joyner ((1987) 390) has written:

> Political science can gain from international law by accepting the proposition that the law is a significant means for organizing political forces, for setting perceptions of national interests, and for promoting ways to attain those national interests.

The expression 'universalising public interest phenomenon' is attributed to Allott. For written variations see Allott (1992) 774–9; and Allott (1995). See similarly Villiger (1985) 38–9; and Charney (1993) 540. The 'common interest' is not a new concept in international law. For instance, it was explicitly recognised as being the underlying concern of the Charter of the United Nations, which states in its preamble that 'armed force shall not be used, save in the common interest'. Given that the primary goal of the drafters of the Charter was to prevent the use of armed force by States except in self-defence, this concession to the common interest is a significant one. See Art. 2 of the Charter, where five out of seven principles deal with the use of force, or intervention more generally; and, on the historical background to the Charter, Grewe (1994).

[36] See Keohane (1989b) 2–3; and pp. 27–9 above.

This explanation does not suggest that the process of customary international law facilitates co-operation in a manner which maximises absolute gains without regard to the relative positions of different States, which is a criticism that has been levied against institutionalist explanations of international relations.[37] If enough States regard a putative rule which seeks to promote the general interest as likely to have detrimental effects on their relative position *vis-à-vis* other States, they may choose to oppose it, and thus prevent that putative rule from acquiring the force of law. But if only one or a few States perceive such detrimental effects, opting out of the rule through persistent objection might damage the relative positions of those few States more than if they were to accept its application to themselves.[38]

Finally, this explanation of the customary process as a 'universalising public interest phenomenon' which determines, protects and promotes the common interests of most and sometimes all States, would seem to fit comfortably within recent literature, in the disciplines of both international relations and international law, concerning 'compliance'.[39] For example, Chayes and Chayes have explained, in respect of treaties, that:

> [I]f the agreement is well-designed – sensible, comprehensible, and with a practical eye to probable patterns of conduct and interaction – compliance problems and enforcement issues are likely to be manageable. If issues of noncompliance and enforcement are endemic, the real problem is likely to be that the original bargain did not adequately reflect the interests of those that would be living under it, rather than mere disobedience.[40]

The process of customary international law would appear to be a good example of compliance theory in action. It operates in a manner which ensures that the interests of all States are taken into account and that rules are developed only when they are in the interests of most if not all States, as those States perceive and manifest those interests to be. The process is designed and controlled by the international society of States, it operates continuously, and a preference is even manifest, in the concept of persistent objection, for the exclusion of opposing States rather than the risk of non-compliance. Along with the ongoing interest that all States have in the customary process as a functioning institution, it may be this careful tailoring of individual rules to the interests of States, as expressed through their behaviour, which best explains the high degree of compliance which

[37] See Grieco (1988); and Grieco (1990).

[38] See pp. 102–5 above. In this and other ways the process of customary international law may sometimes *transform* State interests, rather than just respond to them. See, in respect of the interest transforming abilities of international institutions generally, Wendt (1992).

[39] See, e.g., Young (1979); Chayes and Chayes (1993); Mitchell (1994); Chayes and Chayes (1995); and Koh (1997).

[40] Chayes and Chayes (1993) 183.

exists in respect of most customary rules. The fact that all States continue to rely on customary rules indicates that, in this instance, a careful balance has been struck between the relative power positions of States and the interest that all States have in a stable, predictable, yet responsive international legal system.

## 'Cost' and the identification of legally relevant State practice

Earlier in this chapter it was suggested that the decisive factor distinguishing legally relevant from legally irrelevant State practice is the context in which the practice takes place. For the purposes of determining whether and to what degree an instance of State practice is legally relevant, it is not particularly important whether that practice involves statements or acts.[41] Instead, the most significant contextual issue concerns the cost that is entailed by the instance of State practice in question, for, as has already been explained, the process of customary international law weighs different instances of State practice in terms of their relative cost.[42] Even diplomatic statements usually entail some cost, enabling them to be weighed alongside other forms of State practice in the process of customary international law.[43]

It would seem important that States, in general, are aware of the State practice in question. Behaviour of which States are not aware should not subsequently be held to impose legal obligations on them, because their failure to support or oppose that behaviour does not necessarily reflect their interests. On the other hand, wilful blindness to the behaviour of other States may reflect a State's interests to some degree. Furthermore, the practice should be engaged in publicly, such that attempts at concealment or denial work only to establish the illegality of the concealed or denied action.[44]

The resolutions and declarations of international organisations have become important forms of State practice over the course of the last fifty years, a change which itself is indicative of other changes in the international system, and most significantly of a substantial increase in the number of relatively less-powerful States.[45] As with any form of State practice, resolutions and declarations may be considered legally relevant as long as they entail some cost, however minor that cost may be.[46] Cost in these instances may be associated with political rather than legal com-

[41] See pp. 133–6 above. [42] See pp. 151–6 above.

[43] See, e.g., *Nuclear Tests Cases*, note 9, p. 107 above, where the International Court of Justice held that a unilateral declaration could, in itself, be legally binding.

[44] See p. 149 above and pp. 168–9 below. [45] See pp. 40–3 above.

[46] See pp. 151–4 above.

mitment, such that the failure to fulfil such a commitment is somehow detrimental to a participating State's future international relations, for example, in affecting its credibility.

In the vast majority of instances resolutions and declarations should probably not be considered a separate form of practice on the part of the organisation in question, because member States usually decide individually whether to vote in favour of, or against, a particular resolution or declaration.[47] Instead, the individual votes themselves will be the legally relevant practice, provided that the text of the resolution or declaration provides some substance for the supporting States' commitments.[48] The situation may be more complicated when a group of States, such as the members of the United Nations Security Council, exercises a kind of delegated authority on behalf of other States.[49]

Although on this analysis many resolutions and declarations involve State practice, that practice will frequently carry little weight in the customary process. For instance, a failure to uphold the commitments associated with supporting or opposing votes will not generally give rise to State responsibility, that is, a legal obligation to make reparation or provide another suitable remedy for a breach of international law.[50] Similarly, although the use of 'consensus' as a means of agreement in many international organisations does not mean that opposition to, or even support for, a consensus position imposes no cost, the cost involved in such instances may be extremely small.[51] The contribution of these kinds of State practice to the customary process may, in many cases, effectively be outweighed by the acts of a small number of opposing States. Such acts – especially those involving significant costs – may create serious obstacles for those States which seek, by way of widely supported resolutions or declarations, to develop or change rules of customary international law.[52]

## Repetition and relative resistance to change

It was explained earlier in this chapter that a rule of customary international law either develops, continues or changes when most States behave as if they would like to see that happen, or at least do not object thereto. It

[47] See pp. 40–3 above.

[48] For this reason Thirlway has suggested that the negotiations leading up to a resolution (or declaration), and the statements made on behalf of member States in those negotiations, 'will almost always be of greater relevance than the final resolution'. Thirlway (1972) 65–6.

[49] See p. 78 above.

[50] On State responsibility, see generally the citations at note 36, p. 83 above.

[51] On the use of consensus as a means of agreement in international organisations, see generally Cassese (1986) 195–8.

[52] See, e.g., the discussion of human rights, pp. 43–5 above; and the discussion of the development of the right of satellite overflight in D'Amato (1971) 88–9.

was suggested that the development, maintenance or change of a particular customary rule consequently involves an implicit weighing of supporting, ambivalent and opposing State practice.[53] Such a weighing process would seem to begin when behaviour which could support a particular rule, or modified rule, first appears.

The following, simple examples may help to clarify this suggestion. Suppose that State A would like a new rule to develop and therefore acts in accordance with, or issues a statement in support of, its preferred new rule. State B is ambivalent towards the new rule and does nothing. State C does not want the new rule to develop and therefore acts in a way which would be in violation of the new rule, were it to develop, or issues a statement objecting to it. Suppose too, that all other States are in the position of State A, State B or State C. Now, if there are many State As, some State Bs, and no or only a few State Cs, the proposed rule will become a rule of customary international law and any State Cs may – at least temporarily – become persistent objectors.[54] If there are few State As, some State Bs and many State Cs, the proposed rule will not develop. In either case the State As, had they acted in violation of an existing rule in order to indicate their support for a new rule, would have violated customary international law. However, the fact that widespread support is required for a new rule to develop makes it unlikely that a successful State A would be regarded as legally responsible for such a violation, except perhaps by persistently objecting States, if there are any. The question becomes more one of opposability than of breach.

The examples above are relatively straightforward. Frequently the balance between supporting and opposing States is not so clear, or the different kinds of State practice do not fall within three strictly definable groups. For example, the strength with which a State voices its opposition or actively opposes a potential, emerging or existing rule may vary, depending on the importance which the State attaches to the outcomes it desires. In such situations it may be more difficult, among other things, to determine whether a rule has developed or changed. The different weights accorded to different acts, omissions and statements in different contexts may further complicate matters, as may the passage of time, the conspicuous character of some common interests and the relative resistance to change of existing customary rules.[55]

The repetition of instances of State practice must be an important factor in a process which involves the weighing of supporting, ambivalent and opposing behaviour – provided that there is a conflict of interests and

[53] See pp. 151–6 above; and Akehurst (1974–75a) 13–14.

[54] On persistent objection, see pp. 102–5 above.

[55] For a discussion of the conspicuous character of some common interests, see pp. 162–5 below.

therefore a lack of uniformity in the behaviour of States in respect of a particular issue. According to both D'Amato and Akehurst, the customary process involves the making of arguments in the context of disputes between States, with each State involved in a dispute attempting to cite as much past practice as possible in support of the potential, emerging or existing rule which most favours its position.[56]

There is, therefore, always the theoretical possibility that one State will be unable to refer to any past practice which supports its position. Both authors have suggested that, should this happen, the other State may be able to 'win' the argument and 'prove' the existence of a customary rule by citing only one instance of past practice which supports it.[57] Moreover, in such a situation – where there is only one instance of past practice in support of a rule – any State may be able to nullify that rule simply by engaging in one act or failure to act in violation of it, or perhaps even by making a statement in support of that rule's nullification or replacement by a new rule. Consequently, rules based on a limited number of instances of State practice are inherently unstable and relatively vulnerable to change.

Most customary rules have at least some resistance to change as a result of repetitive and cumulative instances of supporting State practice. In order to change any such rule, that threshold of resistance first has to be overcome. This means, in Akehurst's words, that 'the amount of practice needed to establish a new rule which conflicts with the previously accepted rule is much greater than the amount of practice needed to establish a new rule *in vacuo*'.[58] Conversely, and as D'Amato explained, repetition of practice in support of an existing rule 'serves to enhance the rule significantly', thus shielding it from extinction or modification.[59]

All of this suggests that a rule which every State has supported, towards which no State has been ambivalent, and which none has opposed should, at least in the absence of a fundamental change of circumstances, be extremely difficult to change. Although it is conceivable that enough opposing State practice could occur to destroy the most resistant of rules, this is only a theoretical possibility in respect of a number of particularly well-established principles of international law.[60] Such principles, although derived from the process of customary international law (or at

[56] D'Amato (1971) 91; and Akehurst (1974–75a) 13.
[57] D'Amato (1971) 91; and Akehurst (1974–75a) 13.
[58] Akehurst (1974–75a) 13; see also at 18–19; and pp. 109–20 above.
[59] D'Amato (1971) 94.
[60] It would, however, remain a possibility, albeit one which might threaten the current international legal system, contrary to the interests of at least the more powerful States. Such a possibility might also necessitate the development of new principles to replace those destroyed. For similar views as to the mutability of 'constitutional' rules in national legal systems, see Sartorius (1971) 158–9; Simmonds (1990) 77–9; and Simmonds (1991) 320–1. For a contrary view, see Hart (1961) 89–96. For a strong suggestion that Hart's approach might be appropriate in international legal theory, see Pellet (1992) 39–40.

least an earlier process akin to it), now provide a structure for the international legal system. Part 2 considered how four of these principles – jurisdiction, personality, reciprocity and legitimate expectation – fulfil such a role by, among other things, qualifying applications of power within the process of customary international law.

### Time and repetition

Time is also an important factor in the customary process because it normally takes time for State practice to accumulate in support of, or in opposition to, any particular rule.[61] D'Amato, however, has been justifiably critical of formulations which attempt to impose rigid requirements of duration, density and consistency on acts which may be creative of customary rules. He identified one problem with such requirements as the difficulty involved in applying them to failures to act, and suggested that States should have a reasonable amount of time in which to respond to an act or omission which supports a rule they oppose.[62] Only if they do not respond in some concrete way within that period can that act or omission contribute to the development of a new rule. Thus, '[t]he idea of communication or notice . . . may be more basic to custom than the mere fact of duration'.[63]

Modern technology and permanent multilateral diplomacy may greatly reduce the time within which it is reasonable for States to respond to a potential or emerging customary rule. The effects of international organisation on the customary process were recognised by Judge Tanaka in his dissenting opinion in the 1966 *South West Africa Cases (Second Phase)*:

> A State, instead of pronouncing its view to a few States directly concerned, has the opportunity, through the medium of an organization, to declare its position to all members of the organization and to know immediately their reaction on the same matter. In former days, practice, repetition and *opinio juris sive necessitatis*, which are the ingredients of customary international law might be combined together in a very long and slow process extending over centuries. In the contemporary age of highly developed techniques of communication and information, the formulation of a custom through the medium of international organizations is greatly facilitated and accelerated.[64]

Some writers have asserted that rules of customary international law may develop so quickly that they become, in effect, 'instant' customary

[61] See Akehurst (1974–75a) 15–16. On time and international law, see generally Higgins (1997).

[62] D'Amato (1971) 58–61. See also Danilenko (1993) 97.

[63] D'Amato (1971) 59.

[64] (1966) *ICJ Reports* 6, at 250, 291. See also the dissenting opinion of Judge Tanaka in the *North Sea Continental Shelf Cases*, note 15, p. 38 above, at 177; Akehurst (1974–75a) 15–16; Raman (1976) 387; Villiger (1985) 24; and Higgins (1994) 22–3.

international law.[65] Many such assertions rely on the following statement in the International Court of Justice's judgment in the 1969 *North Sea Continental Shelf Cases*:

> Although the passage of only a short period of time is not necessarily, or of itself, a bar to the formation of a new rule of customary international law . . . an indispensable requirement would be that within the period in question, short though it might be, State practice, including that of States whose interests are specially affected, should have been both extensive and virtually uniform . . . and should moreover have occurred in such a way as to show a general recognition that a rule of law or legal obligation is involved.[66]

The most serious problem with the idea of 'instant' customary international law may be that States which would otherwise oppose emerging rules might not have sufficient time to become aware that those rules are emerging, and to express their opposition.[67] By requiring State practice to have been 'both extensive and virtually uniform', the judgment in the *North Sea Continental Shelf Cases* went some way to addressing this problem. Yet this requirement seems to have been overlooked by some writers, including several who suggested that individual State consent, whether explicit or inferred, is no longer a necessary requirement because customary international law may be based on 'consensus' rather than consent.[68]

It is also possible that, in the weighing of supporting, ambivalent and opposing State practice, the customary process will accord more weight to recent practice than to practice which has occurred further in the past. Recent practice may be more likely to reflect a State's current interests, especially if there has been a significant change in the circumstances surrounding a particular issue.

A significant change in circumstances may, in addition to altering State interests, also alter how States perceive those interests, as well as how they perceive the legal relevance of previous instances of supporting, ambivalent and opposing State practice. At times a new, widely shared perception may result in previous instances of State practice being considered of little or no relevance to the development of a new rule.[69] An example of this

[65] See, e.g., Cheng (1965); and Abi-Saab (1987) 60. See also the dissenting opinion of Judge Tanaka in the *South-West Africa Cases (Second Phase)*, note 65, p. 160 above, at 250, 292, to the effect that resolutions are a 'middle way between legislation by convention and the traditional process of custom making'.

[66] Note 15, p. 38 above, at 43 (para. 74).

[67] See Villiger (1985) 4.

[68] See, e.g., Abi-Saab (1987); Chodosh (1991); and Charney (1993). See also the discussion of Stern's approach, at pp. 131–2 above.

[69] Fitzmaurice ((1953) 31) wrote:

> A new rule of customary international law based on the practice of States can in fact emerge very quickly, and even almost suddenly, if new circumstances have arisen that imperatively call for legal regulation – though the time factor is never wholly irrelevant.

would seem to have occurred during the First World War, when the rule allowing aircraft overflight changed very quickly to one of complete territorial sovereignty – in response to technological changes and a sudden realisation of the implications of those changes for national security.[70]

In some situations the tendency to accord greater weight to recent practice may, however, be offset by the high degree of legitimate expectation which might be associated with a well-established rule.[71]

## The conspicuous character of some common interests

As was explained earlier in this chapter, one of the determinative factors in the development, maintenance and change of customary rules is the relative degree of supporting as compared to opposing practice which has taken place in respect of those rules.[72] The matter is complicated by the fact that customary rules appear to differ from each other on the basis of the relative amounts of supporting, as compared to opposing, practice needed for them to develop, to continue or to change. Some writers have pointed to international human rights as one area where rule creation involves a lower behavioural threshold, or at least a lower burden of proof.[73]

Koskenniemi, when suggesting that customary international law in the human rights field is determined, not by formal tests of legal validity, but by an 'anterior – though in some respects largely shared – criterion of what is right and good for human life',[74] made a point which, intuitively, must be correct:

> Some norms seem so basic, so important, that it is more than slightly artificial to argue that states are legally bound to comply with them simply because there exists an agreement between them to that effect, rather than because, in the words of the International Court of Justice, noncompliance would 'shock . . . the conscience of mankind' and be contrary to 'elementary considerations of humanity'.[75]

Schachter, for his part, has identified the rules against aggression and on self-defence as also having required little State practice (on the basis of a restrictive conception of that term) to come into force.[76]

[70] In 1950 Brierly suggested to the International Law Commission that 'in regard to the air, the moment the 1914 war broke out, the principle of sovereignty, which had been a matter of opinion up to then, was settled at once' (1950) 1 *Yearbook of the International Law Commission* 5. See also McNair (1964) 5; and Matte (1964) 111–12.

[71] See pp. 106–26 above.

[72] See pp. 157–60 above; and Akehurst (1974–75a) 13–14.

[73] See, e.g., Meron (1989) 113; Schachter (1991) 336; and Schachter (1996) 538–40.

[74] Koskenniemi (1990a) 1953. See pp. 45–6 above.

[75] Koskenniemi (1990a) 1946–7 (footnotes omitted, quoting from the *Advisory Opinion on Reservations to the Convention on the Preservation and Punishment of the Crime of Genocide* and the judgment in the *Corfu Channel Case*).

[76] Schachter (1989) 734. See also Kirgis (1987) 149.

The fact that the development, maintenance and change of customary rules is based on an implicit weighing of relative amounts of supporting as compared to ambivalent and opposing State practice, does not explain why some rules – especially human rights rules – appear to require relatively less supporting practice than other rules to develop, to continue or to change. For Koskenniemi, the existence of such rules is additional proof that the customary process is little more than a facade for the imposition of subjective, political preferences.[77]

Schachter has suggested that one reason for these differences may be that it is difficult to ascertain actual conduct in respect of some rules, such as the rules that make up the humanitarian law of armed conflict.[78] In making this suggestion, he relied for support on the decision of the Appeals Chamber of the United Nations Tribunal for the Former Yugoslavia in the *Tadic Case*, where the Chamber wrote:

> When attempting to ascertain State practice with a view to establishing the existence of a customary rule or a general principle, it is difficult, if not impossible, to pinpoint the actual behaviour of the troops in the field for the purpose of establishing whether they in fact comply with, or disregard, certain standards of behaviour. This examination is rendered extremely difficult by the fact that not only is access to the theatre of military operations normally refused to independent observers (often even to the ICRC) but information on the actual conduct of hostilities is withheld by the parties to the conflict; what is worse, often recourse is had to misinformation with a view to misleading the enemy as well as public opinion and foreign Governments. In appraising the formation of customary rules or general principles one should therefore be aware that, on account of the inherent nature of this subject-matter, reliance must primarily be placed on such elements as official pronouncements of States, military manuals and judicial decisions.[79]

An additional, or alternative, explanation may also be available if the customary process is understood, from an international relations perspective, as a regime or institution which determines the common interests of most, if not all, States, and then protects and promotes those common interests with rules.[80] The weighing of supporting, ambivalent and opposing State practice may be seen as a facilitative, and not as a compulsory, exercise. In other words, although the interests of States will usually become clear only through a careful examination of their actions and statements, in some instances their interests may be so obvious that such a careful examination of State practice is not required.

This would appear to be the case with many of those customary rules having a peremptory or *jus cogens* character, such as the most fundamental

[77] See generally: Koskenniemi (1990a). [78] Schachter (1996) 539.

[79] *Prosecutor* v. *Tadic* (Appeal on Jurisdiction, 2 October 1995), para. 99, reproduced in (1996) 35 ILM 32, 63. [80] See pp. 147–57 above.

of human rights or the prohibition against aggression.[81] It may also help to explain why, in the 1986 *Nicaragua Case (Merits)*, the International Court of Justice did not feel it necessary to examine the past actions of States in respect of the rules prohibiting intervention and aggression.[82] Schachter has written:

> States and tribunals do not question the continued force of those rules [on self-defence and against aggression, genocide, torture, etc.] because of inconsistent or insufficient practice . . . This is not because the rules express 'noble aspirations' . . . but . . . because they express deeply held and widely shared convictions about the unacceptability of the proscribed conduct.[83]

Furthermore, if all States have these conspicuous common interests, this might account for the ease and frequency with which natural law arguments are applied in support of *jus cogens* rules, and help to explain the *erga omnes* character which it is frequently asserted that such rules have.[84]

Other customary rules, including most other international human rights, would also appear to benefit from the conspicuous character of some common interests.[85] For example, the relatively conspicuous character of a common interest might reduce the amount of supporting State practice needed to create a rule, even if that conspicuous character were not sufficiently clear to create the rule by itself. The conspicuous character of some common interests may thus work together with State practice to develop, maintain or change rules of customary international law. In such cases, the State practice may help to guard against problems of cultural relativism, as evidence that the interests in question really are widely shared. Consequently, although there is clearly something different about how some customary rules – and especially human rights rules – arise, this difference may be understood as working with, rather than against, the normal process of customary international law; a process which usually, but not necessarily, weighs supporting, ambivalent and opposing State practice to determine common interests before protecting and promoting those interests through law.

This explanation of the role played by the conspicuous character of some common interests may have implications for problems relating to

[81] See pp. 12–13 above and pp. 183–95 below. [82] See p. 135 above.
[83] Schachter (1989) 734.
[84] For explanations that *jus cogens* rules are derived from natural law, see, e.g., *U.N. Conference on the Law of Treaties* (New York: United Nations, 1969) especially statements by Italy (311); Ecuador (320); Monaco (324); and de Visscher (1971). On the *erga omnes* character of *jus cogens* rules see, e.g., Meron (1986a) 187; Macdonald (1987) 138; Simma (1989) 825; Byers (1997a); and pp. 195–203 below.
[85] See also, in this context, the discussion in Chayes and Chayes ((1993) 198–200) on treaties and 'acceptable levels of compliance', where they suggested that those levels may 'shift according to the type of treaty, the context, the exact behavior involved, and over time' (at 198).

time and repetition. The previous section of this chapter explained that the passage of time is a factor in the development, maintenance and change of most customary rules.[86] When rules arise as a result of the conspicuous character of common interests, it may be possible to have something which approaches 'instant' customary international law.[87] Such extremely rapid developments or changes in rules would probably only occur in response to sudden developments of a technological or environmental character, when the international society of States collectively becomes aware of new interests, and the need for new rules, without having the time to engage in the sort, and degree, of supporting State practice that is normally required. The development of national air space and the rules concerning the use of outer space and celestial bodies might constitute examples of such developments, as might the prohibition on atmospheric nuclear testing.[88]

This explanation of the role played by the conspicuous character of some common interests may also have implications for our understanding of fundamental principles of international law. Although these principles have all received overwhelming support from State practice, their high degree of resistance to change – and therefore their ability to qualify applications of power in the process of customary international law – may have been increased further by the fact that all of them are conspicuously in the common interest of most if not all States. In short, they are entailed, or necessarily implied, by an international legal system in which the principal actors are sovereign States.[89]

Finally, some conspicuous common interests might be labelled values.[90] However, it is an objective, and not a subjective, phenomenon which is being described here.

[86] See pp. 160–2 above. [87] See pp. 160–1 above.

[88] See McNair (1964) 5; Matte (1964) 111–12; Cheng (1965); and arguments of Australia in *Nuclear Tests Case* (1973) 1 *ICJ Pleadings* 502.

[89] See Thirlway (1972) 28; and pp. 10–13 above.

[90] See Koskenniemi's comments on p. 162 above.

# 10 Related issues

The previous chapter has explained *opinio juris* as being those shared understandings which enable States to distinguish between legally relevant and legally irrelevant State practice. This explanation of *opinio juris* was then developed in terms of its implications for several other, fundamental problems associated with the process of customary international law. This chapter extends the analysis yet further by exploring the insights that might be derived, on the basis of such an explanation, in respect of four other, related issues of importance: (i) the relationship between customary international law and treaties; (ii) the concept of persistent objection; (iii) *jus cogens*; and (iv) the relationship between *jus cogens* and *erga omnes* rules.

### Customary international law and treaties

It is generally accepted that there are three primary sources of international law, namely, treaties, customary international law and general principles of law.[1] Of these three sources, the first two – treaties and customary international law – are considered much the more important.

Like the process of customary international law, treaties are a kind of regime or institution.[2] Consequently, to study the relationship between treaties and customary international law is to study the relationship between two different kinds of regimes or institutions. This is something which most international relations scholars have yet to do, having instead focused their attention on the relationship between particular regimes or institutions and States.[3] In contrast, international lawyers have devoted a great deal of attention to the relationship between treaties, rules of customary international law and certain other kinds of institutions, such as, the United Nations and other international organisations.[4] However, rel-

[1] See Art. 38(1) of the Statute of the International Court of Justice; Brownlie (1990) 1–31; Danilenko (1993); and Dinh *et al.* (1994) 111–390. [2] See pp. 24–31 above.

[3] See note 19, p. 25 above.

[4] See, e.g., Kelsen (1951); Bowett (1982b); Charpentier (1991); and Simma (1994).

atively few international lawyers have examined rigorously the relationship between treaties and the *process* of customary international law, as opposed to individual customary rules.[5] The relative lack of attention has become more apparent since the International Court of Justice split on this issue in the 1986 *Nicaragua Case (Merits)*.[6]

One of the problems associated with the relationship between treaties and customary international law concerns the question of what weight, if any, should be attributed to treaties as instances of State practice. Some writers, such as Wolfke and Charney, have maintained that treaties cannot constitute State practice for the purposes of customary international law.[7] This position stands in stark contrast to that adopted by the International Court of Justice when, in its judgment in the 1969 *North Sea Continental Shelf Cases*, it addressed the issue of whether treaty provisions may generate customary international law:

> There is no doubt that this process is a perfectly possible one and does from time to time occur: it constitutes indeed one of the recognized methods by which new rules of customary international law may be formed. At the same time this result is not lightly to be regarded as having been attained.[8]

D'Amato, although unwilling to consider that statements, resolutions and declarations may constitute State practice,[9] has been prepared to accord treaties that status. He argued, first, that the language of treaty provisions can supply the 'articulation' of the rules set out in those provisions, and, secondly, that a State's commitment to act in accordance with its treaty obligations may then constitute the necessary quantitative element – the State practice – for customary international law.[10]

In fact, D'Amato contended that most rules of customary international law begin as provisions in treaties.[11] He even suggested that 'the rule that treaties are binding might itself have resulted from provisions in early treaties containing solemn vows that the treaties were binding'.[12] However, it was D'Amato's view that '[n]ot every variety of treaty *can* give rise to a rule of customary law; rather, only those bilateral or multilateral treaties that contain generalisable rules can have this effect'.[13]

Akehurst, while acknowledging that he had 'no difficulty in regarding treaties as State practice', argued that 'the fact that States are permitted by treaty to act in a particular way does not necessarily justify the

[5] Such studies include: Baxter (1970); Thirlway (1972); Kontou (1994); and Sinclair, note 19, p. 25 above. [6] Note 16, p. 8 above. See pp. 171–2 below.
[7] Wolfke (1993a) 68–72; and Charney (1987) 160 and 163.
[8] Note 15, p. 38 above, at 41 (para. 71). [9] See p. 134 above.
[10] D'Amato (1971) 89–90 and 160. [11] D'Amato (1987b) 125.
[12] D'Amato (1982) 1131.
[13] D'Amato (1971) 105 (emphasis in original). See also D'Amato (1982) 1131; and D'Amato (1987b) 126.

inference that States claim to be entitled to act in that way in the absence of a treaty'.[14] Instead, those invoking treaties in support of customary rules 'often seem to find it necessary to justify such invocation by saying that the treaty is declaratory of customary law'.[15] According to Akehurst, one must, therefore, look to the language of the treaty and to its *travaux préparatoires* to see if the parties considered the treaty to be declaratory of customary international law. Moreover, that language and those *travaux préparatoires* 'constitute State practice and evidence of *opinio juris* even if the treaty never comes into force; the same is true of statements made during negotiations which do not succeed in producing a treaty'.[16]

Weisburd, for his part, took issue with what he considered to be some scholars' over-emphasis on treaties, to the neglect of other forms of State practice, especially acts, when determining the existence and content of customary rules. He was particularly critical of reliance on treaties such as the 1966 International Covenant on Civil and Political Rights and the 1984 Convention Against Torture and Other Cruel, Inhuman or Degrading Treatment or Punishment, which, while imposing legal obligations on States, 'expressly or by necessary implication limit the right of parties . . . to inquire into one another's observance of [their] . . . terms and foreclose the availability of any legal remedies for breach of treaty obligations'.[17] These treaties, Weisburd claimed, 'cannot represent practice informed by *opinio juris* and can contribute little to establishing their prohibitions as rules of customary international law',[18] because legal obligations imply a concurrent right to make inquiry and a concurrent duty to make reparation in the event of a breach.[19] Instead:

> [T]he fact of contrary practice – since the state risks no legal sanctions for violating the treaty and has by its conduct manifested at least some intention of behaving in a fashion contrary to the treaty rules – means that the best prediction is that the state will violate the treaty rule, not adhere to it.[20]

D'Amato responded to this latter point by stating, with specific reference to the Torture Convention:

> It seems . . . important to ask whether the states that engage in torture are (a) disclosing that they are torturing people, (b) proclaiming that what they are doing is legally justified, and (c) implicitly inviting other states to do likewise on the ground that, if torture is legally permissible for them, it is legally permissible for all states.[21]

[14] Akehurst (1974–75a) 43, note 6.
[15] Akehurst (1974–75a) 47. [16] Akehurst (1974–75a) 45, note 4.
[17] Weisburd (1988) 25. See note 39, p. 84 above; and note 39, p. 84, respectively.
[18] Weisburd (1988) 29. [19] Weisburd (1988) 23–5.
[20] Weisburd (1988) 37–8. [21] D'Amato (1988) 466.

D'Amato asserted that instead the 'objective evidence shows hiding, cover-up, minimization, and non-justification – all the things that betoken a violation of law'.[22]

Weisburd may be correct in asserting that it is important to examine closely what treaties actually say when relying on them to help determine the existence and content of rules of customary international law. Moreover, it may be that the character of the treaty provisions in question affects their ability to generate customary international law. Are they, for example, permissive or prescriptive; do they work with or against the presumption in favour of State freedom to act?[23]

Yet treaties of the type to which Weisburd refers are, together with their ambiguities and limitations on the right of inquiry and the availability of legal remedies for breach, the exception rather than the rule. Many treaties, especially bilateral treaties, are remarkably clear, both in respect of the specific obligations they impose and in respect of the consequences of breach. Moreover, sometimes treaties carry a great deal more weight than they may appear to on first inspection. The International Covenant on Civil and Political Rights, for example, does not depend solely on States' ratification of its Optional Protocol to have significant effects on how States behave, and therefore to create real or potential costs or benefits for States parties. For example, Article 40 of the Covenant sets out a reporting obligation for all States parties. A main function of the Human Rights Committee established under Articles 28 to 39 is to study these reports, consult other agencies of the United Nations when it feels that this is appropriate, and to make its views known both to the United Nations Economic and Social Council and to the United Nations General Assembly.[24] It may be observed that the 'cost' which is of importance in these situations is not the report itself, but rather the negative consequences that may flow from its being made public.

Many treaties have an impact which is felt outside compensable or verifiable legal bounds. It is accepted that human rights treaties in general play a role in the 'marshalling of shame' against those States which consistently violate human rights.[25] The fact that States have taken the trouble to negotiate these treaties and the standards they set out may support this general conclusion.

In many ways then, treaties would seem to be similar to resolutions and declarations as instances of legally relevant State practice. Like resolutions and declarations, they are often adopted in the context of

[22] D'Amato (1988) 469. See p. 149 above.
[23] See Higgins (1994) 31; and *Lotus Case*, quotation, p. 142 above.
[24] Note 39, p. 84 above, at Arts. 40(4) and 45 respectively.
[25] See generally Humphrey (1984); and Henkin (1990) 29.

international organisations and generally set out a series of closely related rights and obligations in written form. Yet, unlike resolutions and declarations, treaties often give rise to State responsibility, if and when violated.[26] In many cases, therefore, treaties may entail greater costs, or at least greater potential costs, than resolutions and declarations. It may be that treaties generally carry more weight in the customary process as a result. Moreover, even if certain acts contrary to a treaty do not give rise to State responsibility, for example if the relevant provision has been the subject of reservations, then as long as *some* cost – such as damage to reputation – is entailed, the treaty may still have some effect as relevant State practice.

As with most resolutions and declarations, the vast majority of treaties should probably not be considered an independent kind of practice on the part of international organisations, even if they are often negotiated in that context. They remain a collection of individual State commitments which are given a common substance by the text of the relevant treaty. That said, it is by way of treaties that States sometimes create international organisations, and it is possible that certain organisations may sometimes engage in legally relevant practice of their own. It is difficult to regard behaviour on the part of bodies such as the United Nations High Commissioner for Refugees, the World Trade Organisation or the organs of the European Communities, as in all cases the behaviour of States.

Generally speaking, however, international organisations remain far less important to the process of customary international law than States. For one thing, they engage in far less practice. Their lack of territory and nationals means that the scope of their activity is generally much more limited than that of States. This is one of the reasons why this book focuses on the customary process as it involves States, rather than including international organisations and other non-State actors within the scope of its analysis.[27]

A second, perhaps more important, issue concerning the relationship between customary international law and treaties was identified by Akehurst in a passage quoted earlier in this chapter.[28] It involves the problem that practice in fulfilment of a treaty obligation will generally be directed at that treaty obligation and may therefore lack the necessary *opinio juris* – *vis-à-vis* any parallel customary rule – to enable it to contribute to the development, maintenance or change of customary international law. One of the possible consequences of this problem was explained by Baxter:

[26] See generally Art. 3 of the ILC Draft Articles on State Responsibility (Part One), note 14, p. 14 above, at 30; Brownlie (1983) 85; and Dinh *et al.* (1994) 734.
[27] See pp. 12–13 above. [28] See pp. 167–8 above.

As the express acceptance of the treaty increases, the number of States not parties whose practice is relevant diminishes. There will be less scope for the development of international law *dehors* the treaty, particularly if the non-parties include many States with relatively few international links.[29]

He added:

[A]s more and more States become parties it is virtually impossible to say what the law would be in the absence of the treaty . . . And if little or no customary international practice is generated by the non-parties, it becomes virtually impossible to determine whether the treaty has indeed passed into customary international law.[30]

This apparent paradox may have been decisive in the International Court of Justice's judgment in the 1969 *North Sea Continental Shelf Cases*, where it wrote:

[O]ver half the States concerned, whether acting unilaterally or conjointly, were or shortly became parties to the Geneva Convention [on the Continental Shelf], and were therefore presumably, so far as they were concerned, acting actually or potentially in the application of the Convention. From their action no inference could legitimately be drawn as to the existence of a rule of customary international law in favour of the equidistance principle.[31]

The Court would seem to have since reassessed its position on this issue. At one point in its judgment in the 1986 *Nicaragua Case (Merits)*, it focused on the possible existence of a customary rule prohibiting aggression. After referring to Article 2(4) of the Charter of the United Nations and a number of resolutions of the United Nations General Assembly, all of which supported a prohibition on aggression, the Court wrote:

The effect of consent to the text of such resolutions cannot be understood as merely that of a 'reiteration or elucidation' of the treaty commitment undertaken in the Charter. On the contrary, it may be understood as an acceptance of the validity of the rule or set of rules declared by the resolution by themselves . . . It would therefore seem apparent that the attitude referred to expresses an *opinio juris* respecting such rule (or set of rules), to be thenceforth treated separately from the provisions, especially those of an institutional kind, to which it is subject on the treaty-law plane of the Charter.[32]

[29] Baxter (1970) 73. [30] Baxter (1970) 96. See also Villiger (1985) 195–6.

[31] Note 15, p. 38 above, at 43 (para. 76). See also Villiger (1985) 11–12. However, somewhat contradictorily the Court alluded, in the same judgment, to the possibility of transforming widely accepted treaties into rules of customary international law. See the quotation on p. 167 above.

[32] Note 16, p. 8 above, at 100 (para. 188). See also, albeit less unequivocally, *Nicaragua Case (Jurisdiction)* (1984) *ICJ Reports* 392, 424 (para.73).

The Court concluded that 'customary international law continues to exist and to apply, separately from international treaty law, even where the two categories of law have an identical content'.[33]

This judgment in the *Nicaragua Case* would seem to be consistent with several developments in the law of treaties, most notably Article 43 of the 1969 Vienna Convention on the Law of Treaties.[34] Article 43 recognises the possibility of parallel treaty and customary rules:

> The invalidity, termination or denunciation of a treaty, the withdrawal of a party from it, or the suspension of its operation, as a result of the application of the present Convention or of the provisions of the treaty, shall not in any way impair the duty of any State to fulfil *any obligation embodied in the treaty to which it would be subject under international law independently of the treaty*.[35]

A third, related problem concerns whether customary international law is able to modify treaty rules, and, if it is able to do so, how such modifications occur.[36] There is some evidence that customary modifications of treaty rules do take place.

A suggestion to this effect was made in the arbitral decision concerning the *Air Services Agreement of 27 March 1946* between France and the United States, where the Tribunal wrote:

> [A]ccount has to be taken of the practice of the Parties in the application of the Agreement, as a supplementary means of interpreting this instrument. This method may be susceptible of either confirming or contradicting, *and even possibly*

[33] Note 16, p. 8 above, at 96 (para. 179). Compare the dissenting judgment of Judge Jennings, note 16, p. 8 above, at 528. Brownlie ((1995) 39–40) has noted a potentially important difference between the two situations, such that the *North Sea Continental Shelf Cases* concerned 'an area of law in which new rules were emerging', as opposed to the relatively well-established area of law which concerns the use of force. The Court, it should also be noted, found itself in a highly unusual situation in the *Nicaragua Case*. As a result of a reservation by the United States to its declaration under the 'Optional Clause' (Art. 36(2) of the Statute of the International Court of Justice) the Court was precluded from applying multilateral treaty rules. On parallel treaty and customary rules, see generally Kontou (1994).

[34] Note 10, p. 36 above. See also the virtually identical Art. 43 of the 1986 Vienna Convention on the Law of Treaties between States and International Organizations or between International Organizations, reproduced in (1986) 25 ILM 543.

[35] Emphasis added. See also Art. 38 of both Vienna Conventions (again virtually identical as between the two Conventions) which may be read as also suggesting the possibility of parallel rules. Art. 38 of the 1969 Convention reads:

> Nothing in articles 34 to 37 precludes a rule set forth in a treaty from becoming binding upon a third State as a customary rule of international law, recognized as such.

It might, however, be argued that this article does not represent a rejection of the 'Baxter paradox', that the treaty obligations it refers to may only be found in treaties which are not designed for, or have not achieved, widespread participation.

[36] On this problem, see generally Danilenko (1993) 162–72.

*of correcting*, the conclusions furnished by the interpretations based on an examination of the text and the preparatory work, for the purposes of determining the common intention of the Parties when they concluded the Agreement.[37]

Similarly, in the 1971 *Namibia Advisory Opinion* South Africa objected that, as a result of abstentions by the Soviet Union and the United Kingdom, Security Council Resolution 284 lacked the concurring votes of the permanent members as required by Article 27(3) of the Charter of the United Nations. The International Court of Justice responded:

[T]he proceedings of the Security Council extending over a long period supply abundant evidence that presidential rulings and the positions taken by members of the Council, in particular its permanent members, have consistently and uniformly interpreted the practice of voluntary abstention by a permanent member as not constituting a bar to the adoption of resolutions . . . This procedure . . . has been generally accepted by Members of the United Nations and evidences a general practice of that Organization.[38]

Likewise, in its judgment in the 1962 *Temple of Preah Vihear Case (Merits)*, the International Court of Justice wrote:

The Court considers that the acceptance of the Annex I map by the Parties caused the map to enter the treaty settlement and to become an integral part of it . . . In other words, the Parties at that time adopted an interpretation of the treaty settlement which caused the map line, in so far as it may have departed from the line of the watershed, to prevail over the relevant clause of the treaty.[39]

However, these three examples could concern either the interpretation of treaties or the modification of the internal procedures of an international organisation by its member States, rather than recognition of the possibility of the customary process modifying treaty rules through subsequent State practice.[40] More convincing is the situation involving Article 5(5) of the 1958 Geneva Convention on the Continental Shelf, which requires States parties to remove from the continental shelf any oil platforms which they choose to abandon.[41] The subsequent behaviour of States parties soon indicated their support for a different rule, to the effect that abandoned platforms may be left where they are providing that

[37] (1969) 38 ILR 182, 245–6 (emphasis added); in French at (1965) 69 *Revue générale de droit international public* 189, 246. [38] (1971) *ICJ Reports* 16, 22 (para. 22).

[39] Note 8, p. 107 above, at 33–4.

[40] See Frowein (1989). Compare the comments (on the *Temple Case*) of Waldock, acting as Special Rapporteur on the Law of Treaties, in (1966) 1(2) *Yearbook of the International Law Commission* 168 (para. 63).

[41] (1958) 499 UNTS 311, 316. Art. 5(5) reads (emphasis added):

> Due notice must be given of the construction of any such installations [necessary for the coastal State's exploration and exploitation of its natural resources], and permanent means for giving warning of their presence must be maintained. Any installations which are abandoned or disused must be *removed entirely*.

appropriate safety measures are taken.[42] This change in State practice was later reflected, at least to some degree, in Article 60(3) of the 1982 United Nations Convention on the Law of the Sea, which foresees that in some circumstances abandoned platforms may be left on the continental shelf.[43] It may therefore be that the obligations arising under Article 5(5) of the 1958 Geneva Convention have been modified as a result of changing customary international law.

A similar modification to the 1958 Geneva Convention on the Continental Shelf and the 1958 Geneva Convention on the High Seas may have occurred as a result of the subsequent development, in customary international law, of a twelve-mile breadth to the territorial sea.[44] Although this customary development did not change the provisions of those treaties, it would seem to have reduced the geographic scope of their application. The development of the 200-mile exclusive economic zone as a rule of customary international law may have had similar effects.[45]

The International Law Commission, in its 1966 Draft Articles on the Law of Treaties, seems to have anticipated that treaty rules could be modified through subsequent State practice, at least in so far as that practice established the agreement of States parties to the relevant modifications. Draft Article 38 reads: 'A treaty may be modified by subsequent practice in the application of the treaty establishing the agreement of the parties to modify its provisions.'[46] This provision was omitted from the 1969 Vienna Convention.[47] However, another provision remains

[42] See Churchill and Lowe (1988) 129; and Higgins (1994) 31–2.

[43] Note 29, p. 41 above. Art. 60(3) reads (rather contradictorily) (emphasis added):

> Due notice must be given of the construction of such artificial islands, installations or structures, and permanent means for giving warning of their presence must be maintained. Any installations or structures which are abandoned or disused shall be removed to ensure safety of navigation, taking into account any generally accepted international standards established in this regard by the competent international organization. Such removal shall also have due regard to fishing, the protection of the marine environment and the rights and duties of other States. *Appropriate publicity shall be given to the depth, position and dimensions of any installations or structures not entirely removed.*

[44] See pp. 114–20 above. For the High Seas Convention, see note 31, p. 62 above.

[45] See Danilenko (1993) 168–9. For this and other examples concerning the law of the sea, see Kontou (1994).

[46] *Report of the ILC on the Work of its 18th Session* (1966) 2 *Yearbook of the International Law Commission* 172, 182. See Villiger (1985) 211. An earlier draft (of then Art. 68) went even further, foreseeing that a treaty could be modified by the 'subsequent emergence of a new rule of customary law relating to matters dealt with in the treaty and binding upon all the parties'. See (1966) 1(2) *Yearbook of the International Law Commission* 163 and subsequent discussions of the ILC members at 163–9, 220–2 and 266–7; and Villiger (1985) 208–10.

[47] Note 10, p. 36 above.

which indicates that at least one potential category of customary rules may have significant effects on pre-existing treaties. Article 64 of the 1969 Vienna Convention reads: 'If a new peremptory norm of general international law emerges, any existing treaty which is in conflict with that norm becomes void and terminates.'[48] Furthermore, a number of writers have acknowledged the possibility of changes occurring to treaty rules through the process of customary international law.[49] Yet none of the explanations as to how such changes occur has been widely accepted.

It may prove helpful to consider these changes in terms of the interaction of power and obligation. It has already been suggested that the customary process is a regime or institution which transforms State practice into obligation in the form of customary rules.[50] Some of the rules which result from the process of customary international law make up the law of treaties,[51] and that particular set of customary rules could itself be considered a distinct regime or institution. In Keohane's terms the customary international law of treaties is a persistent and connected set of informal rules which prescribe behavioural roles, constrain activity and shape expectations.[52] Perhaps more importantly, States regularly use the law of treaties to create other regimes and institutions, including international organisations, through the processes of negotiation and signature or ratification.[53]

The basal rule within the law of treaties is *pacta sunt servanda*, which prescribes that treaty obligations must be fulfilled in good faith.[54] Yet this fundamental rule may be only one part of a more general principle, namely, that of legitimate expectation, which also subsumes the principles of consent and estoppel.[55]

The question whether treaty provisions may be modified by subsequent State practice may become easier to answer if the rule of *pacta sunt servanda* is viewed in this context, that is to say, as part of the more general principle of legitimate expectation. It is possible that, in each case of potential modification, the legitimate expectations associated with the

[48] Note 10, p. 36 above. See Danilenko (1993) 165. For a discussion of whether peremptory or *jus cogens* rules are in fact rules of customary international law, see pp. 183–95 below.

[49] See, e.g., Fitzmaurice (1957) 225; Bowett (1976–7) 84; and Sur (1990) 1er cahier, 9.

[50] See pp. 147–57 above.

[51] The customary rules on the law of treaties were codified in the 1969 Vienna Convention on the Law of Treaties, note 10, p. 36 above. However, that Convention does not apply retrospectively (Art. 4), nor are all States party to it. On the customary international law of treaties, see generally McNair (1961); and Reuter (1995).

[52] See p. 27 above.

[53] See generally Keohane (1989e); Young (1989); Franck (1995) 265–6; and p. 170 above.

[54] See Art. 26 of the Vienna Convention on the Law of Treaties, note 10, p. 36 above; and Lachs (1984).

[55] See pp. 106–7 above.

treaty, and with any subsequent practice consistent with that treaty, are weighed against those legitimate expectations which result from subsequent, inconsistent instances of State practice.

The *pacta sunt servanda* rule has acquired weight through countless instances of supporting State practice, and through the conspicuous common interest which States have in this particular rule. In cases of potential modification of treaties, this weight will give rise to a strong presumption in favour of the continuing applicability of treaty provisions, and against their modification by way of the process of customary international law.[56] Yet there are several reasons why it would seem that the possibility of modifying treaty provisions through subsequent practice must exist, why legitimate expectations resulting from subsequent, inconsistent instances of State behaviour should in some situations prevail.

First, in some situations States parties may find it extremely difficult, if not impossible, to negotiate changes, or even an end, to treaties which no longer serve their common interests.[57] In some cases treaties may instead be allowed to fall into desuetude, whereupon States parties are released from their treaty obligations as a result of long periods of collective disregard for those instruments, which lead to inferred terminations by consent.[58]

Secondly, situations may arise where rules of customary international law become so well established that States do not consider it necessary to ratify treaties which replicate those rules, or to change old treaties which conflict with them. For example, the 1933 Montevideo Convention on Rights and Duties of States sets out what are widely accepted as being the requirements of statehood in international law.[59] However, only sixteen States have ever ratified that treaty.[60] In such a situation a lack of ratifications may be indicative of the strength, and not the weakness, of the corresponding customary rules. However, it should be noted that this suggestion is contrary to the position taken by the International Court of Justice in the 1950 *Asylum Case*, where it considered that the claim that a treaty is declaratory of customary international law is weakened if that treaty has only been ratified by a limited number of States.[61] There may in

[56] See Villiger (1985) 222–3. Such a presumption might also be seen as one which operates in favour of explicit as opposed to inferred consent. See pp. 142–6 above. Akehurst ((1974–75b) 275) wrote: '[S]ubsequent custom can terminate a treaty only when there is clear evidence that that is what the parties intended.' [57] See pp. 107–9 above.

[58] On desuetude, see generally Commentary (para. 5) to Art. 39 of the 'ILC Draft Articles on the Law of Treaties', in *Report of the ILC on the Work of the 2nd Part of its 17th Session* (1966) 2 *Yearbook of the International Law Commission* 169, 237; McNair (1961) 516–18; Vamvoukos (1985) 219–303; Plender (1986) 138–45; and Brownlie (1990) 617–18.

[59] 165 LNTS 19; reproduced in (1934) 28 *American Journal of International Law Supplement* 75.

[60] The ratifying States were the United States and fifteen Latin American States.

[61] Note 4, p. 130 above, at 277.

fact be different phases of legal development involved here, beginning with patterns of legally relevant State practice, which lead to customary rules, and continue through codification before returning to patterns of legally relevant State practice as the customary rules grow so strong that codification becomes a redundant and unnecessary exercise.

Thirdly, as was recognised by Judge Hudson in his individual opinion in the 1937 *River Meuse Case*, an important principle of equity holds that:

> [W]here two parties have assumed an identical or a reciprocal obligation, one party which is engaged in a continuing non-performance of that obligation should not be permitted to take advantage of a similar non-performance of that obligation by the other party.[62]

This means that if one party to a treaty has itself engaged in subsequent, inconsistent State practice, it will not be able to rely on the treaty provision in question as the basis for a claim against another State. In such a situation the effect on the treaty provision will be that it becomes unopposable, at least as between those two States. This application of equity thus supports the legitimate expectations of States which are developed in response to the subsequent practice of other States parties to treaties, rather than those developed in response to treaty provisions which those other States parties clearly no longer respect.

Fourthly, those who argue that the customary process cannot modify treaty provisions through subsequent State practice would seem to ignore the role and purpose of those many treaties which codify customary international law. Codification aims to clarify rules of customary international law, to render them more accessible and therefore easier for States to follow and use in co-operative activities and dispute resolution.[63] If codifying treaties are part of a larger endeavour to promote co-operation and the peaceful resolution of disputes, they should not bind States to outmoded statements of customary international law in areas where the interests of most States, as manifested through their practice, have clearly and significantly changed. Although a presumption in favour of *pacta sunt servanda* promotes stability, strict adherence to that principle would have the opposite effect by putting pressure on States to violate international law in certain circumstances.

It is possible that a State could persistently object to the customary modification of a treaty provision. South Africa's argument in the 1971 *Namibia Advisory Opinion* might be regarded as such an attempt, although it would seem that South Africa did not adopt this position early enough. Moreover, it is possible that the desired effect of South Africa's

[62] (1937) PCIJ Reports, Ser. A/B, No. 70, 73, 77.

[63] See Art. 13 of the Charter of the United Nations; Art. 1 of the Statute of the ILC, UNGA Res. 174 (II), in (1947–8) *Yearbook of the United Nations* 211; and Rosenne (1992).

objections could not have been bilateralised, in that they related to the operation of the Security Council as a whole.[64] Yet even if a State could persistently object to the customary modification of a treaty provision, the pressures to conform in such a situation, as in any situation of attempted persistent objection, are likely eventually to force the objecting State to concede.[65]

Certain other limitations would also seem to exist in respect of the ability of subsequent State practice to modify or change treaty provisions. For example, it would seem that a treaty provision could not be modified by the subsequent practice of States *in general* if the treaty in question was entered into for the purposes of creating a legal exception to an otherwise generally applicable rule. Instead, such a treaty provision could only be modified by a new treaty provision or by subsequent State practice *as between* the parties to that treaty. The situation would thus appear to resemble that which concerns rules of special customary international law.[66] Although a rule of special customary international law cannot be modified by the practice of States in general, it may be modified by the practice of those States which are within the limited group of States it binds.

Since the text of the treaty in question will itself remain unchanged by any modification resulting from the customary process, it is difficult to conceive of how subsequent State practice could actually modify a treaty rule, *strictly speaking*, unless the modification in question were subtle enough to fall within the scope of reasonable interpretation. In such a situation it would appear that a customary rule which is identical in content to the treaty rule must first exist alongside it, and bind the same States.[67] The operation of the customary process might then lead to changes in the interpretation of the treaty rule, although the two regimes or institutions – the customary process and the treaty – would remain distinct.[68]

More significant changes would also depend on subsequent State practice having modified a parallel customary rule having the same content as the treaty rule and binding the same States. However, the modified customary rule and the treaty rule would then be weighed against each other in terms of their relative degrees of associated legitimate expectation in

[64] See note 38, p. 173 and p. 88 above. [65] See pp. 102–5 above.
[66] See generally the citations in note 3, p. 3 above. [67] See pp. 170–2 above.
[68] Kontou ((1994) 30–1) wrote:

> [I]t is doubtful whether new custom necessarily implies a duty to abstain from applying another conventional rule on the same subject-matter . . . Supervening custom and a prior conflicting treaty can exist in parallel if the parties to the treaty wish to continue applying the conventional rule in their *inter se* relations . . . It is, therefore, not appropriate to consider that treaty termination automatically follows the formation of new conflicting custom.

order to determine whether the treaty rule has, in effect, fallen into desuetude, leaving the modified customary rule to stand alone.[69] That said, the treaty rule would only fall into desuetude if States parties failed to invoke it in response to practice by other States parties in violation of that rule.[70] In such situations acquiescence works in two ways, both in developing the customary rule *and* in rendering the treaty rule of no further effect. The treaty would then apply *qua* treaty as between the parties in respect of all of its provisions, except for the rule which has been rendered inapplicable by subsequent State practice. That rule is replaced by a new rule of customary international law as between the parties, and perhaps generally.[71]

It should be noted that if customary rules could not exist in parallel with treaty rules, one might have a situation in which treaty rules were being 'modified' solely as a result of the behaviour of non-parties. State parties could, as a result of their behaviour being considered solely as in fulfilment of their treaty obligations, be precluded from contributing to the development or change of a generally applicable rule. Nevertheless, the legitimate expectations associated with the development or change of such a rule could conceivably modify the treaty's provisions, as long as the treaty was not designed to create an exception to a generally applicable rule, and especially if it had been intended to codify generally applicable customary international law.

The general principle of consent indicates,[72] and a corollary of the more specific rule that treaties cannot create rights and legal obligations for third States without their consent suggests,[73] that this cannot be the

[69] For support of this proposition, see Giraud (1961) 49; and Friedmann (1964) 132. Thirlway ((1972) 131) and Kontou ((1994) 20) have relied on the general principle that *lex posterior derogat priori* to explain why treaties may be modified by subsequently developed rules of customary international law. Such an explanation appears unsatisfactory in that it fails to explain the basis, which is both legal *and* sociological, of the *lex posterior* rule, i.e. legitimate expectation. Villiger ((1985) 216), for his part, argued that 'the obligation to derogate from a conventional rule in favour of applying a customary rule is made possible because there is no hierarchy of sources in international law' and that 'the obligation to adhere only to the customary rule is essential, since it entails and ensures that the latter shall command the necessary general and uniform State practice'. These two arguments are similarly unconvincing. The former is based on the fact that such an obligation 'is made possible', with no evidence being provided that it is a logical or necessary conclusion, whereas the latter is a policy argument. Other scholars have relied on the *rebus sic stantibus* rule. For commentary, see Kontou (1994) 32–5.

[70] See Kontou (1994) 25.

[71] In some exceptional cases where the customary rule in question has generated an exceptionally high degree of legitimate expectation, as with rules of *jus cogens*, the treaty as a whole may fall. See Art. 64 of the Vienna Convention on the Law of Treaties, note 10, p. 36 above; and pp. 183–95 below.

[72] See pp. 142–6 above.

[73] See Art. 34 of the Vienna Convention on the Law of Treaties, note 10, p. 36 above and Art. 34 of the Vienna Convention on the Law of Treaties Between States and International Organizations or Between International Organizations, note 34, p. 172 above.

case. Some participation on the part of States parties to the treaty would be required, although acquiescence in the development or change of the generally applicable rule might suffice.[74]

## The persistent objector

States which have not acquiesced in the development or change of customary rules, but which have instead attempted and failed through objections or opposition to prevent such developments or changes, occasionally refuse to accept that those new rules apply to them. It is possible to argue that, because these States have consented to the process of customary international law, they are bound by any rule which results from that process.[75] Yet States are unlikely consistently to oppose the development or change of a rule unless they perceive that development or change to be significantly detrimental to their interests. This means that an insistence on system consent in these situations may encourage law-breaking by opposing States. The doctrine of persistent objection has been developed to deal with these types of situations and allows a State which has consistently objected to or opposed the development or change of a customary rule to avoid being bound by that rule in its relations with all other States.[76]

The International Court of Justice's first apparent endorsement of the doctrine of persistent objection appeared in its judgment in the 1950 *Asylum Case*:

> [E]ven if it could be supposed that such a custom existed . . . it could not be invoked against Peru which, far from having by its attitude adhered to it, has, on the contrary, repudiated it by refraining from ratifying the Montevideo Conventions of 1933 and 1939, which were the first to include a rule concerning the qualification of the offence in matters of diplomatic asylum.[77]

Then, in the 1951 *Anglo-Norwegian Fisheries Case*, the Court stated:

> [A]lthough the ten-mile rule has been adopted by certain States both in their national law and in their treaties and conventions, and although certain arbitral decisions have applied it as between these States, other States have adopted a

[74] See 1977 *Delimitation of the Continental Shelf* (United Kingdom/France), reproduced in (1979) 18 ILM 397. The Court of Arbitration in this dispute accepted (at 417 (para. 47)) that 'a development in customary international law may, under certain conditions, evidence the assent of the States concerned to the modification, or even termination, of previously existing treaty rights and obligations'. Yet it required 'the most conclusive indications of the intention *of the parties*' (*ibid.*, emphasis added).

[75] See pp. 143–5 above.

[76] See generally Akehurst (1974–75a) 23–7; Stein (1985); and Colson (1986). Compare Charney (1985).

[77] Note 4, p. 130 above, at 277–8.

different limit. Consequently, the ten-mile rule has not acquired the authority of a general rule of international law.

In any event the ten-mile rule would appear to be inapplicable as against Norway inasmuch as she has always opposed any attempt to apply it to the Norwegian coast.[78]

The Court may appear to have adopted the opposite position in a *dictum* in its judgment in the 1969 *North Sea Continental Shelf Cases*, where it stated that customary international law 'cannot . . . be the subject of any right of unilateral exclusion exercisable at will by any [State] in its own favour'.[79] This statement, however, refers to unilateral exclusions attempted *after* a rule had come into force.

There would seem to be at least one important, unanswered question about the doctrine of persistent objection: is persistent objection ever realistically available as a long-term option to States? There appears to be no evidence of any State having persistently objected to a customary rule for an indefinite period of time. For example, non-industrialised States and socialist States eventually accepted the doctrine of restrictive State immunity from jurisdiction, notwithstanding their earlier opposition to that rule.[80] And although South Africa attempted to persistently object to the prohibition on *apartheid*, this attempt was never accorded legal effect by other States.[81] Even the most powerful of the maritime States – the United States, the United Kingdom and Japan – eventually abandoned their persistent objection to the development of the twelve-mile territorial sea as a rule of customary international law.[82]

In chapter 6 it was suggested that States which attempt persistently to object gain little thereby because they are forced by the principle of reciprocity to accord the same exceptional right which they claim (i.e., not to be bound by the new or modified rule) to other States. Moreover, other States consistently take advantage of their strength in numbers and, in some cases, of the principle of jurisdiction, by refusing to recognise the claims of persistent objectors.[83] In so doing they indicate a preference for society interests and society rules, that is, for the 'universal public interest', over *ad hoc*, unilaterally created exceptions.

The pressures brought to bear on States to conform in such situations may be considerable. As Stern suggested, the consent of the 'silent majority' is conditioned by the behaviour of other, frequently more powerful

[78] Note 23, p. 134 above, at 131.
[79] Note 15, p. 38 above, at 38 (para. 63). See Koskenniemi (1989) 345. On the application of the distinction between *ratio decidendi* and *obiter dicta* to international law, see Jennings (1996); and Shahabuddeen (1996) 152–64.
[80] See pp. 110–14 above. [81] See pp. 194–5 below. [82] See p. 104 above.
[83] See pp. 102–5 and 114–17 above.

States.[84] The result is the adoption of a rule by 'consensus', which, 'en dépit de l'*apparente unanimité* qui le consacre . . . constitue un instrument de coalition contre les isolés'.[85] Charney and Danilenko have recognised the role played by power in these situations and have questioned '[w]hether at this stage . . . such a limitation [on persistent objection] may be described as a legal one'.[86] However, the interaction of the principles of reciprocity and jurisdiction with applications of power in these instances indicates that, when attempts at persistent objection are abandoned, this is at least partly the result of the influence of obligation in the form of customary rules.[87]

However, in contrast to their reaction to attempts at persistent objection, States generally tolerate the creation of legal exceptions by way of treaties or rules of special customary international law. They appear to do so for two, related reasons. First, such exceptions are not imposed unilaterally on other States, but instead involve the consent of all those States which are bound by those exceptions in any way. This is not the case with exceptions created by way of persistent objection, where the existing rights and obligations of the objecting State are preserved despite the wishes of all or most other States to create a new, generally applicable rule.

Secondly, exceptions created by way of treaty or rules of special customary international law apply only as between the States which are party to the relevant treaty, or as between the members of the particular group of States which is governed by the relevant rule of special customary international law. Such exceptions do not affect the rights and obligations of the excepted States *vis-à-vis* the rest of international society under generally applicable customary rules. Exceptions created by way of treaty or rules of special customary international law do not therefore pose a serious challenge to society interests and society rules. Rather, they reflect the fact that smaller societies of States exist within the larger international society, and that these smaller societies sometimes have common interests unique to themselves which require special rules among their own members.

Despite the fact, then, that States never persistently object for

[84] Stern (1981) 498. See pp. 132–3 above.

[85] Stern (1981) 497, quoting from and adding emphasis to Reuter (1976) 26. My translation reads: 'in spite of the *apparent unanimity* to which it is devoted . . . constitutes an instrument of coalition against isolated States'.

[86] Charney and Danilenko (1995) 28. Danilenko ((1993) 112) has elsewhere made the slightly different – and in this case unquestionably valid – point that 'the possibility of effective preservation of the persistent objector status should not be confused with the legally recognized right not to agree with new customary rules'.

[87] See pp. 102–5 above.

indefinite periods of time, persistent objection remains important in terms of its systemic effects. Persistent objectors play a dialectical role in the development, maintenance and change of customary rules, similar to an opposition party in a national legislature. They draw attention to changes being made in the law and to problems associated with those changes, thus encouraging other States to consider their actions carefully. Moreover, if a persistently objecting State can convince enough other States to adopt similar positions, it may be able to block, reverse, or at least modify the substance of, those changes.[88] Perhaps most importantly, a persistent objector, even if it is unsuccessful, may end up buying itself time by postponing the application of the new, generally applicable rule to itself and thus what it perceives to be the deleterious effects thereof.

## Jus cogens

The example of South Africa's unsuccessful attempt at persistent objection to the prohibition on *apartheid* leads into a second problem associated with the doctrine of persistent objection: the question whether States are ever able to 'opt out' of the development or change of *jus cogens* rules. The answer to this question would seem to depend, in turn, on the source of *jus cogens* rules.

The concept of *jus cogens* has long been part of international law.[89] However, most of the attention paid to the concept in recent years has resulted from its inclusion in two separate provisions of the 1969 Vienna Convention on the Law of Treaties.[90] The first of these provisions, Article 53, deals with the effect of existing *jus cogens* rules on treaties which, at the time of their conclusion, conflict with those rules. It reads:

> A treaty is void if, at the time of its conclusion, it conflicts with a peremptory norm of general international law. For the purposes of the present Convention, a peremptory norm of general international law is a norm accepted and recognized by the international community of States as a whole as a norm from which no derogation is permitted and which can be modified only by a subsequent norm of general international law having the same character.

The second of these provisions, Article 64, deals with those situations where such a *jus cogens* rule emerges, and comes into conflict with a pre-existing treaty. It reads:

> If a new peremptory norm of general international law emerges, any existing treaty which is in conflict with that norm becomes void and terminates.

[88] See Charney (1993) 540; and Charney and Danilenko (1995) 50.
[89] See Byers (1997a) 213–14. [90] Note 10, p. 36 above.

In both instances, the *jus cogens* rule trumps the relevant treaty, rendering it void in its entirety.

Today, there is widespread acceptance among international lawyers of the concept of *jus cogens*. It has been widely discussed by writers and was included in the 1986 Vienna Convention on the Law of Treaties Between States and International Organizations or Between International Organizations.[91] The International Court of Justice mentioned the concept in its judgment in the 1969 *North Sea Continental Shelf Cases*[92] and, in its judgment in the 1986 *Nicaragua Case (Merits)*, quoted with approval the following statement by the International Law Commission:

> [T]he law of the Charter concerning the prohibition of the use of force in itself constitutes a conspicuous example of a rule in international law having the character of *jus cogens*.[93]

There has also been a growing trend of thought which considers that *jus cogens* rules have unusual effects on more than just conflicting treaties. This trend is consistent with Article 53 of the 1969 Vienna Convention, which states that *jus cogens* rules permit 'no derogation'.[94] For instance, the International Law Commission may have adopted the concept, or at least some variant of it, in distinguishing between international crimes and international delicts in its work on State responsibility. International crimes are breaches by States of obligations which are 'essential for the protection of fundamental interests of the international community', whereas international delicts are all other 'internationally wrongful' acts.[95]

[91] For scholarly support for the concept, see, e.g., Verdross (1966); Virally (1966); Mosler (1968a); Onuf and Birney (1974); Macdonald (1987); Hannikainen (1988); Parker and Neylon (1989); Danilenko (1991); and Kadelbach (1992). For scepticism, see, e.g., Schwarzenberger (1965); Sztucki (1974); Weil (1983); Hartmann (1983); and Weisburd (1995). For the 1986 Vienna Convention, see note 34, p. 172 above. Articles 53 and 64 of this treaty are identical to Articles 53 and 64 of the 1969 Vienna Convention.

[92] Note 15, p. 38 above, at 42 (para. 72).

[93] Note 16, p. 8 above, at 100 (para. 190) (quoting from the commentary of the ILC to Art. 50 of its Draft Articles on the Law of Treaties, in *Report of the ILC on the Work of its 18th Session* (1966) 2 *Yearbook of the International Law Commission* 172, 247). For scholarly support for this conclusion, see, e.g., Verdross (1966) 60; Virally (1966) 28; Crawford (1979) 106; and Hannikainen (1988) 323–56.

[94] For the text of Art. 53, see p. 183 above.

[95] See Art. 19 of the Draft Articles on State Responsibility (Part One), note 14, p. 14 above, at 32; and Weiler *et al.* (1989). The distinction is important in terms of the scope of injury in the event of a breach. In short, only international crimes constitute violations of *erga omnes* rules. It is therefore probably more accurate to describe the concept of international crimes as a variant of the concept of *erga omnes*. See Art. 5(3) of the Draft Articles on State Responsibility (Part Two), note 36, p. 83; and pp. 195–203 below. The ILC clearly did not consider international crimes and *jus cogens* rules to be exactly the same thing. In its commentary to Art. 19 it wrote (*ibid.*, 120):

> [O]bligations whose breach is a crime will 'normally' be those deriving from rules of *jus cogens*, though this conclusion cannot be absolute . . . the category of inter-

It has also been suggested that treaty provisions which potentially limit the application of *jus cogens* rules without being in violation of them might not apply in such situations.[96] Similarly, an action which, although taken pursuant to a legal treaty, is nonetheless in violation of a *jus cogens* rule would clearly be contrary to international law notwithstanding the legality of the treaty.[97] It was on the basis of such reasoning that Judge *ad hoc* Lauterpacht, in his 1993 separate opinion on a request for provisional measures in the *Case Concerning Application of the Convention on the Prevention and Punishment of the Crime of Genocide*, applied the concept of *jus cogens* to the question of the legality of the arms embargo which had been imposed on Bosnia-Herzegovina by the United Nations Security Council.[98] The Security Council had been acting under Chapter VII of the Charter of the United Nations. Lauterpacht wrote:

> The concept of *jus cogens* operates as a concept superior to both customary international law and treaty. The relief which Article 103 of the Charter may give the Security Council in case of conflict between one of its decisions and an operative treaty obligation cannot – as a matter of simple hierarchy of norms – extend to a conflict between a Security Council resolution and *jus cogens*. Indeed, one only has to state the opposite proposition thus – that a Security Council resolution may even require participation in genocide – for its unacceptability to be apparent.[99]

If Lauterpacht's analysis is correct, a *jus cogens* rule may thus override even the most authoritative form of executive action known to

national obligations admitting of no derogation is much broader than the category of obligations whose breach is necessarily an international crime.

It is perhaps significant that Art. 19 of the Draft Articles on State Responsibility (Part One) does not refer explicitly to the concept of *jus cogens* (or 'peremptory norm'), whereas Arts. 18(2), 29(2) and 33(2)(a) do. In addition, it is unclear whether the concept is required in respect of unilateral acts. The concept of *jus cogens* is essentially a 'conflict of law' rule which operates between customary rules of a fundamental, public policy character and treaties and other objective regimes. Rules having a *jus cogens* character are not needed to control the actions of individual States because States cannot create treaties and objective regimes on their own. See Marek (1968) 441.

[96] See Brownlie (1990) 613, note 49. Brownlie referred to Art. 102(2) of the UN Charter, which reads: 'No party to any such treaty or international agreement which has not been registered . . . may invoke that treaty or agreement before any organ of the United Nations.' He asked: 'If the instrument is part of the *jus cogens*, should non-registration have this effect?'

[97] See Schachter (1991) 343–4.

[98] (1993) *ICJ Reports* 325, 407. The arms embargo extended to the rest of the former Yugoslavia.

[99] *Ibid.*, 440 (para. 100). For support for the prohibition against genocide being a *jus cogens* rule see, e.g., *Report of the ILC on the Work of its 18th Session*, note 93, p. 184 above, at 248; Virally (1966) 11; Ago (1971) 324, note 37; and Alexidze (1981) 262. It might be argued that the prohibition against genocide is in this respect an unusual *jus cogens* rule and that the Security Council is explicitly authorised to act contrary to another *jus cogens* rule, namely the prohibition on the use of force. However, this latter rule is constrained in scope and only concerns the aggressive use of force, i.e. force which is used neither in self-defence nor with the authorization of the Security Council. Moreover, the Security Council was created to enforce this rule, not to act contrary to it.

international society, should that authority be exercised in violation of that rule.[100]

*Jus cogens* are sometimes thought to preclude persistent objection, as well as the establishment of other legal exceptions through the creation of rules of special customary international law.[101] They may also play a role with regard to questions of statehood and territorial acquisition, such that they make it more difficult for the principles of effectiveness and extinctive prescription to operate in situations where territory has been occupied in a manner which violates one or more *jus cogens* rules.[102] Their violation might also result in the loss of certain privileges, such as the rule that belligerent States are not responsible for damage caused to subjects of neutral States by military operations.[103] Finally, the existence of *jus cogens* rules would seem to provide a strong guide to the interpretation of treaties, so that conflicts between such rules and treaties are avoided wherever possible.[104]

In addition to the prohibitions on aggression and genocide, rules which are today widely accepted as being rules of *jus cogens* include the prohibitions on slavery, torture and *apartheid*.[105] These rules play an essential

[100] However, it is not clear whether Lauterpacht's analysis would apply if the Security Council were violating a *jus cogens* rule in order to prevent the violation of either that same rule, or another *jus cogens* rule. Given that many Security Council actions address acts of aggression, and therefore violations of a *jus cogens* rule, the analysis would seem to require expansion to include an examination of the effectiveness of any such action in support of one *jus cogens* rule, at the expense of another. That said, the Security Council's actions to prevent genocide in Bosnia-Herzegovina were clearly ineffective.

[101] On the preclusion of persistent objection, see M. K. Yasseen (Chair of the Drafting Committee), *U.N. Conference on the Law of Treaties, Official Records* (1st Session 1968) (New York: United Nations, 1969) 472; Rozakis (1976) 78; Alexidze (1981) 246–7 and 258; Brownlie (1990) 514; and *Case 9647 (United States)* (Inter-American Commission of Human Rights), in Buergenthal and Norris (1988) 61, 78–9. Compare Schwarzenberger (1965) 459–60; and Cassese (1986) 178. On persistent objection more generally, see pp. 180–3 above. On special customary international law, see the citations, note 3, p. 3 above.

[102] See Jennings (1965) 70–8; Crawford (1976–7) 148; Crawford (1979) 81–4 and 420; Brownlie (1990) 80; and the discussion of the *East Timor Case* at note 166, p. 201 below.

[103] See Schwarzenberger (1957) 646; and Brownlie (1990) 514. Article 33(2)(a) of the ILC Draft Articles on State Responsibility (Part One), note 14, p. 14 above, at 33, reads:

> In any case, a state of necessity may not be invoked by a State as a ground for precluding wrongfulness: (a) if the international obligation with which the act of the State is not in conformity arises out of a peremptory norm of general international law.

[104] See Art. 31(3)(c) of the 1969 Vienna Convention on the Law of Treaties, note 10, p. 36 above; and McNair (1961) 383–5.

[105] On the prohibition against slavery, see Hannikainen (1988) 444–7; Brownlie (1990) 513; Kadelbach (1992) 296–7. On the prohibition against torture, see Higgins (1976–7) 282; Rodley (1987) 70; Hannikainen (1988) 499–513; and Kadelbach (1992) 291–4. On the prohibition against *apartheid*, see Dugard (1987) 156–8; Hannikainen (1988) 467–89; and Kadelbach (1992) 277–82.

role in the international legal system by defining certain key aspects of that system and making it extremely difficult for States to change the way these rules apply to them. In this way *jus cogens* rules would appear to resemble – at least to some degree – the fundamental principles of international law the effects of which were examined in Part 2.

There is, however, some uncertainty as to the source of *jus cogens* rules. There are serious problems associated with assertions that *jus cogens* rules could be the result of one or any of the generally accepted primary sources of international law (treaties, customary international law, general principles of law), or perhaps natural law.[106]

There are two reasons why treaties could, at best, only be contributing factors in the development of *jus cogens* rules. First, a treaty cannot bind its parties not to modify its terms, nor to relieve themselves of their legal obligations under it, through a subsequent treaty to which all the parties to the first treaty have consented.[107] Secondly, it appears that all existing, generally accepted *jus cogens* rules apply universally and none of the treaties which have codified these rules has been universally ratified.[108] No treaty which has not been universally ratified, not even the Charter of the United Nations, can – in and of itself – establish a rule of general international law, for treaties can only create legal obligations as between their parties.[109]

Customary international law may likewise seem a problematic source for *jus cogens* rules because customary international law is generally considered to be based on State consent, even though this consent may take the form of a diffuse consensus, or of a general consent to the process of customary international law, as distinct from specific consent to individual rules.[110] It is therefore considered that individual States are able to create legal exceptions to customary rules if they so choose. Even a

[106] For a suggestion that *jus cogens* rules may be derived from either treaties, customary international law or general principles of law, see *Report of the ILC on the Work of its 18th Session*, note 93, p. 184 above, at 248. For assertions that they are rules of customary international law see, e.g., Brownlie (1990) 513; Paust (1991); and Kadelbach (1992) 186. For assertions that they are derived from natural law, see, e.g., *U.N. Conference on the Law of Treaties, Official Records* (1st Session, 1968) (New York: United Nations, 1969), statements by Italy (311); Ecuador (320); and Monaco (324). See subsequently de Visscher (1971). On the different sources of international law, see Art. 38(1) of the Statute of the International Court of Justice; Brownlie (1990) 1–31; Danilenko (1993); and Dinh *et al.* (1994) 111–390.

[107] See Art. 39 of the Vienna Convention on the Law of Treaties, note 10, p. 36 above; and Art. 29(1) of the ILC Draft Articles on State Responsibility (Part One), note 14, p. 14 above, at 32.

[108] See Danilenko (1991) 63; and Danilenko (1993) 246–7.

[109] See Art. 34 of the Vienna Convention on the Law of Treaties, note 10, p. 36 above; and Sur (1990) 1er cahier, 13. A widely ratified treaty could play an important role in the development of a generally applicable rule of customary international law. See pp. 167–70 above.

[110] See pp. 142–5 above.

general consent does not in itself preclude the creation of such exceptions.

*Jus cogens* rules would also seem to preclude the establishment of legal exceptions through the creation of rules of special customary international law and the conclusion of treaties, as well as, perhaps, persistent objection.[111] These former two kinds of exception operate on the basis of new rules applicable only as between the States which are subject or party to them. Most writers agree, and the 1969 Vienna Convention on the Law of Treaties confirms, that *jus cogens* rules deny the second of these options, namely the creation of exceptions through treaties.[112] Many writers consider that *jus cogens* rules also deny the other two options, namely the creation of rules of special customary international law, and persistent objection.[113] Therefore, since the creation of legal exceptions is precluded, *jus cogens* rules might appear to lack the consensual basis which is generally associated with customary international law. For this reason it is sometimes assumed that such rules cannot be the result of the customary process.[114]

Another possible explanation is that *jus cogens* rules are derived from general principles of law, in the sense identified by Article 38(1)(c) of the Statute of the International Court of Justice. For example, in 1953 Hersch Lauterpacht, as Special Rapporteur on the Law of Treaties, included an article on *jus cogens* rules in his report to the International Law Commission.[115] In his commentary to that article he stated:

> [T]he test whether the object of the treaty is illegal and whether the treaty is void for that reason is not only inconsistency with customary international law pure and simple, but inconsistency with such overriding principles of international law

[111] See pp. 180–3 above.

[112] See, e.g., Verdross (1966); Virally (1966); Mosler (1968a); Hannikainen (1988); Danilenko (1991); Kadelbach (1992); and Arts. 53 and 64 of the Vienna Convention on the Law of Treaties, note 10, p. 36 above.

[113] See, e.g., Rozakis (1976) 78; Alexidze (1981) 246–7 and 258; and Brownlie (1990) 514.

[114] See, e.g., Weil (1983) 425–9; Sur (1990) 1er cahier, 13 and 2e cahier, 8; Danilenko (1991) 47*ff*; and to some degree Onuf and Birney (1974). Compare *Report of the ILC on the Work of its 18th Session*, note 93, p. 184 above, at 248, where the ILC stated its intent to leave the full content of the *jus cogens* concept 'to be worked out in State practice and in the jurisprudence of international tribunals'; 'Commentary to the ILC Draft Articles on State Responsibility', in *Report of the ILC on the Work of its 28th Session* (1976) 2(2) *Yearbook of the International Law Commission* 75, 85–6 (para. 21); Brownlie (1990) 513; Danilenko (1993) 247; and, by implication, *Nicaragua Case (Merits)*, note 16, p. 8 above, at 100–1 (para. 190).

[115] (1953) 2 *Yearbook of the International Law Commission* 90, 93. The article in question was Art. 15:

> A treaty, or any of its provisions, is void if its performance involves an act which is illegal under international law and if it is declared so to be by the International Court of Justice.

which may be regarded as constituting principles of international public policy (*ordre international public*). These principles need not necessarily have crystallized in a clearly accepted rule of law . . . They may be expressive of rules of international morality so cogent that an international tribunal would consider them as forming part of those principles of law generally recognized by civilized nations which the International Court of Justice is bound to apply . . . The voidance of contractual agreements whose object is illegal is a general principle of international law.[116]

Yet general principles of law have only rarely been invoked explicitly by international tribunals, and, when invoked, have never had their basis fully explained.[117] Moreover, there are a number of reasons why general principles of law are problematic as a potential source of *jus cogens* rules, with these reasons differing according to which of two possible understandings of general principles of law is adopted.

First, general principles may be considered a kind of natural law.[118] From this perspective the possible status of some general principles as *jus cogens* rules, or as bases for *jus cogens* rules, may fall victim to the following problem. Natural law scholars generally consider that rules of international law are, at least to some degree, part of an established order which necessarily predated the development of any contemporary legal system.[119] Yet societies are dynamic, even if the fundamental rules which structure their legal systems purport not to be. In the absence of an overarching sovereign the international legal system may be considered a particularly dynamic legal system. At some point its members may therefore conceive – or perhaps they have already conceived – differently of their requirements in terms of fundamental, peremptory rules. Most international lawyers would accept that *jus cogens* rules themselves have not always existed. As a result, it would seem that *jus cogens* rules cannot be rules of natural law, nor be based on such rules.[120]

Secondly, it is possible to understand general principles of law as being a kind of customary law based on the general principles, constitutional and statutory provisions, and court judgments of different national legal

[116] *Ibid.*, 155. See also Verdross (1937) 572–3.

[117] See *Chorzow Factory Case* (1928) PCIJ Reports, Ser. A, No. 17, 29; the individual opinion of Judge Hudson in the *River Meuse Case*, note 62, p. 177 above, at 76–7; and *Effect of Awards of Compensation made by the U.N. Administrative Tribunal, Advisory Opinion* (1954) *ICJ Reports* 47, 53.

[118] See Cavaglieri (1929); Salvioli (1932); and Verdross (1935) 195–206.

[119] See generally Verdross and Koeck (1983).

[120] See Commentary to Art. 50 of the 'ILC Draft Articles on the Law of Treaties with Commentaries,' in *United Nations Conference on the Law of Treaties: Official Records (Documents of the Conference)* (New York: UN, 1971) 7, 68 ('[I]t would clearly be wrong to regard even rules of *jus cogens* as immutable and incapable of modification in the light of future developments'); Terz (1978) 620; and Kreca (1982) 27 and 32.

systems as forms of State practice.[121] Although *jus cogens* rules deny the right to create legal exceptions,[122] there are several reasons why Lauterpacht's and most other people's understanding of general principles of law may be seen as at least partly subsumed by the larger process of customary international law, and why explanations which consider *jus cogens* rules to be derived from general principles of law should therefore be treated as locating those rules within the customary process.

To the degree that they concern issues of an international character, general principles of law, like rules of customary international law, may serve to protect and promote the common interests of most if not all States. One of the clearest manifestations of a State's interests may be how it regulates itself and its citizens through its own national laws. If one State's national laws were to indicate that State's particular interests, the national laws of all States might, in so far as they concerned an issue of an international character, collectively provide a reasonable indication of the common interests of most, if not all, of the members of the international society of States.[123] Since national laws have long played a role in the customary process as instances of relevant State practice, looking to national laws to determine whether most States have a common interest in *jus cogens* rules would seem to be consistent with *jus cogens* rules being rules of customary international law.[124]

Alternatively, if Lauterpacht's explanation is read to mean only that general principles of law are in some way conspicuous, or, in his terms, 'cogent', rather than being derived from the general principles, constitutional and statutory provisions, and court judgments of national legal systems, his understanding of general principles of law might still be regarded as being subsumed by the process of customary international law. In this case the explanation provided in the previous chapter of the role played by the conspicuous character of some common interests would seem to apply.[125] Much of the confusion about the source of *jus cogens* rules – and tendencies to look to natural law-based explanations – may result from the effect that the conspicuous character of some common interests has in diminishing or eliminating the need to weigh

[121] See Guggenheim (1953) Tome 1, 149–53; and Cheng (1953) 23–6.

[122] See pp. 183–7 above.

[123] In respect of some issues divergences in national laws will preclude the determination of common interests in this way. Yet comparative law studies aimed at resolving questions of international law sometimes produce convincing results. See, e.g., Fox and Nolte (1995) (on international law and the right of democratic States to impose limits on democratic participation).

[124] National legislation and national court judgments have been particularly important in the development and change of customary rules concerning State immunity. See generally Sucharitkul (1979); Emanuelli (1984); Trooboff (1986); and pp. 110–14 above.

[125] See pp. 162–5 above.

supporting, ambivalent and opposing State practice in this context. Translated literally, '*jus cogens*' means 'compelling law', and the peremptory character of many widely accepted *jus cogens* rules is clearly in the interests of most, if not all, States, as those States see and manifest those interests to be. In short, most States consider rules like the prohibitions on aggression and genocide, both of which protect the foundations of the modern nation-State, to be so important as to allow of no exceptions.

The language of Article 53 of the 1969 Vienna Convention on the Law of Treaties may also provide evidence that *jus cogens* rules are the result of the customary process rather than derived from general principles of law (of the natural law kind), in that it conforms more closely to Article 38(1)(b) of the Statute of the International Court (on custom) than to Article 38(1)(c) of the Statute (on general principles).[126] Although the Vienna Convention should not be regarded as the definitive statement on *jus cogens* rules, in part because it deals with those rules solely in the context of treaties, Article 53 requires that such rules be 'accepted and recognized by the international community of States as a whole'. Article 38(1)(b) of the Statute speaks similarly of 'a general practice accepted as law'. Article 38(1)(c), on the other hand, does not speak of acceptance as such, but of recognition. Moreover, its 'general principles' must only be 'recognised by civilised nations', a phrase which, despite its roots in a past colonial era, might still limit the requirement of recognition to something less than the 'international community of States as a whole' as required by Article 53.[127]

An explanation of *jus cogens* rules as being derived from the customary process would seem to differ in only one respect from explanations which base those rules on general principles of law (of the non-natural law kind). An explanation based on the process of customary international law would accommodate situations where a *jus cogens* rule, such as the prohibition on aggression, has not been widely incorporated into national legal systems, where States have instead expressed their interests in other ways. Some issues of an essentially international character just might not be dealt with at the national level, despite their importance to States.

However, this explanation still does not resolve the apparent problem

[126] For the Vienna Convention, see note 10, p.36 above.

[127] Compare: Cheng (1953) 25. He wrote (footnote omitted, emphasis in original):

> [T]he word *nation* was originally used in the sense of 'people' rather than 'State'. The qualifying epithet 'civilised' was, therefore, necessary in order to exclude from consideration systems of law of primitive communities which were not yet civilised. At a later stage, however, it would seem that the term was sometimes understood in the sense of States, in which case the word 'civilised' must be considered as merely redundant, since any State which is a member of the international society must be considered as civilised.

of consent which arises as a result of *jus cogens* rules denying the possibility of legal exceptions.[128] In addressing this problem it may be helpful to distinguish between two aspects of any *jus cogens* rule: first, the substantive rule itself; and, secondly, the imperative character of that rule, which renders it non-derogable and gives it peremptory effect.[129] It is the latter aspect which is at the heart of the problem, for it remains to be explained how the process of customary international law could give rise to the peremptory character of *jus cogens* rules, as opposed to their substantive content.

Mosler accounted for the non-derogable character of certain rules of international law in the following way:

> In any legal community there must be a minimum of uniformity which is indispensable in maintaining the community. This uniformity may relate to legal values which are considered to be the goal of the community or it may be found in legal principles which it is the duty of all members to realise. It may relate to legal rules which are binding within the community. The whole of this minimum can be called a common public order (ordre public international). The international community cannot dispense with this minimum of principles and rules as without them it would cease to exist.[130]

Mosler's argument may be challenged on the basis that it is possible to imagine an international society in which many States did not have a common interest in certain rules being invulnerable to the creation of exceptions, either through treaties, rules of special customary international law or persistent objection. The key point, however, is that in contemporary international society most States appear to have such a common interest. As was suggested above, States may consider rules like the prohibitions on aggression and genocide to be so important as to allow of no exceptions.

The existence and ongoing development of such common interests may be implicitly recognised by Article 53 of the 1969 Vienna Convention, which affirms that a *jus cogens* rule 'can be modified only by a subsequent norm of general international law having the same character'.[131] Although this fact does not address the larger issue of principle –

[128] See p. 183 above. [129] See Sur (1990) 1er cahier, 13.

[130] Mosler (1974) 33 (footnote omitted). See also Verdross (1937) 572. Verdross wrote:

> [E]very judicial order regulates the rational and moral coexistence of the members of a community. No judicial order can, therefore, admit treaties between juridical subjects, which are obviously in contradiction to the ethics of a certain community.

[131] Note 10, p. 36 above. This requirement may be overly strict, for it implies that a *jus cogens* rule can only be replaced by another *jus cogens* rule, rather than by a non-*jus cogens* rule of general application. As Virally ((1966) 18–19, note 13) pointed out, likening *jus cogens* rules to constitutional rules: there must be some mechanism whereby constitutional

i.e., as to whether *jus cogens* rules are inconsistent with consent-based theories of international law – it suggests that new or modified *jus cogens* rules will not be imposed lightly on non-consenting States.

The larger issue of principle is addressed by the fact that, if most States have common interests in non-derogable rules, there would seem to be no reason why the process of customary international law could not give rise to rules having a *jus cogens* character. States may behave in accordance with the potential or emerging peremptory character of a new or existing rule, if they so choose, and accept that their behaviour is consistent with or creative of that character, thus fulfilling the traditional requirements of both State practice and *opinio juris*.[132] If most or nearly all States behaved and accepted the effects of their behaviour in this way, or at least did not oppose this development, the non-derogable character – and not just the substance of the rule – would seem to become part of customary international law.[133]

Such rules would remain open to change, although it bears repeating that in most instances they would have received so much support from States that such changes would be unlikely to occur.[134] This degree of resistance to change may be heightened further by the fact that there is only one kind of State practice in which States wishing to support a change to a *jus cogens* rule may legally engage, namely, the making of

rules may be 'de-constitutionalised'. See also Riesenfeld (1966) 514–15; and Akehurst (1974–75b) 285, note 5. It is interesting to note that, as with changes to *jus cogens* rules, amendments to constitutional rules in national legal systems usually require larger majorities than amendments to ordinary legislation.

[132] See p. 130 above.

[133] See Virally (1966) 27–8; and Higgins (1994) 21–2.

[134] See pp. 157–60 above. One consequence of this explanation may be that it dispels claims that *jus cogens* rules occupy a higher place than other rules in a new 'normative hierarchy'. For such a claim see Weil (1983). As Virally (1966) 18 explained:

> [L]es normes du droit international général se distribuent en deux classes, les normes du *jus cogens* et les normes de *jus dispositivum*, la différence entre les deux catégories tenant à la validité ou, au contraire, à la nullité des traités particuliers qui prétendraient déroger à leurs dispositions. La véritable hiérarchie qu'introduit le *jus cogens* – et elle est très nouvelle – est donc une hiérarchie entre, d'une part, les normes du droit international général, qui présentent ce caractère, et, d'autre part, les normes du droit international particulier, régional, local ou bilatéral.

My translation reads:

> Norms of general international law distribute themselves into two classes, norms of *jus cogens* and norms of *jus dispositivum*. The difference between the two categories concerns the validity or, to the contrary, the nullity of particular treaties which purport to derogate from their dispositions. The effective hierarchy that is introduced by *jus cogens* – and it is very new – is thus a hierarchy between, on the one hand, norms of general international law, which exhibit this characteristic, and, on the other hand, norms of a particular, regional, local or bilateral international law.

statements. Unlike non-peremptory rules of customary international law, which only render conflicting acts illegal, the effect of *jus cogens* rules extends to treaties and other objective regimes.[135] States may nevertheless choose to create such illegal regimes, and these regimes may then contribute as State practice to a possible change in a *jus cogens* rule. Yet States will probably be less willing to engage in these particular forms of practice if they are illegal, even if they are forms of practice which, in other instances, may be quite influential in the development, maintenance and change of customary rules.

Nevertheless, some international lawyers have difficulty accepting that the customary process is the source of *jus cogens* rules because they assume that when a State adopts an opposing stance in respect of a potential or emerging customary rule it is withholding its consent to be bound by that rule, should that rule come into force, and certainly not conceding its ability to make certain legal exceptions (i.e., by way of treaty or special customary international law) to any such rule in the future.[136] The answer to this apparent conundrum may be that, in an international society which is based on the rule of law, the members of that society recognise that certain fundamental rules must bind them all equally.[137] States, by participating in the customary process, may therefore be consenting to that process, to any existing customary rules, to any subsequently developed customary rules the development of which they have not opposed, and to any *jus cogens* rules *even if* they have opposed their development.[138]

There is a final consideration which suggests that the process of customary international law is the source of *jus cogens* rules. It would appear that *opinio juris*, or something like *opinio juris*, is at the root of the peremptory character of these rules. As has already been suggested, the interests protected and promoted by *jus cogens* rules go to the heart of the character of the international society of States and, specifically, to how that society comes to define itself. Something like *opinio juris* appears to be involved in protecting these key interests because States, quite simply, do not believe that it is possible to contract out of *jus cogens* rules, or to persistently object to them. State practice which would otherwise contribute to the creation of legal exceptions is consequently not regarded as relevant to the customary process nor capable of generating legal effects.

A good example of this phenomenon may be international society's reaction to South Africa's former racist policies, the issue with which this

[135] See pp. 183–7 above. [136] See pp. 180–3 above. [137] See pp. 10–13 above.

[138] See pp. 142–6 above. As was explained in the previous section of this chapter, persistent objectors to rules which are not of a *jus cogens* character may eventually abandon their objections for other reasons. See pp. 102–5 above.

section began.[139] It seems that other States never contemplated the possibility of South Africa establishing itself as a persistent objector to the prohibition against *apartheid*, which they regarded as a *jus cogens* rule.[140]

The principal source of *jus cogens* rules may thus be identified as the customary process, and the peremptory character of such rules explained in a manner which is consistent with the traditional bipartite conception of customary international law. One consequence of this conclusion may be that States cannot 'opt out' of the concept of *jus cogens*, just as they cannot opt out of individual *jus cogens* rules.[141] France, in particular, has asserted that it is not subject to the *jus cogens* character of any rules, if rules with such a character exist, because it never consented to the development of that concept.[142] The concept of *jus cogens*, however, is not a rule as such. It is instead a description of certain characteristics held by particular rules which have themselves been developed or changed through the long accepted, and generally accepted, process of customary international law. France has long accepted the process of customary international law and therefore, it would seem, the source of *jus cogens* rules.

## Jus cogens and erga omnes rules

Very shortly after the concept of *jus cogens* was included in the 1969 Vienna Convention on the Law of Treaties,[143] the International Court of Justice brought another, related concept to the forefront of international law. In a *dictum* in the 1970 *Barcelona Traction Case* the Court referred to obligations (and therefore rules) *erga omnes*, which, translated literally, means 'as against all':

> [A]n essential distinction should be drawn between the obligations of a State towards the international community as a whole, and those arising *vis-à-vis* another State in the field of diplomatic protection. By their very nature the former are the concern of all States. In view of the importance of the rights involved, all States can be held to have a legal interest in their protection; they are obligations *erga omnes*.
>
> Such obligations derive, for example, in contemporary international law, from the outlawing of acts of aggression, and of genocide, as also from the principles and rules concerning the basic rights of the human person, including protection from slavery and racial discrimination. Some of the corresponding rights of

[139] See generally Bissell (1977); and Özgur (1982).

[140] See, e.g., Art. 5(3) of the International Convention on the Suppression and Punishment of the Crime of Apartheid, UNGA Res. 3068 (XXVIII) (1973); UNGA Res. 33/183 (1979); and Dugard (1987) 156–8.

[141] See Danilenko (1993) 236–8.

[142] See Deleau (1969) 14–17 and 23; and Weil (1983) 428.

[143] See pp. 184–5 above.

protection have entered into the body of general international law . . . others are conferred by international instruments of a universal or quasi-universal character.
Obligations the performance of which is the subject of diplomatic protection are not of the same category.[144]

Although some of the rules which the Court identified as being *erga omnes* rules may also be considered *jus cogens* rules, the Court in this passage was clearly referring to a characteristic distinct from that of non-derogability. It focused on the fact that some rules give rise to a generality of standing – amongst all States bound by those rules – to make claims in the event of a violation. Generality of standing, rather than non-derogable character, is the essence of *erga omnes* rules.

A similar reference was made by the Court in its judgment in the 1974 *Nuclear Tests Cases*, where it analysed certain unilateral statements made by French government officials as having been made *erga omnes*, and held those statements to be legally binding.[145] More recently, in the 1995 *East Timor Case* the Court accepted that the right of self-determination is a rule which has an '*erga omnes* character'.[146] And in its 1996 judgment on preliminary objections in the *Case Concerning Application of the Convention on the Prevention and Punishment of the Crime of Genocide* the Court affirmed that 'the rights and obligations enshrined by the Convention are rights and obligations *erga omnes*'.[147]

The concept of *erga omnes* rules has been endorsed by numerous States, organisations and writers.[148] For example, the International Law Commission, in Article 5(3) of Part Two of its Draft Articles on State Responsibility, stated that 'if the internationally wrongful act constitutes an international crime' the injured States include 'all other States'.[149]

[144] Note 1, p. 3 above, at 32 (paras. 33–5). With this *dictum* the Court was effectively reversing its judgment in the *South West Africa Cases (Second Phase)*, note 64, p. 160 above. In that case Ethiopia and Liberia had argued that they had standing to bring an action because they, as members of the (former) League of Nations, had a legal interest in the enforcement of South Africa's mandate over South West Africa. The Court responded (at 47, para. 88):

> [T]he argument amounts to a plea that the Court should allow the equivalent of an '*actio popularis*', or right resident in any member of a community to take legal action in vindication of a public interest. But although a right of this kind may be known to certain municipal systems of law, it is not known to international law as it stands at present; nor is the Court able to regard it as imported by the 'general principles of law' referred to in Article 38, paragraph 1(c), of its Statute.

[145] Note 9, p. 107 above, at 269–70 (paras. 50–1).
[146] (1995) *ICJ Reports* 90, 102 (para. 29). See also the dissenting opinion of Judge Weeramantry, *ibid.*, 139, 172–3 and 213–16.
[147] 11 July 1996, General List No. 91, 23 (para. 31); http://www.icj-cij.org/idecis.htm.
[148] See generally Schachter (1991) 208–13; Frowein (1994b) 405–22; and Annacker (1994). For a criticism of the concept see Weil (1983) 431–3.
[149] See p. 184 above. See also note 36, p. 83 above.

However, the relationship between *erga omnes* rules and *jus cogens* rules remains unclear. Some writers have suggested that the concepts involve different aspects of the same rules,[150] and the terms have been used interchangeably in debates of the International Law Commission.[151] Others have suggested that the concept of *erga omnes* is wider than that of *jus cogens*.[152]

In chapter 6 it was suggested that international law is made up of a multitude of bilateral legal relationships between States, and that, if all rules of international law are composed of bilateral legal relationships, an *erga omnes* rule might be considered to involve a series of identical bilateral relationships between every possible pair of States.[153] However, such an explanation of *erga omnes* rules fails to satisfy because a violation of the bilateral relationship between two States would not give other States any right to make a legal claim. The obligations existing between the violating State and those other States would remain fulfilled.

*Erga omnes* rules are therefore best seen as being more than just rules whose bilateral relationships have been fully generalised. As was explained by the International Court of Justice in the *Barcelona Traction Case*, there are two parts to every *erga omnes* rule.[154] First, as with ordinary rules, each *erga omnes* rule contains a series of rights and corresponding obligations concerning its substantive content. It is these rights and obligations which form the principal bilateral relationships between any of the many pairs of States which are subject to the rule. Secondly, each State has, in the words of the Court, a 'corresponding right of protection'. In other words, each State not only has rights and obligations in respect of the substantive content of the rule, giving rise to State responsibility *vis-à-vis* injured States in the event of a violation, but it is also subject to a series of additional, bilateralised rights and obligations. The additional rights enable it to make claims against any State which is bound by and violates the substantive rule, while the additional obligations require that it not violate that same substantive rule in its relations with any other similarly bound State.[155]

The creation of an *erga omnes* rule is, therefore, a two-step process involving, first, the creation of a rule, and, secondly, the creation of additional bilateralised rights and obligations which confer standing, in the

150 See, e.g., Simma (1989) 825.
151 See, e.g., (1986) 1 *Yearbook of the International Law Commission* 247–53.
152 See, e.g., Meron (1986a) 187; and Macdonald (1987) 138.
153 See pp. 88–9 above. 154 See quotation at pp. 195–6 above.
155 As with all violations of international law, violations of these additional rights and obligations engage the responsibility of the violating State and must therefore be remedied. However, as these specific violations are of rights of protection, remedies will frequently be limited to declarations of responsibility. Reparations will generally not be available.

event of any violation, on *any* of the States subject to that rule.[156] It may be possible for these two steps to occur simultaneously.

Unlike the explanation of *jus cogens* rules advanced in the previous section of this chapter, this explanation of *erga omnes* rules does not preclude the possibility of persistent objection, nor the possibility of *erga omnes* rules which are created by treaty and limited in scope to those States which are party to the relevant treaty.[157] Similarly, this explanation does not preclude the customary development of *erga omnes* rules which are limited in applicability to a group of States. Although it is generally assumed that *erga omnes* rules apply universally, the right of protection associated with a rule having an *erga omnes* character is a right which is held by all States *bound by that rule*. Persistent objectors and any other States which might be outside the scope of that rule cannot be affected by its *erga omnes* character.[158]

As importantly, pairs (and multiple pairs) of States which are bound by a rule having an *erga omnes* character are not prevented from subsequently contracting out of that rule as between themselves, although that rule will remain applicable *erga omnes* between them and all other similarly bound States. This is because the conclusion of a treaty or the development of a rule of special customary international law in an area governed by a more

[156] For an explanation of the concept of *erga omnes* which is very different from that provided here, see Annacker (1994). Annacker claimed (at 136) that the 'distinguishing feature of an *erga omnes* obligation is its non-bilateralizable structure'. Yet after examining the background to Article 5 of the ILC Draft Articles on State Responsibility (Part Two) (note 36, p. 83 above) she admitted that the ILC had come to the opposite conclusion. See Annacker (1994), 142–8. In addition, widespread use of the phrase 'obligations *erga omnes*' rather than '*erga omnes* rules' may facilitate a distinction between substantive rights and obligations and those rights and obligations which confer standing, in the event of a violation, on States which would otherwise not have a claim. And in the *East Timor Case* (note 146, p. 196 above) Portugal argued on the basis of '*erga omnes* rights'. But, as Judge Weeramantry pointed out in his dissenting opinion (note 146, p. 196 above, at 215), an *erga omnes* right is the corollary of an obligation *erga omnes*. The terminology adopted here – of *erga omnes* rules – encompasses both rights and obligations.

[157] On the latter point, see Schachter (1991) 209–10.

[158] This (potential) limitation is reflected in Art. 5(2)(e) of the ILC Draft Articles on State Responsibility (Part Two) (note 36, p. 83 above), which reads, *inter alia*:

> In particular, 'injured State' means . . .
> (e) if the right infringed by the act of a State arises from a multilateral treaty or from a rule of customary international law, any other State party to the multilateral treaty or bound by the relevant rule of customary international law, if it is established that:
> (i) the right has been created or is established in its favour,
> (ii) the infringement of the right by the act of a State necessarily affects the enjoyment of the rights or the performance of the obligations of the other States parties to the multilateral treaty or bound by the rule of customary international law . . .

general rule does not normally violate that more general rule in and of itself. Instead, it creates a legal exception to that more general rule. The rights of protection held by the other States which are bound by the general rule do not come into play *unless* that general rule is actually violated, and only if the *erga omnes* rule is also a *jus cogens* rule will the creation of such legal exceptions be precluded.

It seems unlikely, but is nevertheless conceivable, that a *jus cogens* rule could also apply to a limited number of States. It seems unlikely because *jus cogens* rules are the result of the process of customary international law developing fundamental rules within a society of States, and both that customary process and the legal system of which it is a part are today predominantly global in scope. It would seem conceivable because societies of States may exist or develop which are distinct and closely knit enough to want to preclude exceptions to certain rules amongst themselves, while accepting that those rules do not apply, or do not have peremptory effects, in respect of States on the 'outside'.[159]

It is also conceivable that such developments occurred in the past. At one point in time Latin American States had developed a number of rules of special customary international law which, potentially, could have acquired a *jus cogens* character within that limited group of States.[160] It is possible that such rules exist today, such as in the concept of a 'public order' within European law,[161] and assertions by 'liberal' scholars of international law may point towards such developments in the future.[162]

However, the strongest possibility of non-derogable rules which are limited in scope exists within the context of human rights treaties, as States parties appear to be unable to create legal exceptions to many of the rules set out in such treaties.

[159] See Kadelbach (1992) 203–4. However, such a 'special' *jus cogens* rule would be unable to derogate from a *jus cogens* rule which was general in application. See Virally (1966) 14.

[160] See the comments of Mr Belaunde (Peru), 915th meeting of the Sixth Committee (1966) UN GAOR, 21st Session, A/C/.6/SR/915, 87 (para. 15); the 1987 decision of the Inter-American Commission of Human Rights, note 101, p. 186 above, which held that 'in the member States of the OAS there is recognized a norm of *jus cogens* which prohibits the State execution of children'. On Latin American special customary international law generally, see Alvárez (1910); *Asylum Case*, note 4, p. 130 above, at 276–7 and dissenting opinion of Judge Alvárez, 290, 293–4; and Barberis (1983) 222.

[161] See, e.g., *Austria* v. *Italy* (*South Tyrol Case*) (1962) 4 *Yearbook of the European Convention on Human Rights* 116, 140 (European Commission on Human Rights); *Chrisostomos et al.* v. *Turkey* (1991) 12 *Human Rights Law Journal* 113, 121 (para. 22) (European Commission on Human Rights); Mosler (1968b), especially 532; and Verdross and Simma (1984) 333.

[162] See, e.g., Slaughter Burley (1993); and Slaughter (1995). For a critical analysis of this approach, see Kingsbury (1994).

Human rights treaties may be understood as involving two kinds of rights. First, there are rights which are held by individuals or groups. These rights may exist independently of the treaty (as rules of customary international law) or they may have been created by the treaty as a kind of third party right, or '*stipulation pour l'autrui*'.[163] States have corresponding obligations – to those individuals or groups – not to violate these rights. Secondly, there are rights of protection. These rights are created by the treaty and are held by the States parties. They apply *erga omnes* and allow any State party to make a claim in the event that any other State party violates the rights of an individual or group under the treaty.

These rules appear to be non-derogable because the primary rights and obligations do not exist between States, but rather between States and individuals or groups. Consequently, legal exceptions to these rules cannot be created by States but instead require the consent of the individual or group holders of the rights. This consent is extremely unlikely to be forthcoming given the numbers of individuals or groups which are usually involved. Yet, because it is at least conceivable that these individuals or groups could consent to the creation of exceptions, and because such exceptions would then appear to be valid, these rules are in fact derogable and should therefore not be referred to as *jus cogens* rules.[164]

Despite the possibility that *jus cogens* rules and *erga omnes* rules might sometimes apply to limited numbers of States, such situations are unlikely to arise. Both types of rules exist to protect and promote common interests, and although groups of States frequently have their own, unique common interests international society is today more and more defining itself as universal, at least in terms of its most fundamental rules.

It follows that particularly 'weighty' rules of international law are usually both *jus cogens* and *erga omnes* in character.[165] Moreover, *jus cogens* rules necessarily apply *erga omnes*. Illegal treaties and illegal rules of

[163] On human rights in customary international law, see Meron (1989); and Schachter (1991) 335–42. On the third party rights of individuals, see Chinkin (1993) 13–15 and 120–33.

[164] Some human rights are designated by treaties as being 'non-derogable', in that they cannot be overridden during 'states of emergency'. See generally Higgins (1976–7). It is possible that these particular rights are also inalienable, although derogation with the consent of the right holder is very different from derogation in the absence of consent. On the relationship between the concept of *jus cogens* and rules which are designated by treaties as being non-derogable, see Meron (1986b) 15–19.

[165] See Frowein (1994b) 405–6.

special customary international law would never be struck down as being inconsistent with *jus cogens* rules unless those rules also gave standing to other States.[166] States which enter into illegal treaties or otherwise attempt to create illegal exceptions to general rules are normally not interested in challenging the validity of those exceptions.[167] However, *erga omnes* rules are not necessarily also of a *jus cogens* character.[168] As was explained earlier in this section, there is nothing which prevents States from opting out of *erga omnes* rules unless those rules are also *jus cogens* rules, for claims by third States must be based on violations of rules and not the creation of legal exceptions.[169]

One type of situation where *erga omnes* rules might not at the same time be *jus cogens* rules is where the *erga omnes* rules in question apply to individuals, or other non-State entities, rather than to States. Rules

[166] There is, it should be noted, an important difference between an *erga omnes* rule and the jurisdiction of international courts or tribunals. Although a State may be subject to an *erga omnes* rule it still cannot be subject to judicial proceedings in the absence of its consent. See *East Timor Case*, note 146, p. 196, at 102 (para. 29); and de Hoogh (1991) 196.

In the *East Timor Case* this issue arose because Indonesia had not consented to the jurisdiction of the Court and, as had been established in the *Monetary Gold Case* ((1954) *ICJ Reports* 19, 32), the Court cannot decide issues which concern the legal interests of third States as the 'very subject matter of the decision' when those third States are not themselves before it. Portugal attempted to get around this principle by arguing that Australia had violated the right of the East Timorese to self-determination, that the Court had jurisdiction because Australia had violated that right independently of Indonesia's actions, and that Portugal had standing, either as the administering power over the non-self-governing territory, or on the basis that the right of self-determination was a 'right *erga omnes*'. The problem with these arguments was that any violation by Australia of the right to self-determination in this instance was still closely linked to, and highly dependent on, Indonesia's role as occupying power.

Portugal did not make any arguments based on the concept of *jus cogens*. However, it could have argued that Australia had violated Portugal's rights – as administering power – by entering into the treaty because Indonesia's violation of the *jus cogens* rule prohibiting aggression had prevented Indonesia from establishing effective title over East Timor, and that Indonesia consequently lacked the legal capacity to enter into a treaty concerning that territory. See p. 186 above. Although the legality of Indonesia's actions would still have been an issue, Australia's actions – in entering into a treaty which was in violation of Portugal's rights – would then have formed 'the very subject matter of the decision', thus allowing Portugal to sidestep the principle from the *Monetary Gold Case*. This argument could perhaps have been buttressed by an argument that the *Monetary Gold Case* principle cannot serve to protect third States which have violated *jus cogens* rules, in that such rules override the principle of State consent in this context as well as in regard to attempts to create legal exceptions.

[167] This lack of interest in challenging illegal treaties or other illegal exceptions on the part of States involved in their creation was demonstrated in the *East Timor Case* (note 146, p. 196 above), where it was a State not party to the relevant treaty, i.e., Portugal, which challenged its validity before the International Court of Justice.

[168] For scholarly support for this proposition, see the citations in note 152, p. 197 above.

[169] See pp. 198–9 above.

prohibiting war crimes appear to be the best examples of rules which apply in this way.[170] In such situations the particular rule in question may be of a kind which cannot bind States, although it may give all States a right – and perhaps impose an obligation – to enforce that rule.[171]

It is true that, were two States to enter into a treaty the effect of which was to assist individuals in committing war crimes, that treaty would almost certainly be rendered void for being in violation of a *jus cogens* rule. However, the *jus cogens* rule having the effect in that instance would be a rule prohibiting State complicity in those individual acts, rather than a *jus cogens* rule directed at the individuals committing them.[172] The obligation to enforce a rule prohibiting war crimes would remain unaffected by the treaty, but it would do so as an *erga omnes* rule, and not as a *jus cogens* rule.

Most rules which are generally accepted as being *erga omnes* in character are rules the violations of which are not readily subject to inter-State claims by directly injured States, or by States on behalf of their own directly injured nationals. In situations involving violations of the most fundamental of human rights a claim on the basis of diplomatic protection is generally precluded because the State committing the violation is usually – although not necessarily – also the victim's State of nationality.[173] Similarly, a State which is subjected to an armed attack may not be able to protect itself through the invocation of international law to the same extent as it might be protected by other States, were those other States to have rights of protection which were violated as a result of the attack. Although the attacked State may invite other States to come to its assistance, and the United Nations Security Council can always take action under Chapter VII of the Charter, the violation of an *erga omnes* rule may give those other States another option, namely that of engaging

[170] See generally: S/RES/827 (1993) (Security Council Resolution Establishing an International Tribunal for the Prosecution of Persons Responsible for Serious Violations of International Humanitarian Law Committed in the Territory of the Former Yugoslavia), note 18, p. 79 above; *Report of the Secretary-General Pursuant to Paragraph 2 of Security Council Resolution 808 (1993)*, note 18, p. 79 above; S/RES/955 (1994) (Security Council Resolution Establishing the International Tribunal for Rwanda), note 18, p. 79 above; the Rome Statute of the International Criminal Court, note 18, p. 79 above; and Bassiouni (1986).

[171] On the right ('universal jurisdiction'), see Akehurst (1972–3) 160–6; Bowett (1982a) 11–14; and p. 64 above. On the obligation, see *Report of the Secretary-General Pursuant to Paragraph 2 of Security Council Resolution 808 (1993)*, note 18, p. 79, at Arts. 9 and 29; S/RES/955 (1994) (Security Council Resolution Establishing the International Tribunal for Rwanda), note 18, p. 79, at Arts. 8 and 28; ILC Draft Statute for an International Criminal Court, note 18, p. 79, at Arts. 58 and 63.

[172] There would be no point in having rules with a *jus cogens* character which were directed solely at individuals. Individuals cannot modify, persistently object, or otherwise create exceptions to rules of international law. See pp. 78–9 above.

[173] See pp. 82–6 above.

in countermeasures against the attacking State even if the victim of the aggression has not requested assistance.[174]

The International Court's of Justice's *dictum* in the *Barcelona Traction Case* seems to have been directed at redressing situations like these, on the basis that rules of international law should be capable of supporting inter-State claims and allow for effective enforcement opportunities if they are to have any effect.[175] *Erga omnes* rules expand the scope of possible claimants in certain situations, to protect key common interests where traditional rules of standing are insufficient to do so.

Like *jus cogens* rules, *erga omnes* rules are not the result of a *sui generis* mechanism of law creation. Most *erga omnes* rules are best explained as being derived from the long-established process of customary international law, although it is possible that some such rules may be created by treaty. Although the effects of these rules are exceptional, their origins are not, and they should not be explained – or feared – on that basis.

[174] See generally Schachter (1991) 196–8; Frowein (1994b); and Annacker (1994) 159–60. The issue of what limits necessarily exist on the rights of States, including third States, to engage in countermeasures in response to international crimes is currently the subject of much debate in the ILC. See, e.g., Arangio-Ruiz, *Seventh Report on State Responsibility*, note 33, p. 62 above; Symposium (1994) (including comments from several members of the ILC). This proposition might seem to have been rejected by the International Court of Justice in the *Nicaragua Case (Merits)* (note 16, p. 8 above, at 127) when it stated that: 'They [the acts of which Nicaragua was accused] could not justify counter-measures taken by a third State, the United States, and particularly could not justify intervention involving the use of force.' However, it may be that the Court was merely defining limits on the right to engage in countermeasures, much as the ILC is attempting to do. As Nicaragua did not launch an armed attack (in the sense of Art. 2(4) of the Charter) but rather only supported the actions of private persons and thus violated only the rule of non-intervention, third States could not resort to countermeasures involving the use of force. For an extended analysis of the concept of *erga omnes* in the context of situations like that in the *Nicaragua Case*, see Kress (1995) 332 *ff.*

[175] See quotation on pp. 195–6 above.

# 11 Conclusions

An interdisciplinary approach to the study of customary international law may offer many ideas and insights both to international lawyers and to international relations scholars. It may, for example, enable us better to understand the origins of the process of customary international law – and thus of obligation within the international legal system – by seeing that process as but one of many similar customary processes which have existed, and continue to exist, in many different societies, at various levels of social, political and legal development.[1]

More specifically, an interdisciplinary approach to customary international law may change the way we think about 'system consent', that is, the idea that States have consented to the entire process of customary international law rather than to each individual rule by which they are bound.[2] The members of the various societies within which customary processes operate clearly have differing degrees of awareness as to their own participatory role in the development, maintenance and change of customary rules. In some societies such 'law-makers' may only become aware that a customary law process is operating once other law-makers begin to rely on some of the resulting rules in contentious situations. It is therefore possible that customary processes do not even need to be based on the consent of the law-maker to a pre-existing set of 'secondary' or 'constitutional' rules.[3] Instead, a customary law process may be seen to evolve out of a social process, as a society creates a legal system and thereby recreates itself.[4] If the process of customary international law developed in this way, the reliance by States on customary rules – and their acknowledgment of the possible validity of other States' claims

[1] For studies of customary legal processes other than the process of customary international law see, e.g., Reid (1980); Comaroff and Roberts (1981); Reisman (1983); and Weyrauch and Bell (1993). [2] See pp. 142–6 above.

[3] See pp. 142–6 above. Lowe ((1983a) 209) has written, in respect of the international legal system, that '[t]he secondary rule of law-creation in question will itself be a rule of customary international law derived . . . from state practice'.

[4] See generally: Allott (1990).

based on similar rules – may be sufficient to signal their consent, not only to those specific rules, but also to the customary process as a whole.

However, the most important insight offered by an interdisciplinary approach to customary international law may well concern the role of shared understandings. Although shared understandings are an important component of any social system, the role they play is not readily acknowledged within traditional, positivist conceptions of law and legal systems. In chapter 9 it was explained that shared understandings of legal relevance enable States, judges and other international actors to distinguish behaviour which contributes to the customary process from behaviour which does not. Shared understandings of legal relevance thus constitute a key element in the transformation of State practice into obligation in the form of customary rules.

This book, by considering the customary process to be a regime or institution which is based upon shared understandings of legal relevance, takes an approach which differs from that taken by most works on customary international law. Instead of explaining how judges and lawyers determine the existence and content of individual rules, it has sought to explain the process which gives rise to those rules. And in doing so it has had to deal with a factor with which most international lawyers, most of the time, justifiably do not concern themselves. That factor is, of course, power.

In chapter 1 it was suggested that 'powerful' States often find it easier than less powerful States to engage in practice which will significantly affect the development, maintenance and change of customary rules. For example, powerful States generally have large, well-financed diplomatic corps which are able to follow international developments globally across a wide spectrum of issues. This enables those States to object, in a timely fashion, to developments which they perceive as being contrary to their interests. Similarly, powerful States, as a result of their greater military, economic and political strength, are usually better able to enforce jurisdiction claims, impose trade sanctions and dampen or divert international criticism.[5] These differing abilities to engage in State practice are important because, as many international lawyers have acknowledged, the development, maintenance and change of customary rules usually involves a weighing of supporting, ambivalent and opposing State practice.[6] Indeed, a number of international lawyers have indicated that this quantitative aspect must favour powerful States, that in this way the customary process 'gives weight to effective power and responsibility'.[7]

[5] See pp. 35–40 above. [6] See, e.g., Akehurst (1974–75a) 13–14; and pp. 151–7 above.
[7] Schachter (1989) 721. See pp. 37–40 above.

In chapter 1 it was also explained that the process of customary international law involves the transformation of power into obligation in the form of customary rules, and that at least some of those rules may then qualify *subsequent* applications of power within that very same process.[8] The customary process thus involves at least two different aspects of the relational character of power. First, it involves inter-State power relationships of the kind traditionally studied by international relations scholars, namely, the relative abilities of States to control or influence directly how other States behave.

Secondly, and perhaps more importantly, the customary process also involves the relative ability of power and obligation to affect each other in the development, maintenance and change of customary rules. One of this book's central arguments is that the interaction of these two kinds of 'power' within the customary process produces different results depending on the different sources of power that are involved in each particular interaction, as well as on the particular context within which that interaction takes place. Part 2 considered a number of the factors which may affect the development, maintenance and change of customary rules, while focusing on the effects that four particular principles of international law have on applications of power within the customary process. By doing so it demonstrated that the influence of powerful States on customary law-making is not always decisive, that the 'power of rules' sometimes affects how even the most powerful of States behave, and what they are able to accomplish, when they seek to develop, maintain or change rules of customary international law.

Although in some situations the interests of powerful States might be better served were they to apply power without considering the process of customary international law, all States, and powerful States in particular, generally act in ways which support and maintain the customary process. This suggests that there are reasons for compliance which outweigh the short-term benefits that may be associated with ignoring customary international law, that legal obligation provides a degree of stability and predictability to international relations, which is regarded as essential by all States.[9]

This book, by breaking out of the positivist mould and seeking to explain the customary process as a complex interaction of power and obligation, takes an approach which is similar to, and yet distinct from, two other approaches to international legal theory that have been developed in the second half of the twentieth century. The first of these

[8] See pp. 18–20 above.

[9] See the discussions of recent literature on the English school of international relations theory, at pp. 31–2 above, and compliance at p. 155 above.

approaches is that of the 'New Haven School' of Lasswell, McDougal, Reisman and their 'associates'; the second is that of the Critical Legal Studies scholars, represented most effectively in international law by the work of Koskenniemi. It is appropriate, at this concluding stage, to consider how this book has differed from these other approaches.

## Distinguishing the 'New Haven School'

It would be difficult to conclude an examination of the role played by power in the process of customary international law without at least considering the work of Lasswell, McDougal, Reisman and the other members of the New Haven School. In the 1950s and 1960s the New Haven School represented a revolutionary approach to international legal scholarship. It broke out of the constraints imposed by traditional, positivist approaches to the discipline by applying Lasswell's social science methodology – a methodology he had originally developed for the study of national politics – to international law.

The approach taken by the New Haven School differs from that adopted here because it constitutes a purely sociological approach to the study of international law – one which does not distinguish between power and legal obligation. Thus, from the perspective of the New Haven School, power finds expression in, and is to some degree derived from, the authority and control exercised by decision-makers.[10] It is this exercise of authority and control in the decision-making process which gives rise to law, or in the case of customary international law, to the State practice that creates law.[11] Law is strictly a product of the decision-making process, and the 'decision-makers' are those individuals whose decisions turn out to be 'authorising and controlling'. Although decisions are, or should be, made on the basis and in consideration of values in pursuit of common interests or goals, the legal system *itself* places no restrictions and apparently has no qualifying effects on this process.[12]

The differences between the approach taken by the New Haven School and that adopted in this book are perhaps best exposed through an examination of McDougal's explanation of the process of customary

[10] For a concise and comprehensible explanation of the New Haven School approach, see Reisman (1992). [11] See Raman (1967); and Raman (1976).

[12] The values, as defined by the New Haven School, are power, entitlement, wealth, skill, well-being, affection, respect and rectitude. The most important of the common interests or goals is the furtherance of 'human dignity'. For applications of this approach to specific areas of international law, see, e.g., McDougal and Feliciano (1961); McDougal and Burke (1962); McDougal *et al.* (1963); and McDougal *et al.* (1967). For a recent application of the New Haven School approach (albeit without most of its specialised vocabulary) to international law as a whole, see Higgins (1994).

international law – an explanation which, at least superficially, is very similar to that advanced here. McDougal wrote the following passage in 1955 about the customary international law of the sea:

From the perspective of realistic description, the international law of the sea is not a mere static body of rules but is rather a whole decision-making process, a public order which includes a structure of authorized decision-makers as well as a body of highly flexible, inherited prescriptions. It is, in other words, a process of continuous interaction, of continuous demand and response, in which the decision-makers of particular nation states unilaterally put forward claims of the most diverse and conflicting character to the use of the world's seas, and in which other decision-makers, external to the demanding state and including both national and international officials, weigh and appraise these competing claims in terms of the interests of the world community and of the rival claimants, and ultimately accept or reject them. As such a process, it is a living, growing law, grounded in the practices and sanctioning expectations of nation-state officials, and changing as their demands and expectations are changed by the exigencies of new interests and technology and by other continually evolving conditions in the world arena.[13]

In short, McDougal considered rules of customary international law to result from the interaction of decision-makers as they assert and assess claims in an attempt to make laws which further some sort of 'common interest'. Perhaps most importantly, he recognised that customary international law is the result of a *process*, and that the process is a kind of dialogue among States. This book agrees with McDougal to that extent.[14]

However, its approach differs from his approach in several ways. First, this book suggests that States' interests are themselves indicated through 'claims' and other forms of State practice, and are therefore not a separate element in terms of which competing claims are weighed and appraised. McDougal, in contrast, was not prepared to leave the determination of interests, and thus the substance of rules, to a legal process such as the process of customary international law. Instead, determining the rules which result from the customary process meant imposing interests – and thus 'policy purposes' – on States. For example, in the context of the law of the sea the relevant policy purpose was, 'not merely the negation of unnecessary restrictions upon navigation and fishing, but also the effective promotion of the fullest, peaceful, and conserving use and development by all peoples'.[15]

To his credit, McDougal recognised that no matter how precisely articulated a policy purpose may be, different decision-makers will interpret that purpose in different ways depending on their own particular interests and perspectives. He therefore devised an additional, generally applicable

[13] McDougal (1955) 356–7.
[14] See also, e.g., Sur (1990) 1er cahier, 8; and Danilenko (1993) 75–129.
[15] McDougal (1955) 358.

test, whereby differences in interpretation are resolved on the basis of 'reasonableness'. He explained:

For all types of controversies the one test that decision-makers have in fact invoked and applied is that simple and ubiquitous, but indispensable, standard of what, considering all relevant policies and variables in context, is *reasonable* as between the parties; and for the clarification of detailed policies in ascribing meaning to particular prescriptions and terms, such decision-makers have habitually turned to all those sources authorized for the International Court of Justice, including not only 'international conventions, whether general or particular,' but also 'international custom, as evidence of a general practice accepted as law,' 'the general principles of law recognized by civilized nations,' 'judicial decisions and the teachings of the most qualified publicists,' and considerations '*ex aequo et bono.*'[16]

In short, McDougal advocated the application of one enormous 'shared understanding' to all of international law, the outcomes of which may then be justified by recourse to the traditional 'sources' of international law. It is well known that there is a high risk of subjective application associated with this approach. For example, in his 1955 article McDougal determined that it was 'reasonable' for the United States to engage in atmospheric nuclear tests 'in preparation for the defense of itself and its allies and of all the values of a free world society', and he did so without any (explicit) consideration of the behaviour of other States.[17]

McDougal's reliance on reasonableness bears some resemblance to this book's description of the conspicuous character of some common interests and its capacity to contribute to the development, maintenance and change of customary rules.[18] However, this book does not suggest that such conspicuous common interests will be determined without any reference to State practice. It would seem that conspicuous common interests will always, at least to some degree, be expressed through behaviour, and it may be the character of that expression which makes a full consideration of all instances of State practice unnecessary, by indicating clearly that most other States are likely to share the particular interest which is being expressed, and that few or any States are or will be opposed to the putative rule in question. Even then, in cases of disagreement among States as to the conspicuous character of different interests, or the existence of rules based on State practice more generally, it is not the interpretation of any one State, or scholar, which determines the existence or non-existence of a rule. In some cases a neutral third party might be required to determine whether a particular rule exists. As MacGibbon has pointed out:

[16] McDougal (1955) 359 (footnotes omitted).
[17] McDougal (1955) 361.
[18] See pp. 162–5 above.

Although claims may be made and may be accepted because they are reasonable, it is going too far to say that they are held valid or decided in every case on grounds of reasonableness . . . the decision-makers entitled to apply the test of reasonableness are the intermediate decision-makers, the State officials, and not the final arbiters, the tribunal which ultimately sets the seal of legality on a disputed practice.[19]

A second, even more fundamental difference between McDougal's explanation of customary international law and the approach taken here concerns the role of legal obligation. As has already been explained, the New Haven School adopts a purely sociological approach to international law. As a result, its members have not considered legal obligation; although reasonableness falls within the scope of their studies, the 'power of rules' does not. From their perspective, law is strictly a *product* of the exercise of authority and control in the decision-making process. It may, or may not, have independent force.[20]

In contrast, this book focuses on how the international legal system, and more specifically the process of customary international law, accords or withholds legitimacy from the *results* of decision-making processes. Unlike the New Haven School, it considers the basis of customary international law from a universalised perspective which is above the level of the individual State. In doing so it distinguishes between fact and norm by focusing on how the process of customary international law gives rules a legal *specificity* which distinguishes them from other social resultants, and enables those rules to qualify subsequent applications of power in important ways which the New Haven School has failed to acknowledge.

## A response to Koskenniemi

In chapter 3 it was explained that Critical Legal Studies scholars, and most notably Koskenniemi, have sought to expose the myths of objectivity, of value-freedom and of determinacy in international law and in processes of international law creation by deconstructing legal texts, thus demonstrating that the international legal system is neither self-contained nor politically neutral. Instead, Koskenniemi and his colleagues have maintained that the international legal system is based on tensions inherent in liberal ideology between, for example, the community and the individual, or positivism and naturalism.[21]

[19] MacGibbon (1957) 134.

[20] Higgins has gone further than any other member of the New Haven School in asserting that 'law as process does *not* entail a rejection of that core predictability that is essential if law is to perform its functions in society'. Higgins (1994) 8 (emphasis in original).

[21] See pp. 45–6 above.

This book's explanation of the customary process as a means of identifying State interests through behaviour, and in particular of the roles played by shared understandings of legal relevance and the conspicuous character of some common interests, responds to these concerns. Koskenniemi has summarised his position as follows:

> The dynamics of international legal argument are provided by the constant effort of lawyers to show that their law is either concrete or normative and their becoming thus vulnerable to the charge that such law is in fact political because apologist or utopian. Different doctrinal and practical controversies turn on transformations of this dilemma. It lies behind such dichotomies as 'positivism' / 'naturalism', 'consent' / 'justice', 'autonomy' / 'community', 'process' / 'rule', etc., and explains why these and other oppositions keep recurring and do not seem soluble in a permanent way. They recur because it seems possible to defend one's legal argument only by showing either its closeness to, or its distance from, state practice.[22]

A number of points may be made about this passage. First, Koskenniemi seems to have confused international legal processes with the product of those processes, whereas the two are distinct. For example, the process of customary international law may be complex, and its operation may in many cases be ambiguous, but the legal rules which result from its operation are nevertheless very real, and have tangible results. Their normative value is not diminished by the possible indeterminacy of the arguments which may be used to establish their existence and content. Although this book steps behind customary legal rules to examine the process out of which they arise, it maintains that those rules may nevertheless be effectively determined and applied, at least in most instances.

The second point relates to this book's explanation of the role played by conspicuous common interests in the development, maintenance and change of some customary rules. If, as this book suggests, the closeness to or distance from State practice depends on the conspicuous or non-conspicuous character of States' interests in a particular rule, then Koskenniemi's apologetic/utopian dilemma may be nothing more than Simmonds' positivist/idealist tension playing itself out on the international plane.[23] The customary process, by seeking to identify common interests, will necessarily deal with an extremely wide range of State interactions, some of which are relatively more 'subjective' and relatively less 'practical', or objectively determinable than others. By adopting different methods of determining common interests, the customary process is responding to social complexity, rather than being arbitrary, subjective or overly political.

22 Koskenniemi (1990b) 8.

23 See Simmonds (1991); and the quotation, note 21, p. 150 above.

Although Koskenniemi has viewed the situation as proof of the incoherence and political subjectivity of international law, this book prefers the approach adopted by Simmonds in respect of general legal theory. Simmonds, in contrast to Koskenniemi, has embraced and celebrated the complexity of legal systems as truly reflective of human society.[24]

There would also appear to be a third, important respect in which Koskenniemi's analysis does not stand up to the explanation of the customary process which is advanced in this book. This book seeks to break out of the State practice–*opinio juris* epistemological circle, and thus, again, out of the tension between 'apology and utopia'.[25] It seeks to show that it is possible – at least for explanatory purposes – to eliminate the traditional requirement of an identifiable element of *opinio juris* without sacrificing the stability and determinacy of international law.

*Opinio juris* has traditionally served two closely related functions. First, it was used to distinguish legally relevant from legally irrelevant State practice. Secondly, and perhaps less obviously, it was used to control the abuse of power by States within the process of customary international law. In short, the requirement of *opinio juris* meant that only some instances of State practice counted for the purposes of the customary process, since a State had to believe that its behaviour was already required by customary international law. This test controlled the abuse of power, and promoted stability and determinacy, by excluding a great deal of State practice which might otherwise have contributed to the development, maintenance or change of customary rules. It thus fulfilled what would appear to be an essential function within any developed society, that of socialising the behaviour of society's members by imposing the framework of a legal system upon them, of enabling them to think rationally about the future and not to focus on short-term calculations of interest and risk.

The exclusionary function of the traditional requirement of *opinio juris* may explain why so many scholars have proposed alternative formulations which, for example, allow a State to 'articulate' the legality of its actions, or to have its behaviour considered legally relevant as long as it has indicated a desire that a rule consistent with that behaviour comes into force.[26] Yet even these alternative formulations have imposed controls on the abuse of power by States. Under these formulations a State wishing to develop or change a customary rule still has to take a public position in favour of that development or change.

[24] See Simmonds (1991).
[25] On the epistemological circle, see pp. 136–41 above.
[26] See pp. 132–3 above.

Viewed from this perspective the process of customary international law as traditionally understood is, at least to some degree, stable and determinate. Koskenniemi's charge that the customary process is a camouflage for subjective, political decisions rests on the fluctuation of emphasis which occurs, between the two elements of State practice and *opinio juris*, whenever the traditional bipartite conception is applied or otherwise relied on in different situations. And it is true that, regardless of whether *opinio juris* imposes some degree of stability and determinacy, if the *degree* of determinacy depends on the will of the States concerned in any particular situation, political preferences will at least have the potential to overwhelm any essentially stable and determinate factor.

Of the alternative conceptions provided by other writers, only D'Amato and Wolfke's separation of State behaviour into two distinct categories – acts as State practice and statements as evidence of *opinio juris* – breaks out of the epistemological circle and evades this aspect of Koskenniemi's criticism. But, as chapter 8 explained, D'Amato and Wolfke's approach is unacceptable for other reasons.[27]

This book breaks out of the epistemological circle by relying on Haggenmacher's suggestion and explaining *opinio juris* as a diffuse consensus, or set of shared understandings, as to the legal relevance or irrelevance of different instances of State practice in different situations.[28] A relatively high degree of stability and determinacy may exist under this conception as a result of two factors. First, these shared understandings of legal relevance would, for the most part, seem highly resistant to opportunistically motivated short-term change. Proving the content of these shared understandings in any given situation may be difficult, but their substance remains relatively stable because they are part of the shared 'conceptual universe' of States. This inherently social aspect would seem to make these shared understandings largely immune to short-term manipulation by individual States, or groups of States.

Secondly, and perhaps more importantly, Part 2 demonstrated that applications of power within the customary process – as a regime or institution based upon shared understandings of legal relevance – are qualified by a number of fundamental principles of international law. These principles ensure that customary rules are not strictly the result of short-term political preferences. They thus allow international lawyers – as international lawyers – to consider the effects of that very factor, i.e. power, which Koskenniemi has condemned as being responsible for the incoherence and instability of international law.

[27] See p. 134 above. [28] See pp. 140–1 and 147–9 above.

## The interdisciplinary enterprise

This book has sought to demonstrate that the process of customary international law is what international relations scholars would regard as a regime or institution, and that it transforms applications of power by States into obligation in the form of customary rules. It has also sought to explain how certain, well-established customary rules of a general character qualify applications of power within the customary process.

This explanation confirms what many international relations scholars have been arguing for a number of years.[29] Regimes and international institutions matter a great deal, and the study of how they promote co-operation and affect State behaviour is therefore a worthwhile and necessary enterprise.

It is therefore somewhat surprising that most international relations scholars have yet to consider the process of customary international law or, indeed, most other regimes or institutions of an informal character. Such informal regimes and institutions are a vital part of international society, enabling States better to protect and promote their interests while at the same time controlling or influencing how those same States behave. In fact, the process of customary international law may be broader in scope and more fundamental to international society than any formal regime or international institution, including the United Nations.

This book has also explored several possible reasons why so few international lawyers have examined in detail the role played by power in the development, maintenance and change of customary international law. These reasons include the fact that judges and lawyers necessarily focus on determining the existence and content of rules, that some international lawyers worry that considering the role of power might lead judges and lawyers to favour some States over others as they go about determining rules, and that considering the role of power might call into question the stability and determinacy of international law. Another, contributing factor may be a lack of knowledge about the methodologies and conceptual tools used by the discipline of international relations. In any event, it is clearly time for the two disciplines to reach out to each other, so that experience and insights from both fields can be drawn on in co-operative efforts to understand regimes and institutions like the process of customary international law.

Interdisciplinary work may prove valuable in a number of areas. For example, both power and obligation would appear to play a role in the negotiation and interpretation of treaties. How these two factors interact

[29] See pp. 24–34 above.

with each other and influence international actors in the negotiation of treaties, and how they subsequently condition the content ascribed to those treaties, are questions to which it would seem possible to provide adequate answers only by drawing on international relations scholarship in addition to international law. Setear's attempt to apply game theory to the law of treaties is but one step towards a greater interdisciplinary understanding of this complex area.[30]

Humanitarian intervention is another subject which may benefit from interdisciplinary study. The decision to intervene in another State's territory for humanitarian reasons is a decision which, in most cases, would seem to be based primarily if not exclusively on political and moral grounds. However, such decisions are always taken within a framework of treaties and rules of customary international law. Although numerous studies have been conducted in this area by writers from both disciplines, a truly integrated analysis of how the relevant political, moral *and* legal factors interact in specific situations could contribute a great deal to our understanding of how decisions to engage in humanitarian intervention are both taken and implemented.

An interdisciplinary approach would also seem to offer much to the study of international dispute settlement. Relatively few disputes between States are ever brought before courts or tribunals, yet international law would seem to be a factor in virtually every dispute. How States resolve disputes, and why they choose different mechanisms in different situations, are issues which would seem to involve considerations that are both political and legal in character. Thus, a detailed examination of the interaction of power and international law may be called for in this context.[31]

The interdisciplinary enterprise should probably not stop at a limited integration of international relations and international law. Other disciplines, such as history, economics, sociology, linguistics and theology, may also be relevant to an integrated study of international society. To provide but one example in the context of customary international law, it is possible that the ability of States to contribute to the customary process varies, in part, because of the differing traditions and self-perceptions which national societies have of their role in world events.

We clearly need to adopt what Mills referred to as a 'sociological imagination' if we are to understand fully the complex processes which have given rise to, and continue to change, the social world in which we live.[32] Only by perceiving and studying the social world as a totality and by

[30] Setear (1996). See pp. 17–18 above.

[31] For support of this suggestion see Brownlie (1988).

[32] See Mills (1959). For an attempt to revive Mills' approach from within the discipline of international relations, see Rosenberg (1994b).

drawing on the insights, traditions and methods of a variety of intellectual disciplines can we ever hope to understand the complex social, political and legal milieu which surrounds us, and of which we are a part.

## Reconsidering the 'realist' assumptions

This book's examination of how four principles of international law qualify applications of power in the customary process demonstrated that the development, maintenance and change of customary rules is never strictly political nor ever strictly legal in character. It was this demonstration which grounded this book's explanation of the customary process as a regime or institution which first determines common interests, and then protects and promotes those common interests with rules. In turn, the idea that *opinio juris* is a collection of shared understandings of legal relevance was based on the explanation of the customary process as a regime or institution within international society. Such understandings, which seem to be necessarily social in character, have been an important part of other explanations of similar regimes and institutions.[33] The role ascribed by this book to conspicuous common interests, as well as the account of why different customary rules sometimes have differing degrees of resistance to change, were derived on a similar basis.

If power relationships among States play a role in the process of customary international law, it is unlikely that the customary process could ever be the completely neutral, procedurally objective mechanism that some legal scholars seem to claim. Rather, rules of customary international law are the result of an interactive and evolving process whereby different States contribute, in differing ways and degrees, to the ongoing development, maintenance and change of generally applicable rules. However, as part of that interactive and evolving process, the frequently unequal contributions of States occur within, and are qualified by, a structured system of those States' own creation. Social inequality thus interacts directly with sovereign equality in what amounts to a social process of self-regulation.

Such a social process, in this case the social dynamic of customary international law, is difficult, if not impossible, to explain on a traditional, positivist basis. It requires the adoption and application of social science-type conceptions, such as those of institutionalism, shared understanding, social purpose and relative resistance to change. Only by stepping back from the study of 'law as norm' can one begin to account for the full complexity of the interaction of power and obligation in the process of customary international law.

[33] See pp. 24–31, 141 and 147–8 above.

In terms of this book, one of the most important consequences of such an interdisciplinary approach may be that it undermines the 'realist' assumptions which were adopted here. It will be recalled from chapter 1 that three principal assumptions were made: that States are the most important, if not the only, actors operating on the international plane; that States are only bound by those rules of international law to which they have consented; and that States are more-or-less self-interested. However, it was also stated that these assumptions were adopted as 'analytical aids which may later need to be discarded or modified to accommodate further complexities or changes in international society, or in our understandings of it'.[34] Having made a sustained effort to explain the process of customary international law, it is now time to reconsider these three assumptions.

The first realist assumption – the statist assumption – is called into question as soon as an interdisciplinary approach is adopted and an attempt is made to consider the social world in its totality. Although intellectual disciplines such as international relations and international law restrict themselves to, or at least focus their attention at the level of, States, other disciplines such as sociology, linguistics, economics, history and theology cannot thus be confined. Languages do not respect State borders, and neither do cultures, religions, ethnic groups, transnational corporations or currency speculators. From an historical perspective, even the concepts of statehood and the free-market can be seen as relatively new, and therefore highly contingent, creations of the modern world.[35]

Similarly, it is becoming increasingly difficult to maintain the statist assumption in the face of political processes and developments within States, or between individuals or other non-State actors located within different States at a sub-State level. To provide but one example within the context of customary international law, the ability of States to participate in the customary process may sometimes be affected by internal political constraints, such as those which have existed in Japan and Germany in respect of the use of force.

Moreover, although it may be possible to make the statist assumption when considering law, that assumption becomes extremely difficult to sustain when considering power, as opposed to law. Statehood is a structural concept of the international *legal* system, where States are the symbolic holders of rights and obligations and, therefore, of power as it is legally conceived. By deeming States to be the sole holders of legal power, the discipline of international law has avoided important discussions of

[34] See p. 14 above. [35] See Rosenberg (1994a).

power as it is more broadly defined, and failed to consider to what degree the State may be representative of other centres of power, control and decision-making authority. Somewhat ironically, traditional approaches to international relations theory reveal their origins in the discipline of international law by preserving the symbolic baggage of statehood, thus leaving out other actors who, from an empirical perspective, may also be quite important.

If this first, statist assumption is being undermined, then the two subsequent realist assumptions – that States are only bound by rules of international law to which they have consented and that States are more-or-less self-interested – would seem at least inadequate. Both these assumptions are based on the first assumption, and both restrict themselves to States. There seems to be little scope within these assumptions for serious consideration of how individuals, groups and other non-State actors might participate in and influence the process of customary international law. The traditional realist perspective, as a statist perspective, largely excludes the sort of considerations as to other actors, and other factors, which are an implicit part of reaching out to other intellectual disciplines.

However, it is not entirely clear that a 'realist' approach to the study of international society needs to be exclusively statist, and therefore restrictive in its disciplinary scope. Realism purports, above all, to describe things as they are, which is precisely the task an interdisciplinary approach also seeks to facilitate. Nor is it clear that the development of theories which would accommodate non-State actors and transboundary factors at the sub-State level would result in significantly different explanations of all aspects of international society, as that society exists today.

States continue to be by far the most important actors in the international legal system, and therefore also by far the most important participants in the process whereby customary rules are developed, maintained and changed. This is the case, in part, because States have created that legal system by and for themselves. Therefore, an explanation of how that process currently operates may be justified in confining its examination to the interactions of States as the sole holders of full international legal personality, which is precisely what this book has done.

That said, non-State actors sometimes do play a role in the process of customary international law as it operates today. As chapter 5 explained, non-State actors are not only responsible for the internal social and political pressures which motivate most State practice, but sometimes their presence also enables States to participate in the customary process in ways, or to degrees, that they would otherwise not be able to do.

More importantly, it is not at all evident that the current, statist character of the international legal system promotes justice, either for States, or for the individuals and groups who live within States. It is difficult to disagree with Wright's assertion that 'international law, through its privileging of the state, relies on patriarchal and oppressive divisions between public and private spheres'.[36] The fact that civil wars are largely beyond the scope of international law is but one example of how injustices may be permitted and perpetuated in the name of statehood.

Most importantly, the statist character of the international legal system may itself change. By demonstrating that power plays an important role in the process of customary international law as it currently operates, this book has shown that States are probably not subject to that process as the result of some prior, explicit consent. Rather, they may be bound by customary rules because of their long-term participation in a larger, more informal and evolving social process which has little to do with the subjective willing of individual 'sovereigns'. This book has demonstrated that even the most powerful States may in practice be unable, or unwilling, to persistently object to new customary rules for indefinite periods of time, and that certain well-established principles, which are themselves customary in origin, sometimes qualify applications of power by such States in the process of customary international law.

If the process of customary international law is a regime or institution of the kind studied by international relations scholars, and if *opinio juris* is best understood as a set of shared understandings as to the legal relevance of different kinds of behaviour in different situations, then the predominant position of States within the international legal system may be a contingent one. It is entirely possible, as Allott has explained, that the international society of all human beings may at some point realise that the international legal system must be wrested away from the society of States and remade into a legal system which promotes, serves and recreates the ideal order of humanity.[37] Although the complexity and full implications of Allott's ideas deserve a degree of attention that cannot be provided here, his point that 'the international system itself is nothing other than a structure of ideas [that] has been made nowhere else than in the human mind' is compelling and important.[38] If the international system is whatever human beings think it is, then it, or any part of it, is capable of being changed. The fact that States have defined, and continue to play a dominant role in defining, the international legal system is no less a fact as a result of this insight, but it is a fact which may over time be modified, or even, quite abruptly, cast aside by the human beings within whose minds the reality of the State exists.

What is perhaps more likely is that the international system will

[36] Wright (1993) 134. [37] See Allott (1990). [38] Allott (1990) xv–xvi.

become more and more like a federal State, with different powers vested in different levels of government and organisation. Attempts at regional integration, such as those in Europe and North America, as well as the increasing liberalisation of world trade, could be seen as precursors of a more general development in this direction.

In such a situation, factors internal to States will play an increasingly important role in determining international society's 'shared conceptual universe' and, therefore, how States and other actors at the international level behave. Although this book has adopted a statist assumption for the purposes of its analysis, the dynamic character of international society may eventually render this assumption inappropriate even for methodological purposes. Recent developments in the literature of international law and international relations clearly anticipate such a change.[39]

This book's explanation of customary international law has sought to accommodate such eventualities. For example, 'power' has been dealt with here as the ability of a State or States to control or influence directly how other States behave. Today, such an approach is justified, at least *within* the confines of the customary process. Yet, were international society to change, the term 'power' could easily be applied in an expanded manner to include all non-legal forms of power. The identification of non-legal power as an important factor in the customary process will remain valid because non-legal power is not necessarily a statist concept. Indeed, *outside* the process of customary international law it is virtually the only kind of power available to most non-State actors, such as transnational corporations, operating at the international level.

At the beginning of this book it was also explained that power is derived from many sources, including wealth and military strength. Power, generally speaking, may be derived from almost any of the elements which exist in international society at any given time. Although the sources of power which are of greatest importance to the customary process today involve the economic and military abilities of States, and legal obligation in the form of rules and principles of international law, the relative importance of different sources of power could also easily change. Indeed, they will have to change, should the State-centric character of international law be redefined.

An interdisciplinary approach to the process of customary international law has to accommodate the possibility of change because it promotes that possibility of itself. If we open our minds to the complexity of international society, we quickly become aware, not only of international

[39] See Hobe (1997); the citations in note 45, p. 14 above; as well as the literature on epistemic communities cited in note 58, p. 141 above.

society's contingent character, but also of our own role in determining its future. What we do with that awareness is up to us. Yet it may be reassuring to know that the process of customary international law will continue to preserve, remake and recreate the rules of international law, and international society itself, and that it will do so on that, on our society's, terms.

# Bibliography


'Continental Shelf Oil Disasters: Challenge to International Pollution Control', (1969) 55 *Cornell Law Review* 113 (note)

'Countermeasures and Dispute Settlement: The Current Debate within the ILC', (1994) 5 *European Journal of International Law* 20 (symposium)

Abi-Saab, Georges (1968) 'The Development of International Law by the United Nations', (1968) 24 *Revue égyptienne de droit international* 95

(1987) 'La coutume dans tous ses états ou le dilemme du développement du droit international général dans un monde éclaté', in *Le droit international à l'heure de sa codification: Etudes en l'honneur de Roberto Ago* (Milan: Dott. A. Giuffrè Editore, 1987) Vol. 1, 53

Aggarwal, Vinod (1985) *Liberal Protectionism: The International Politics of Organized Textile Trade* (Berkeley: University of California Press, 1985)

Ago, Roberto (1971) 'Droit des traités à la lumière de la Convention de Vienne', (1971-III) 134 *Recueil des cours* 297

(1984) 'Positivism', in Rudolf Bernhardt (ed.), *Encyclopedia of Public International Law* (Amsterdam: North-Holland, 1984) vol. 7, 385

Akehurst, Michael (1972–3) 'Jurisdiction in International Law', (1972–3) 46 *British Yearbook of International Law* 145

(1974–5a) 'Custom as a Source of International Law', (1974–5a) 47 *British Yearbook of International Law* 1

(1974–5b) 'The Hierarchy of the Sources of International Law', (1974–5b) 47 *British Yearbook of International Law* 273

(1992) 'Civil War', in Rudolf Bernhardt (ed.), *Encyclopedia of Public International Law* (Amsterdam: North-Holland, 1992) vol. 1, 597

Alexidze, Levan (1981) 'Legal Nature of *Jus Cogens* in Contemporary International Law', (1981-III) 172 *Recueil des cours* 219

Allott, Philip (1971) 'Language, Method and the Nature of International Law', (1971) 45 *British Yearbook of International Law* 79

(1990) *Eunomia: New Order for a New World* (New York: Oxford University Press, 1990)

(1992) '*Mare Nostrum*: A New International Law of the Sea', (1992) 86 *American Journal of International Law* 764

(1995) 'The International Court and the Voice of Justice', in Vaughan Lowe and Malgosia Fitzmaurice (eds.), *Fifty Years of the International Court of Justice: Essays in Honour of Sir Robert Jennings* (Cambridge: Cambridge University Press, 1995) 17

Alvárez, Alejandro (1910) *Le droit international américain* (Paris: Pedone, 1910)
(1959) *Le Droit international nouveau dans ses rapports avec la vie actuelle des peuples* (Paris: Pedone, 1959)
Amerasinghe, C. F. (1992) 'Issues of Compensation for the Taking of Alien Property in the Light of Recent Cases and Practice', (1992) 41 *International and Comparative Law Quarterly* 22
Annacker, Claudia (1994) 'The Legal Régime of *Erga Omnes* Obligations in International Law', (1994) 46 *Austrian Journal of Public International Law* 131
Arangio-Ruiz, Gaetano (1972) 'The Normative Role of the General Assembly of the United Nations and the Declaration of Principles of Friendly Relations', (1972-III) 137 *Recueil des cours* 419
Arend, Anthony Clark (1996) 'Toward an Understanding of International Legal Rules', in Robert Beck *et al.*, *International Rules* (New York: Oxford University Press, 1996) 289
Asamoah, Obed (1966) *The Legal Significance of the Declarations of the General Assembly of the United Nations* (The Hague: Martinus Nijhoff, 1966)
Austin, John (1832) *The Province of Jurisprudence Determined* (London: Weidenfeld and Nicolson, 1954) (first published in 1832)
Australian Law Reform Commission (1984) *Report No. 24: Foreign State Immunity* (Canberra: Australian Government Printing Office, 1984)
Axelrod, Robert (1984) *The Evolution of Cooperation* (New York: Basic Books, 1984)
Bacchi, Carol (1992) 'Do Women Need Equal Treatment or Different Treatment?' (1992) 8 *Australian Journal of Law and Society* 80
Baker, Blaine (1993) 'Interstate Choice of Law and Early-American Constitutional Nationalism. An Essay On *Joseph Story and the Comity of Errors: A Case Study in Conflict of Laws* (by Alan Watson)', (1993) 38 *McGill Law Journal* 454
Baldwin, Malcolm (1970) 'The Santa Barbara Oil Spill', (1970) 42 *University of Colorado Law Review* 33
Barberis, Julio (1983) 'International Law, American', in Rudolf Bernhardt (ed.), *Encyclopedia of Public International Law* (Amsterdam: North-Holland, 1983) vol. 6, 222
Bardonnet, Daniel (1962) 'La largeur de la mer territoriale', (1962) 66 *Revue générale de droit international public* 34
Barker, Ernest (1918) *The Confederation of Nations* (Oxford: Clarendon, 1918)
Barston, R. (1995) 'United Nations Conference on Straddling and Highly Migratory Fish Stocks', (1995) 19 *Marine Policy* 159
Bassiouni, Cherif (1986) *International Criminal Law* (Dobbs Ferry, NY: Transnational, 1986) vol. 1
Baty, Thomas (1928) 'The Three Mile Limit', (1928) 22 *American Journal of International Law* 503
Baxter, Richard (1970) 'Treaties and Custom', (1970-I) 129 *Recueil des cours* 25
Beck, Robert (1996) 'International Law and International Relations: The Prospects for Interdisciplinary Collaboration', in Beck *et al.*, *International Rules: Approaches from International Law and International Relations* (New York: Oxford University Press, 1996) 3

Beck, Robert, Anthony Arend and Robert Lugt (1996) *International Rules: Approaches from International Law and International Relations* (New York: Oxford University Press, 1996)

Bederman, David (1988) review of David Kennedy, *International Legal Structures*, (1988) 18 *Georgia Journal of International and Comparative Law* 527

Bedjaoui, Mohammed (1979) *Towards a New International Order* (Paris: UNESCO, 1979)

Beesley, Alan (1973) 'The Canadian Approach to International Environmental Law', (1973) 11 *Canadian Yearbook of International Law* 3

Benson, Peter (1982) 'François Gény's Doctrine of Customary Law', (1982) 20 *Canadian Yearbook of International Law* 267

Berger, Peter and Thomas Luckmann (1966) *The Social Construction of Reality* (New York: Anchor Books, 1966)

Bernhardt, Rudolf (1992) 'Customary International Law', in Bernhardt (ed.), *Encyclopedia of Public International Law* (Amsterdam: North-Holland, 1992) vol. 1, 898

Biersteker, Thomas (1993) 'Constructing Historical Counterfactuals to Assess the Consequences of International Regimes', in Volker Rittberger (ed.), *Regime Theory and International Relations* (Oxford: Clarendon, 1993) 315

Bilder, Richard (1970–1) 'The Canadian Arctic Waters Pollution Prevention Act: New Stresses on the Law of the Sea', (1970–1) 69 *Michigan Law Review* 1

Bishop, William (1953) 'New United States Policy Limiting Sovereign Immunity', (1953) 47 *American Journal of International Law* 93

(1965) 'General Course of Public International Law', (1965-II) 115 *Recueil des cours* 147

Bissell, Richard (1977) *Apartheid and International Organizations* (Boulder: Westview, 1977)

Bodansky, Daniel (1995) 'The Concept of Customary International Law', (1995) 16 *Michigan Journal of International Law* 667 (review of Karol Wolfke, *Custom in Present International Law* (2nd ed.))

Bodart, Serge (1995) 'Les réfugiés apolitiques: guerre civile et persécution de groupe au regard de la Convention de Genève', (1995) 7 *International Journal of Refugee Law* 39

Bonin, Jean-François (1986) 'La protection contre la torture et les traitements cruels, inhumains et dégradants: l'affirmation d'une norme et l'évolution d'une définition en droit international', (1986) 3 *Revue québecoise de droit international* 169

Bowett, Derek (1957) 'Estoppel Before International Tribunals and its Relation to Acquiescence', (1957) 33 *British Yearbook of International Law* 176

(1976–7) 'Reservations to Non-Restricted Multilateral Treaties', (1976–7) 48 *British Yearbook of International Law* 66

(1982a) 'Jurisdiction: Changing Patterns of Authority over Activities and Resources', (1982a) 53 *British Yearbook of International Law* 1

(1982b) *The Law of International Institutions* (4th ed.) (London: Stevens, 1982b)

Boyle, Francis (1985) *World Politics and International Law* (Durham, NC: Duke University Press, 1985)

Bray, W. and M. Beukes (1981) 'Recent Trends in the Development of State

Immunity in South African Law', (1981) 7 *South African Yearbook of International Law* 13

Breitmeier, Helmut and Klaus Wolf (1993) 'Analyzing Regime Consequences', in Volker Rittberger (ed.), *Regime Theory and International Relations* (Oxford: Clarendon, 1993) 339

Brierly, James (1958) 'The Basis of Obligation in International Law', in Hersch Lauterpacht and Humphrey Waldock (eds.), *The Basis of Obligation in International Law and Other Papers by the Late James Leslie Brierly* (Oxford: Clarendon, 1958) 1 (original version of the article published in French in (1928-III) 23 *Recueil des cours*)

Broderick, Albert (ed.), (1970) *The French Institutionalists* (Cambridge, MA: Harvard University Press, 1970)

Brower, Charles, Walter Bistline and George Loomis (1979) 'The Foreign Sovereign Immunities Act of 1976 in Practice', (1979) 73 *American Journal of International Law* 200

Brown, Philip (1923) 'The Marginal Sea' (1923) 17 *American Journal of International Law* 89

Brownlie, Ian (1963) *International Law and the Use of Force by States* (Oxford: Oxford University Press, 1963)

(1983) *State Responsibility* (Oxford: Clarendon, 1983)

(1986) 'Remarks', in 'Comparative Approaches to the Theory of International Law', (1986) 80 *American Society of International Law Proceedings* 154

(1988) 'The Relation of Law and Power', in Bin Cheng and Edward Brown (eds.), *Contemporary Problems of International Law: Essays in Honour of Georg Schwarzenberger on His Eightieth Birthday* (London: Stevens, 1988) 19

(1990) *Principles of Public International Law* (4th ed.) (Oxford: Clarendon, 1990)

(1995) 'International Law at the Fiftieth Anniversary of the United Nations: General Course on Public International Law', (1995-I) 255 *Recueil des cours* 9

Buergenthal, Thomas and Robert Norris (eds.) (1988) *Human Rights: The Inter-American System* (Booklet 21.3) (Dobbs Ferry: Oceana, 1988)

Bull, Hedley (1977) *The Anarchical Society: A Study of Order in World Politics* (London: Macmillan, 1977)

Bull, Hedley and Adam Watson (eds.) (1984) *The Expansion of International Society* (Oxford: Oxford University Press, 1984)

Burke, William (1994) *The New International Law of Fisheries* (Oxford: Clarendon, 1994)

Burley, Anne-Marie (1989) 'The Alien Tort Statute and the Judiciary Act of 1789: A Badge of Honor', (1989) 83 *American Journal of International Law* 461

Buzan, Barry (1993) 'From International System to International Society: Structural Realism and Regime Theory Meet the English School', (1993) 47 *International Organization* 327

Byers, Michael (1995) 'State Immunity: Article 18 of the International Law Commission's Draft', (1995) 44 *International and Comparative Law Quarterly* 882

(1997a) 'Conceptualising the Relationship Between *Jus Cogens* and *Erga Omnes* Rules', (1997a) 66 *Nordic Journal of International Law* 211

(1997b) 'Taking the Law out of International Law: A Critique of the "Iterative Perspective"', (1997b) 38 *Harvard International Law Journal* 201

Caflisch, Lucius (1989) 'Land-Locked and Geographically Disadvantaged States', in Rudolf Bernhardt (ed.), *Encylopedia of Public International Law* (Amsterdam: North-Holland, 1989) vol. 11, 169

Caminos, Hugo and Michael Molitor (1985) 'Progressive Development of International Law and the Package Deal', (1985) 79 *American Journal of International Law* 871

Carlier, Jean-Yves and Dirk Vanheule (1994) 'Belgian Bricks for Fortress Europe: Comment on the New Refugee Law after a Judgment of the Cour d'Arbitrage', (1994) 6 *International Journal of Refugee Law* 323

Carr, Edward (1946) *The Twenty Years' Crisis* (2nd ed.) (London: Macmillan, 1946)

Carter, Barry and Phillip Trimble (1991) *International Law* (Boston: Little, Brown, 1991) 550

Carty, Anthony (1986) *The Decay of International Law?: A Reappraisal of the Limits of Legal Imagination in International Affairs* (Manchester: Manchester University Press, 1986)

(1991) 'Critical International Law: Recent Trends in the Theory of International Law', (1991) 2 *European Journal of International Law* 66

Cassese, Antonio (1986) *International Law in a Divided World* (Oxford: Clarendon, 1986)

Castaneda, Jorge (1969) *Legal Effects of United Nations Resolutions* (trans. Alba Amoia) (New York: Columbia University Press, 1969)

Cavaglieri, Arrigo (1929) 'Règles générales du droit de la paix', (1929-I) 26 *Recueil des cours* 544

Charlesworth, Hilary (1992) 'The Public/Private Distinction and the Right to Development in International Law', (1992) 12 *Australian Yearbook of International Law* 190

Charlesworth, Hilary, Christine Chinkin and Shelley Wright, (1991) 'Feminist Approaches to International Law', (1991) 85 *American Journal of International Law* 613

Charney, Jonathan (1985) 'The Persistent Objector Rule and the Development of Customary International Law' (1985) 56 *British Yearbook of International Law* 1

(1987) 'Remarks' in 'Disentangling Treaty and Customary International Law', (1987) 81 *American Society of International Law Proceedings* 157, 159

(1993) 'Universal International Law', (1993) 87 *American Journal of International Law* 529

Charney, Jonathan and Gennady Danilenko (1995) 'Consent and the Creation of International Law', in Lori Damrosch *et al.* (eds.), *Beyond Confrontation: International Law for the Post-Cold War Era* (Boulder: Westview, 1995)

Charpentier, Jean (1991) *Institutions internationales* (10th ed.) (Paris: Dalloz, 1991)

Chayes, Abram and Antonia Chayes (1993) 'On Compliance', (1993) 47 *International Organization* 175

(1995) *The New Sovereignty: Compliance with International Regulatory Agreements* (Cambridge, MA: Harvard University Press, 1995)

Cheng, Bin (1953) *General Principles of Law as Applied by International Courts and Tribunals* (London: Stevens, 1953)
(1965) 'United Nations Resolutions on Outer Space: "Instant" International Customary Law?', (1965) 5 *Indian Journal of International Law* 23
Chinkin, Christine (1992) 'A Gendered Perspective to the International Use of Force', (1992) 12 *Australian Yearbook of International Law* 279
(1993) *Third Parties in International Law* (Oxford: Clarendon, 1993)
Chodosh, Hiram (1991) 'Neither Treaty nor Custom: The Emergence of Declarative International Law', (1991) 26 *Texas International Law Journal* 87
Churchill, Robin and Vaughan Lowe (1988) *The Law of the Sea* (revised edition) (Manchester: Manchester University Press, 1988)
Cobbett, Pitt (1922) *Leading Cases on International Law* (4th ed.) (Hugh Bellot, ed.) (London: Sweet and Maxwell, 1922)
Cohen-Jonathan, Gérard (1961) 'La coutume locale', (1961) 7 *Annuaire français de droit international* 119
Collier, John (1994) *Conflict of Laws* (2nd ed.) (Cambridge: Cambridge University Press, 1994)
Collins, Hugh (1993) *The Law of Contract* (2nd ed.) (London: Butterworths, 1993)
Colombos, Constantine (1924) 'Territorial Waters', (1924) 9 *Transactions of the Grotius Society* 89
(1967) *The International Law of the Sea* (6th ed.) (London: Longman, 1967)
Colson, David (1986) 'How Persistent Must the Persistent Objector Be?', (1986) 61 *Washington Law Review* 957
Comaroff, John and Simon Roberts (1981) *Rules and Processes: The Cultural Logic of Dispute in an African Context* (Chicago: University of Chicago Press, 1981)
Conboy, Martin (1924) 'The Territorial Sea', (1924) 2 *Canadian Bar Review* 8
Cooper, Richard (1975) 'Prolegomena to the Choice of an International Monetary System', (1975) 29 *International Organization* 63
Corbett, Percy (1925) 'The Consent of States and the Sources of the Law of Nations', (1925) 6 *British Yearbook of International Law* 20
Cotterrell, Roger (1992) *The Sociology of Law: An Introduction* (2nd ed.) (London: Butterworths, 1992)
Court of Justice of the European Communities, (1992) *Civil Jurisdiction and Judgments in Europe* (London: Butterworths, 1992)
Cowhey, Peter (1990) 'The International Telecommunications Regime: The Political Roots of Regimes for High Technology', (1990) 44 *International Organization* 169
(1993) 'Domestic Institutions and the Credibility of International Commitments: Japan and the United States', (1993) 47 *International Organization* 299
Crawford, James (1976–7) 'The Criteria for Statehood in International Law', (1976–7) 48 *British Yearbook of International Law* 93
(1979) *The Creation of States in International Law* (Oxford: Oxford University Press, 1979)
(1981) 'Execution of Judgments and Foreign Sovereign Immunity', (1981) 75 *American Journal of International Law* 820

(1983) 'A Foreign State Immunities Act for Australia?', (1983) 8 *Australian Yearbook of International Law* 71

(1989) 'Islands as Sovereign Nations', (1989) 38 *International and Comparative Law Quarterly* 277

(1993) 'Democracy and International Law', (1993) 64 *British Yearbook of International Law* 113

(1995) 'Negotiating Global Security Threats in a World of Nation-States: Issues and Problems of Sovereignty', (1995) 38 *American Behavioral Scientist* 867

Crawford, James and Thomas Viles (1994) 'International Law on a Given Day', in *Völkerrecht zwischen normativem Anspruch und politischer Realität: Festschrift für Karl Zemanek* (Berlin: Duncker and Humblot, 1994) 45

Dahm, Georg (1958) *Völkerrecht* (Stuttgart: Kohlhammer, 1958)

Dallmeyer, Dorinda (ed.) (1993) *Reconceiving Reality: Women and International Law* (Washington, DC: American Society of International Law, 1993)

D'Amato, Anthony (1969) 'The Concept of Special Custom in International Law' (1969) 63 *American Journal of International Law* 211

(1971) *The Concept of Custom* (Ithaca: Cornell University Press, 1971)

(1982) 'The Concept of Human Rights in International Law', (1982) 82 *Columbia Law Review* 1110

(1984–5) 'Is International Law Really "Law"?', (1984–5) 79 *Northwestern University Law Review* 1293

(1987a) 'Trashing Customary International Law', (1987a) 81 *American Journal of International Law* 101

(1987b) *International Law: Prospect and Process* (Dobbs Ferry: Transnational, 1987b)

(1988) 'Custom and Treaty: A Response to Professor Weisburd', (1988) 21 *Vanderbilt Journal of Transnational Law* 459

Danilenko, Gennady (1991) 'International *Jus Cogens*: Issues of Law-Making', (1991) 2 *European Journal of International Law* 42

(1993) *Law-Making in the International Community* (Dordrecht: Martinus Nijhoff, 1993)

Davies, Peter (1995) 'The EC/Canadian Fisheries Dispute in the Northwest Atlantic', (1995) 44 *International and Comparative Law Quarterly* 927

Davies, Peter and Catherine Redgwell (1996) 'The International Legal Regulation of Straddling Fish Stocks', (1996) 67 *British Yearbook of International Law* 199

Dawson, John (1947) 'Economic Duress – An Essay in Perspective', (1947) 45 *Michigan Law Review* 253

Degan, Vladimir-Duro (1981/2) 'Peaceful Change', (1981/2) 16 *Revue belge de droit international* 536

Delaume, Georges (1953) *American–French Private International Law* (New York: Oceana, 1953)

Deleau, Olivier (1969) 'Les positions françaises à la Conférence de Vienne sur le droit des traités', (1969) 15 *Annuaire français de droit international* 7

Dicey, A.V. (1959) *Introduction to the Study of the Law of the Constitution* (10th ed.) (London: Macmillan, 1959)

Dinh, Nguyen Quoc, *et al.* (1994) *Droit international public* (5th ed.) (Paris: Librairie Générale de Droit et de Jurisprudence, 1994)
Dolzer, Rudolf (1981) 'New Foundations of the Law of Expropriation of Alien Property', (1981) 75 *American Journal of International Law* 553
Dominicé, Christian (1968) 'A propos du principe de l'estoppel en droit des gens', in *Recueil d'études de droit international en hommage à Paul Guggenheim* (Geneva: University of Geneva, 1968) 327
Donnelly, Jack (1986) 'International Human Rights: A Regime Analysis', (1986) 40 *International Organization* 599
Donner, Ruth (1994) *The Regulation of Nationality in International Law* (2nd ed.) (Irvington-on-Hudson, NY: Transnational, 1994)
Drachsler, Leo (1960) 'Some Observations on the Current Status of the Tate Letter', (1960) 54 *American Journal of International Law* 790
Dugard, John (1987) *Recognition and the United Nations* (Cambridge: Grotius, 1987)
Dupuy, René-Jean (1974) 'Coutume sage et coutume sauvage', in *Mélanges offerts à Charles Rousseau* (Paris: Pedone, 1974) 75
Dworkin, Ronald (1977) *Taking Rights Seriously* (Cambridge, MA: Harvard University Press, 1977)
Eagleton, Clyde (1953) 'Self-Determination in the United Nations', (1953) 47 *American Journal of International Law* 88
Elias, Olufemi (1995) 'The Nature of the Subjective Element in Customary International Law', (1995) 44 *International and Comparative Law Quarterly* 501
Emanuelli, Claude (1984) 'L'immunité souveraine et la coutume internationale: de l'immunité absolue à l'immunité relative?', (1984) 22 *Canadian Yearbook of International Law* 26
Erasmus, Gerhard (1982) 'Proceedings Against Foreign States – The South African Foreign States Immunities Act', (1982) 8 *South African Yearbook of International Law* 92
Fanon, Frantz (1991) *Les damnés de la terre* (Paris: Gallimard, 1991)
Fatouros, A. A. (1987) 'National Legal Persons in International Law', in Bernhardt (ed.), *Encyclopedia of Public International Law* (Amsterdam: North-Holland, 1987) vol. 10, 299
Fenwick, Charles (1924) *International Law* (New York: Century, 1924)
Fidler, David (1996) 'Challenging the Classical Concept of Custom: Perspectives on the Future of Customary International Law', (1996) 39 *German Yearbook of International Law* 198
Finlayson, Jock and Mark Zacher (1983) 'The GATT and the Regulation of Trade Barriers: Regime Dynamics and Functions', in Stephen Krasner (ed.), *International Regimes* (Ithaca: Cornell University Press, 1983) 273
Finnis, John (1980) *Natural Law and Natural Rights* (Oxford: Clarendon, 1980)
Fitzmaurice, Gerald (1953) 'The Law and Procedure of the International Court of Justice, 1951–54: General Principles and Sources of Law', (1953) 30 *British Yearbook of International Law* 1
(1956) 'The Foundations of the Authority of International Law and the Problem of Enforcement', (1956) 19 *Modern Law Review* 1
(1957) 'The Law and Procedure of the International Court of Justice,

1951–54: Treaty Interpretation and other Treaty Points', (1957) 33 *British Yearbook of International Law* 203

Food and Agriculture Organisation (1985) 'FAO/Australia Workshop on the Management of Penaeid Shrimp/Prawns in the Asia–Pacific Region', (Fisheries Report No. 323) (Rome: FAO, 1985)

Fox, Gregory and Georg Nolte (1995) 'Intolerant Democracies', (1995) 36 *Harvard International Law Journal* 1

Franck, Thomas (1990) *The Power of Legitimacy Among Nations* (New York: Oxford University Press, 1990)

(1992) 'The Emerging Right to Democratic Governance', (1992) 86 *American Journal of International Law* 46

(1995) *Fairness in International Law and Institutions* (Oxford: Clarendon, 1995)

Freid, John (1968) 'How Efficient is International Law?', in Karl Deutsch and Stanley Hoffmann (eds.), *The Relevance of International Law: Essays in Honor of Leo Gross* (Cambridge, MA: Schenkmann, 1968) 93

Friedmann, Wolfgang (1964) *The Changing Structure of International Law* (New York: Columbia University Press, 1964)

Frowein, Jochen (1987) 'Recognition', in Rudolf Bernhardt (ed.), *Encyclopedia of Public International Law* (Amsterdam: North-Holland, 1987) vol. 10, 340

(1989) 'The Internal and External Effects of Resolutions by International Organizations', (1989) 49 *Zeitschrift für ausländisches öffentliches Recht und Völkerrecht* 778

(1994a) 'Demokratie und Völkerrecht in Europa', in *Völkerrecht zwischen normativem Anspruch und politischer Realität: Festschrift für Karl Zemanek* (Berlin: Duncker and Humblot, 1994) 365

(1994b) 'Reaction by Not Directly Affected States to Breaches of Public International Law', (1994-IV) 248 *Recueil des cours* 345

Fuller, Lon (1969) *The Morality of Law* (rev. ed.) (New Haven: Yale University Press, 1969)

Galiani, Ferdinando (1782) *Dei doveri dei principi neutrali* (2nd ed.) (Bologna: Zanichelli, 1942) (first published 1782)

Gayim, Eyassu (1990) *The Principle of Self-Determination* (Oslo: Norwegian Institute of Human Rights, 1990)

Geny, François (1919) *Méthode d'interprétation et sources en droit privé positif* (2nd ed.) (Paris: Librairie Générale de Droit et de Jurisprudence, 1919)

Gilmore, William (1995) 'Hot Pursuit: the Case of *R.* v. *Mills and Others*', (1995) 44 *International and Comparative Law Quarterly* 949

Giraud, Emile (1961) 'Exposé préliminaire. Modification et terminaison des traités collectifs', (1961) 49 *Annuaire de l'institut de droit international* 5

Goedhuis, D. (1978) 'The Changing Legal Regime of Air and Outer Space', (1978) 27 *International and Comparative Law Quarterly* 576

Goode, Roy (1997) 'Usage and its Reception in Transnational Commercial Law', (1997) 46 *International and Comparative Law Quarterly* 1

Goodwin-Gill, Guy (1994) 'Case and Comment: The Haitian *Refoulement* Case', (1994) 6 *International Journal of Refugee Law* 69

(1995) 'Asylum: The Law and Politics of Change', (1995) 7 *International Journal of Refugee Law* 1

Gordon, Ruth (1994) 'United Nations Intervention in Internal Conflicts: Iraq, Somalia, and Beyond', (1994) 15 *Michigan Journal of International Law* 519

Gorove, Stephen (1979) 'The Geostationary Orbit: Issues of Law and Policy', (1979) 73 *American Journal of International Law* 444

Gray, Christine (1987) *Judicial Remedies in International Law* (Oxford: Clarendon, 1987)

Greenwood, Christopher (1993) 'Is There a Right of Humanitarian Intervention?', (February 1993) *World Today* 34

Grewe, Wilhelm (1994) 'The History of the United Nations', in Bruno Simma (ed.), *The Charter of the United Nations* (Oxford: Oxford University Press, 1994) 1

(1999) *The Epochs of International Law* (trans. Michael Byers) (Berlin: Walter de Gruyter, 1999)

Grieco, Joseph (1988) 'Anarchy and the Limits of Cooperation: A Realist Critique of the Newest Liberal Institutionalism', (1988) 42 *International Organization* 485

(1990) *Cooperation Among Nations* (Ithaca: Cornell University Press, 1990)

Guerrero, Gustave (1930) *La codification du droit international* (Paris: Pedone, 1930)

Guggenheim, Paul (1950) 'Les deux éléments de la coutume en droit international', in *La technique et les principes du droit public: Etudes en l'honneur de Georges Scelle* (Paris: Librairie Générale de Droit et de Jurisprudence, 1950) tome 1, 275

(1953) *Traité de droit international public* (Geneva: Librairie de l'Université, 1953)

(1961) 'Lokales Gewohnheitsrecht', (1961) 11 *Österreichische Zeitschrift für öffentliches Recht* 327

(1967) *Traité de droit international public* (2nd ed.) (Geneva: Librairie de l'Université, 1967)

Gunning, Isabelle (1991) 'Modernizing Customary International Law: The Challenge of Human Rights', (1991) 31 *Virginia Journal of International Law* 211

Gupta, R. S. (1986) 'Resolutions of the United Nations General Assembly as a Source of International Law', (1986) 23 *International Studies* 143

Haas, Ernst (1979–80) 'Why Collaborate? Issue-Linkage and International Regimes', (1979–80) 32 *World Politics* 357

Haas, Peter (1992a) 'Knowledge, Power, and International Policy Coordination,' (1992) 46 (1) *International Organization* (special issue)

(1992b) 'Introduction: Epistemic Communities and International Policy Coordination', (1992b) 46 *International Organization* 1

(1993) 'Epistemic Communities and the Dynamics of International Environmental Co-operation', in Volker Rittberger (ed.), *Regime Theory and International Relations* (Oxford: Clarendon, 1993) 168

Haggenmacher, Peter (1986) 'La doctrine des deux éléments du droit coutumier dans la pratique de la cour internationale', (1986) 90 *Revue générale de droit international public* 5

Hannikainen, Lauri (1988) *Peremptory Norms (Jus Cogens) in International Law* (Helsinki: Lakimiesliiton Kustannus, 1988)

Harris, Donald *et al.* (1984) *Compensation and Support for Illness and Injury* (Oxford: Clarendon, 1984)

Hart, H. L. A. (1961) *The Concept of Law* (Oxford: Clarendon, 1961)

(1982) *Essays on Bentham* (Oxford: Clarendon, 1982)

Hartmann, Gode (1983) 'Internationales jus cogens?', (1983) 11(4) *Demokratie und Recht* 390

Harvard Research Project (1935) 'Jurisdiction with Respect to Crime', (1935) 29 *American Journal of International Law Supplement* 435

Haufler, Virginia (1993) 'Crossing the Boundary between Public and Private: International Regimes and Non-State Actors', in Volker Rittberger (ed.), *Regime Theory and International Relations* (Oxford: Clarendon, 1993) 94

Hegel, G. W. F. (1821) *Elements of the Philosophy of Right* (trans. T. M. Knox) (Oxford: Oxford University Press, 1967) (first published in 1821)

Henkin, Louis (1971) 'Arctic Anti-Pollution: Does Canada Make or Break International Laws?', (1971) 65 *American Journal of International Law* 131

(1979) *How Nations Behave* (2nd ed.) (New York: Columbia University Press, 1979)

(1990) *The Age of Rights* (New York: Columbia University Press, 1990)

Higgins, Rosalyn (1963) *The Development of International Law through the Political Organs of the United Nations* (London: Oxford University Press, 1963)

(1976–7) 'Derogations under Human Rights Treaties', (1976–7) *British Yearbook of International Law* 281

(1994) *Problems and Process: International Law and How We Use It* (Oxford: Clarendon, 1994)

(1997) 'Time and the Law: International Perspectives on an Old Problem', (1997) 46 *International and Comparative Law Quarterly* 501

Hobe, Stephan (1997) 'Statehood at the End of the 20th Century – The Model of the "Open State": A German Perspective', (1997) 2 *Austrian Review of International and European Law* 127

Hoffmann, Stanley (1968a) 'International Systems and International Law', in Richard Falk and Wolfram Hanrieder (eds.), *International Law and Organization* (Philadelphia: Lippincott, 1968) 89

(1968b) 'International Law and the Control of Force', in Karl Deutsch and Stanley Hoffmann (eds.), *The Relevance of International Law: Essays in Honor of Leo Gross* (Cambridge, MA: Schenkmann, 1968) 21

Hohfeld, Wesley (1913–14) 'Some Fundamental Legal Conceptions as Applied in Judicial Reasoning', (1913–14) 23 *Yale Law Journal* 16; reproduced in Hohfeld, *Fundamental Legal Conceptions* (New Haven: Yale University Press, 1923) 23

(1916–17) 'Fundamental Legal Conceptions as Applied in Judicial Reasoning (Part 2)', (1916–17) 26 *Yale Law Journal* 710; reproduced in Hohfeld, *Fundamental Legal Conceptions* (New Haven: Yale University Press, 1923) 65

(1923) *Fundamental Legal Conceptions* (New Haven: Yale University Press, 1923)

van Hoof, G. J. H. (1983) *Rethinking the Sources of International Law* (Deventer: Kluwer, 1983) de Hoogh, A. J. J. (1991) 'The Relationship between *Jus Cogens*, Obligations *Erga Omnes* and International Crimes: Peremptory Norms in Perspective', (1991) 42 *Austrian Journal of Public International Law* 183

Humphrey, John (1984) *Human Rights and the United Nations: A Great Adventure* (Epping: Bowker, 1984)

Hurrell, Andrew (1993) 'International Society and the Study of Regimes', in Volker Rittberger (ed.), *Regime Theory and International Relations* (Oxford: Clarendon, 1993) 49

Hurst, Cecil (1923–4) 'Whose is the Bed of the Sea?', (1923–4) 4 *British Yearbook of International Law* 34

Hutchinson, Mark (1993) 'Restoring Hope: UN Security Council Resolutions for Somalia and an Expanded Doctrine of Humanitarian Intervention', (1993) 34 *Harvard International Law Journal* 624

Jabbari, David (1992) 'From Criticism to Construction in Modern Critical Legal Theory', (1992) 12 *Oxford Journal of Legal Studies* 507

Jennings, Robert (1957) 'Extraterritorial Jurisdiction and the United States Anti-trust Laws', (1957) 33 *British Yearbook of International Law* 146

(1965) 'Nullity and Effectiveness in International Law', in *Cambridge Essays in International Law* (London: Stevens, 1965) 64

(1967) 'General Course on Principles of Public International Law', (1967-II) 121 *Recueil des cours* 323

(1981) 'What is International Law and How Do We Tell It When We See It?', (1981) 37 *Schweizerisches Jahrbuch für internationales Recht* 59

(1996) 'The Judiciary, International and National, and the Development of International Law', (1996) 45 *International and Comparative Law Quarterly* 1

Jennings, Robert and Arthur Watts (eds.) (1992) *Oppenheim's International Law* (9th ed.) (Harlow: Longman, 1992) vol. 1

Jessup, Philip (1927) *The Law of Territorial Waters and Maritime Jurisdiction* (New York: Jennings, 1927) vol. 1

Jiménez de Aréchaga, Eduardo (1978) 'International Law in the Past Third of a Century', (1978-I) 159 *Recueil des cours* 1

Jónsson, Hannes (1982) *Friends in Conflict: The Anglo-Icelandic Cod Wars and the Law of the Sea* (London: Hurst, 1982)

Joyner, Christopher (1987) 'Crossing the Great Divide: Views of a Political Scientist Wandering in the World of International Law', (1987) 81 *Proceedings of the American Society of International Law* 385

Kadelbach, Stefan (1992) *Zwingendes Völkerrecht* (Berlin: Duncker and Humblot, 1992)

Kairys, David (ed.) (1990) *The Politics of Law* (rev. ed.) (New York: Pantheon, 1990)

Kaplan, Morton and Nicholas Katzenbach (1961) *The Political Foundations of International Law* (New York: Wiley, 1961)

Kelsen, Hans (1939) 'Théorie du droit international coutumier', (1939) *Revue internationale théorie du droit* 253

(1951) *The Law of the United Nations* (London: Stevens, 1951)

(1952) *Principles of International Law* (New York: Rinehart, 1952)

(1961) *General Theory of Law and State* (New York: Russell and Russell, 1961)

(1966) *Principles of International Law* (2nd ed.) (Robert Tucker, ed.) (New York: Holt, Rinehart and Winston, 1966)

Kennedy, David (1987) *International Legal Structures* (Baden-Baden: Nomos, 1987)

Keohane, Robert (1984) *After Hegemony* (Princeton: Princeton University Press, 1984)

(1986) 'Reciprocity in International Relations', (1986) 40 *International Organization* 1

(1989a) *International Institutions and State Power* (Boulder: Westview, 1989)

(1989b) 'Neoliberal Institutionalism: A Perspective on World Politics', in Keohane, *International Institutions and State Power* (Boulder: Westview, 1989) 1

(1989c) 'The Theory of Hegemonic Stability and Changes in International Economic Regimes, 1967–1977', in Keohane, *International Institutions and State Power* (Boulder: Westview, 1989) 74

(1989d) 'The Demand for International Regimes', in Keohane, *International Institutions and State Power* (Boulder: Westview, 1989) 101

(1989e) 'International Institutions: Two Approaches', in Keohane, *International Institutions and State Power* (Boulder: Westview, 1989) 158

(1993) 'The Analysis of International Regimes', in Volker Rittberger (ed.), *Regime Theory and International Relations* (Oxford: Clarendon, 1993) 23

Keohane, Robert and Joseph Nye (1977) *Power and Interdependence* (Boston: Little, Brown, 1977)

(1987) '*Power and Interdependence* Revisited', (1987) 41 *International Organization* 725

Kingsbury, Benedict (1994) 'The Tuna-Dolphin Controversy, the World Trade Organization, and the Liberal Project to Reconceptualize International Law', (1994) 5 *Yearbook of International Environmental Law* 1

Kirgis, Fredric (1987) 'Custom on a Sliding Scale', (1987) 81 *American Journal of International Law* 146

Kiss, Alexandre and Dinah Shelton (1991) *International Environmental Law* (New York: Transnational, 1991)

Knop, Karen (1993) 'Re/Statements: Feminism and State Sovereignty in International Law', (1993) 3 *Transnational Law and Contemporary Problems* 293

Knopf, Jeffrey (1993) 'Beyond Two-Level Games: Domestic–International Interaction in the Intermediate-Range Nuclear Forces Negotiations', (1993) 47 *International Organization* 599

Koh, Harold (1996) 'Transnational Legal Process', (1996) 75 *Nebraska Law Review* 181

(1997) 'Why Do Nations Obey International Law?', (1997) 106 *Yale Law Journal* 2599

Kokkini-Iatridou, D. and P.J.I.M. de Waart (1983) 'Foreign Investments in Developing Countries – Legal Personality of Multinationals in International Law', (1983) 14 *Netherlands Yearbook of International Law* 87

Kontou, Nancy (1994) *The Termination and Revision of Treaties in the Light of New Customary International Law* (Oxford: Clarendon, 1994)

Kopelmanas, Lazare (1937) 'Custom as a Means of the Creation of International Law', (1937) 18 *British Yearbook of International Law* 127

Koskenniemi, Martti (1989) *From Apology to Utopia* (Helsinki: Lakimiesliiton Kustannus, 1989)

(1990a) 'The Pull of the Mainstream', (1990) 88 *Michigan Law Review* 1946

(1990b) 'The Politics of International Law', (1990) 1 *European Journal of International Law* 4

Krasner, Stephen (1983) 'Structural Causes and Regime Consequences: Regimes as Intervening Variables', in Krasner (ed.), *International Regimes* (Ithaca: Cornell University Press, 1983) 1

(1993) 'Sovereignty, Regimes, and Human Rights', in Volker Rittberger (ed.), *Regime Theory and International Relations* (Oxford: Clarendon, 1993) 139

Kratochwil, Friedrich (1989) *Rules, Norms, and Decisions: On the Conditions of Practical Legal Reasoning in International Relations and Domestic Affairs* (Cambridge: Cambridge University Press, 1989)

(1993) 'Contracts and Regimes', in Volker Rittberger (ed.), *Regime Theory and International Relations* (Oxford: Clarendon, 1993) 73

Kreca, Milenko (1982) 'Some General Reflections on Main Features of Ius Cogens as Notion of International Public Law', in Rafael Girardot *et al.* (eds.), *New Directions in International Law: Essays in Honour of Wolfgang Abendroth* (Frankfurt: Campus, 1982) 27

Kresock, David (1994) '"Ethnic Cleansing" in the Balkans: The Legal Foundation of Foreign Intervention', (1994) 27 *Cornell International Law Journal* 203

Kress, Claus (1995) *Gewaltverbot und Selbstverteidigungsrecht nach der Satzung der Vereinten Nationen bei staatlicher Verwicklung in Gewaltakten Privater* (Berlin: Duncker and Humblot, 1995)

Kunz, Joseph (1953) 'The Nature of Customary International Law', (1953) 47 *American Journal of International Law* 662

Kwakwa, Edward (1987) 'Emerging International Development Law and Traditional International Law – Congruence or Cleavage?' (1987) 17 *Georgia Journal of International and Comparative Law* 431

de Lacharrière, Guy (1983) *La politique juridique extérieure* (Paris: Economica, 1983)

Lachs, Manfred (1984) 'Pacta Sunt Servanda', in Rudolf Bernhardt (ed.), *Encyclopedia of Public International Law* (Amsterdam: North-Holland, 1984) vol. 7, 364

Lagoni, Rainer (1994) 'Article 71', in Bruno Simma (ed.), *The Charter of the United Nations* (Oxford: Oxford University Press, 1994) 902

Lall, K. B. (1974) 'Economic Inequality and International Law', (1974) 14 *Indian Journal of International Law* 7

Lane, Eric (1978) 'Demanding Human Rights: A Change in the World Legal Order', (1978) 6 *Hofstra Law Review* 269

Lansing, Robert (1921) 'Notes on World Sovereignty', (1921) 15 *American Journal of International Law* 13

Lasswell, Harold and Myres McDougal (1992) *Jurisprudence for a Free Society* (New Haven: New Haven Press, 1992)

Laurence, T. J. (1919) *The Society of Nations* (New York: Oxford University Press, 1919)

Lauterpacht, Elihu (1958) 'The Contemporary Practice of the United Kingdom in the Field of International Law: Survey and Comment, VI', (1958) 7 *International and Comparative Law Quarterly* 514

(1960) 'The Contemporary Practice of the United Kingdom in the Field of International Law: Survey and Comment, VIII', (1960) 9 *International and Comparative Law Quarterly* 253

Lauterpacht, Hersch (1933) *The Function of Law in the International Community* (Oxford: Clarendon, 1933)

(1950) *International Law and Human Rights* (London: Stevens, 1950)

Leigh, Monroe (1978) 'Address', in *Proceedings of the 1978 International Law Association Conference on 'State Immunity: Law and Practice in the United States and Europe'*, 7

Lewis, Charles (1990) *State and Diplomatic Immunity* (3rd ed.) (London: Lloyd's, 1990)

Lillich, Richard (1975) 'The Valuation of Nationalized Property in International Law: Toward a Consensus or More "Rich Chaos"?', in Lillich (ed.), *The Valuation of Nationalized Property in International Law* (Charlottesville: University Press of Virginia, 1975) Vol. 3, 183

(1984) *The Human Rights of Aliens in Contemporary International Law* (Manchester: Manchester University Press, 1984)

(1993) 'Humanitarian Intervention through the United Nations: Towards the Development of Criteria', (1993) 53 *Zeitschrift für ausländisches öffentliches Recht und Völkerrecht* 557

(1995/6) 'The Growing Importance of Customary International Human Rights Law', (1995/96) 25 *Georgia Journal of International and Comparative Law* 1

Lillich, Richard and Burns Weston (1975) *International Claims: Their Settlement by Lump Sum Agreements* (Charlottesville: University Press of Virginia, 1975)

Lillich, Richard and Stephen Neff (1978) 'The Treatment of Aliens and International Human Rights Norms: Overlooked Developments at the UN', (1978) 21 *German Yearbook of International Law* 97

Lobo de Souza, I. M. (1995) 'The Role of State Consent in the Customary Process', (1995) 44 *International and Comparative Law Quarterly* 521

Lord, Janet (1995) 'The United Nations High Commissioner for Human Rights: Challenges and Opportunities', (1995) 17 *Loyola of Los Angeles International and Comparative Law Journal* 329

Loring, David (1970–1) 'The United States–Peruvian "Fisheries" Dispute', (1970–1) 23 *Stanford Law Review* 391

Lowe, Vaughan (1981) 'Blocking Extraterritorial Jurisdiction: The British Protection of Trading Interests Act 1980', (1981) 75 *American Journal of International Law* 257

(1983a) 'Do General Rules of International Law Exist?', (1983) 9 *Review of International Studies* 207

(1983b) (ed.) *Extraterritorial Jurisdiction: An Annotated Collection of Legal Materials* (Cambridge: Grotius, 1983)

Luca, Donatella (1993) 'Intervention humanitaire: questions et réflexions', (1993) 5 *International Journal of Refugee Law* 424

Macalister-Smith, Peter (1992) 'Comity', in Rudolf Bernhardt (ed.), *Encyclopedia of Public International Law* (Amsterdam: North-Holland, 1992) vol. 1, 671
Macdonald, Ronald St. J. (1987) 'Fundamental Norms in Contemporary International Law', (1987) 25 *Canadian Yearbook of International Law* 115
Macdonald, Ronald St. J., G. L. Morris and D. M. Johnston (1971) 'The Canadian Initiative to Establish a Maritime Zone for Environmental Protection', (1971) 21 *University of Toronto Law Journal* 247
MacGibbon, Iain (1954) 'The Scope of Acquiescence in International Law', (1954) 31 *British Yearbook of International Law* 143
(1957) 'Customary International Law and Acquiescence', (1957) 33 *British Yearbook of International Law* 115
Maier, Harold (1983) 'Interest Balancing and Extraterritorial Jurisdiction', (1983) 31 *American Journal of Comparative Law* 579
(1984) 'Resolving Extraterritorial Conflicts or There and Back Again', (1984) 25 *Virginia Journal of International Law* 7
Mann, F. A. (1964) 'The Doctrine of Jurisdiction in International Law', (1964-I) 111 *Recueil des cours* 1
(1984) 'The Doctrine of Jurisdiction in International Law Revisited After Twenty Years', (1984-III) 186 *Recueil des cours* 9
Manning, C. A. W. (1962) *The Nature of International Society* (London: London School of Economics, 1962)
Marek, Krystyna (1968) 'Contribution à l'étude du *jus cogens* en droit international', in *Recueil d'études de droit international en hommage à Paul Guggenheim* (Geneva: University of Geneva, 1968) Tome 2, 426
Marks, Susan (1995) 'The European Convention on Human Rights and its "Democratic Society"', (1995) 66 *British Yearbook of International Law* 209
Marston, Geoffrey (ed.) (1985) 'United Kingdom Materials on International Law 1985', (1985) 56 *British Yearbook of International Law* 363
(1996) 'The Incorporation of Continental Shelf Rights into United Kingdom Law', (1996) 45 *International and Comparative Law Quarterly* 13
Matte, Nicolas (1964) *Traité de droit aérien-aéronautique* (2nd ed.) (Paris: Pedone, 1964)
Mayer, Pierre (1994) *Droit international privé* (5th ed.) (Paris: Montchrestien, 1994)
McDougal, Myres (1955) 'The Hydrogen Bomb Tests and the International Law of the Sea', (1955) 49 *American Journal of International Law* 356
McDougal, Myres and William Burke (1962) *The Public Order of the Oceans: A Contemporary International Law of the Sea* (New Haven: Yale University Press, 1962)
McDougal, Myres and Florentino Feliciano (1961) *Law and Minimum World Public Order: The Legal Regulation of International Coercion* (New Haven: Yale University Press, 1961)
McDougal, Myres, Harold Lasswell and Ivan Vlasic (1963) *Law and Public Order in Space* (New Haven: Yale University Press, 1963)
McDougal, Myres, Harold Lasswell and James Miller (1967) *The Interpretation of Agreements and World Public Order: Principles of Content and Procedure* (New Haven: Yale University Press, 1967)

McNair, Arnold (1961) *The Law of Treaties* (Oxford: Clarendon, 1961)
(1964) *The Law of the Air* (3rd ed., Michael Kerr and Anthony Evans, eds.) (London: Stevens, 1964)
Meesen, Karl (1984) 'Antitrust Jurisdiction under Customary International Law', (1984) 78 *American Journal of International Law* 783
von Mehren, Robert (1978) 'The Foreign Sovereign Immunities Act of 1976', (1978) 17 *Columbia Journal of Transnational Law* 33
Meron, Theodor (1986a) *Human Rights Law-Making in the United Nations* (Oxford: Clarendon, 1986)
(1986b) 'On a Hierarchy of International Human Rights', (1986) 80 *American Journal of International Law* 1
(1989) *Human Rights and Humanitarian Norms as Customary Law* (Oxford: Clarendon, 1989)
Mills, C. Wright (1959) *The Sociological Imagination* (Oxford: Oxford University Press, 1959)
Mitchell, Ronald (1994) 'Regime Design Matters: Intentional Oil Pollution and Treaty Compliance', (1994) 48 *International Organization* 425
Molot, H. L. and M. L. Jewett (1982) 'The State Immunity Act of Canada', (1982) 20 *Canadian Yearbook of International Law* 79
Money, Robert (1993) 'The Protocol on Environmental Protection to the Antarctic Treaty: Maintaining a Legal Regime', (1993) 7 *Emory International Law Review* 163
Morgenthau, Hans (1954) *Politics Among Nations* (2nd ed.) (New York: Alfred Knopf, 1954)
Morris, Anne and Susan Nott (1991) *Working Women and the Law: Equality and Discrimination in Theory and Practice* (London: Routledge, 1991)
Mosler, Hermann (1968a) 'Ius Cogens im Völkerrecht', (1968) 25 *Schweizerisches Jahrbuch für internationales Recht* 9
(1968b) 'Der "Gemeinschaftliche Ordre Public" in europäischen Staatengruppen', (1968) *Revista Española de Derecho Internacional* 523
(1974) 'The International Society as a Legal Community', (1974-IV) 140 *Recueil des cours* 1
Nanda, Ved (1967) 'The "Torrey Canyon" Disaster: Some Legal Aspects', (1967) 44 *Denver Law Journal* 400
Nietzsche, Friedrich (1887) *The Genealogy of Morals*, in Oscar Levy (ed.), *The Complete Works of Friedrich Nietzsche* (Edinburgh: Foulis, 1913) (first published in 1887) vol. 13
Nolte, Georg (1993) 'Restoring Peace by Regional Action: International Legal Aspects of the Liberian Conflict', (1993) 53 *Zeitschrift für ausländisches öffentliches Recht und Völkerrecht* 603
Norton, Patrick (1991) 'A Law of the Future or a Law of the Past? Modern Tribunals and the International Law of Expropriation', (1991) 85 *American Journal of International Law* 474
Note (1969) 'Continental Shelf Oil Disasters: Challenge to International Pollution Control', (1969) 55 *Cornell Law Review* 113
Nye, Joseph (1988) 'Neorealism and Neoliberalism', (1988) 40 *World Politics* 235
O'Connell, D. P. (1965) 'Independence and Problems of State Succession', in

William O'Brien (ed.), *The New States in International Law Diplomacy* (London: Stevens, 1965) 7
(1982) *The International Law of the Sea* (Oxford: Clarendon, 1982)
Oda, Shigeru (1988) 'Further Thoughts on the Chambers Procedure of the International Court of Justice', (1988) 82 *American Journal of International Law* 556
Oda, Shigeru and Hisashi Owada (1985) 'Annual Review of Japanese Practice in International Law', (1985) 28 *Japanese Annual of International Law* 59
Ofodile, Anthony (1994) 'The Legality of ECOWAS Intervention in Liberia', (1994) 32 *Columbia Journal of Transnational Law* 381
Onuf, Nicholas (1994) 'Book Review: Karol Wolfke, *Custom in Present International Law* (2nd rev. ed.)', (1994) 88 *American Journal of International Law* 556
Onuf, Nicholas and Richard Birney (1974) 'Peremptory Norms of International Law: Their Source, Function and Future', (1974) 4 *Denver Journal of International Law and Policy* 187
Oppenheim, Lassa (1905) *International Law* (London: Longmans, Green and Co.: 1905)
Ostrihansky, Rudolf (1988) 'Chambers of the International Court of Justice', (1988) 37 *International and Comparative Law Quarterly* 30
Özgur, Özdemir (1982) *Apartheid: The United Nations and Peaceful Change in South Africa* (Epping: Bowker, 1982)
Park, William and Stephen Cromie (1990) *International Commercial Litigation* (London: Butterworths, 1990)
Parker, Karen and Lyn Neylon (1989) '*Jus Cogens*: Compelling the Law of Human Rights', (1989) 12 *Hastings International and Comparative Law Review* 411
Paust, Jordan (1991) 'The Reality of *Jus Cogens*', (1991) 7 *Connecticut Journal of International Law* 81
Pellet, Alain (1992) 'The Normative Dilemma: Will and Consent in International Law Making', (1992) 12 *Australian Yearbook of International Law* 22
Permanent Court of International Justice (1920) Advisory Committee of Jurists, *Procès-Verbaux of the Proceedings of the Committee* (16 June–24 July 1920, with annexes) (The Hague: van Langenhuysen Bros, 1920)
Plender, Richard (1986) 'The Role of Consent in the Termination of Treaties', (1986) 57 *British Yearbook of International Law* 133
Powell, Robert (1994) 'Anarchy in International Relations Theory: The Neorealist–Neoliberal Debate', (1994) 48 *International Organization* 313
Ragazzi, Maurizio (1997) *The Concept of International Obligations Erga Omnes* (Oxford: Clarendon, 1997)
Raman, Venkata (1967) *Prescription of International Law by Customary Practice* (unpublished S. J. D. thesis, Yale Law School, 1967)
(1976) 'Toward a General Theory of International Customary Law', in Michael Reisman and Burns Weston (eds.), *Toward World Order and Human Dignity: Essays in Honor of Myres S. McDougal* (New York: Free Press, 1976) 365
von Ranke, Leopold (1973) *The Theory and Practice of History* (Greg Iggers, ed.) (Indianapolis: Bobbs-Merrill, 1973)

Raul, Alan and Paul Hagen (1973) 'The Convergence of Trade and Environmental Law', (Fall 1993) *Natural Resources and Environment* 3

Rawls, John (1971) *A Theory of Justice* (Cambridge, MA: Harvard University Press, 1971)

Raz, Joseph (1990) *Practical Reason and Norms* (Princeton: Princeton University Press, 1990)

Redfern, Alan and Martin Hunter (1991) *Law and Practice of International Commercial Arbitration* (2nd ed.) (London: Sweet and Maxwell, 1991)

Reid, John (1980) *Law for the Elephant: Property and Social Behaviour on the Overland Trail* (Salt Lake City: Publisher's Press, 1980)

Reisman, Michael (1983) 'Looking, Staring and Glaring: Microlegal Systems and Public Order', (1983) 12 *Denver Journal of International Law and Policy* 165

(1987) 'The Cult of Custom in the Late 20th Century', (1987) 17 *California Western International Law Journal* 133

(1992) 'The View from the New Haven School of International Law', (1992) 86 *American Society of International Law Proceedings* 118

Reuter, Paul (1958) *Droit international public* (Paris: Presses universitaires de France, 1958)

(1961) 'Principes de droit international public', (1961-II) 103 *Recueil des cours* 425

(1976) *Droit international public* (5th ed.) (Paris: Thémis, 1976)

(1995) *An Introduction to the Law of Treaties* (2nd English ed.) (trans. José Mico and Peter Haggenmacher) (London: Kegan Paul, 1995)

Riesenfeld, Stefan (1966) '*Jus Dispositivum* and *Jus Cogens* in International Law: In the Light of a Recent Decision of the German Supreme Constitutional Court', (1966) 60 *American Journal of International Law* 511

Risse-Kappen, Thomas (1994) 'Ideas do not Float Freely: Transnational Coalitions, Domestic Structures, and the End of the Cold War', (1994) 48 *International Organization* 185

Robertson, Aidan and Marie Demetriou (1994) '"But That Was Another Country . . .": The Extra-Territorial Application of the US Antitrust Laws in the US Supreme Court', (1994) 43 *International and Comparative Law Quarterly* 417

Robinson, Davis (1984) 'Expropriation in the Restatement (Revised)', (1984) 78 *American Journal of International Law* 176

Rodley, Nigel (1987) *The Treatment of Prisoners under International Law* (Oxford: Clarendon, 1987)

Rosenberg, Justin (1994) *The Empire of Civil Society* (London: Verso, 1994)

(1994b) 'The International Imagination: IR Theory and "Classic Social Analysis"', (1994) 23 *Millennium* 85

Rosenne, Shabtai (1965) *The Law and Practice of the International Court* (Leyden: Sijthoff, 1965)

(1992) 'Codification of International Law', in Rudolf Bernhardt (ed.), *Encyclopedia of Public International Law* (Amsterdam: North-Holland, 1992) vol. 1, 632

Roth, P. M. (1992) 'Reasonable Extraterritoriality: Correcting the "Balance of Interest"', (1992) 41 *International and Comparative Law Quarterly* 245

Rousseau, Charles (1953) *Droit international public* (Paris: Sirey, 1953)
Rozakis, Christos (1976) *The Concept of Jus Cogens in the Law of Treaties* (Amsterdam: North-Holland, 1976)
Rubin, Alfred (1988) *The Law of Piracy* (Newport: Naval War College Press, 1988)
(1997) *Ethics and Authority in International Law* (Cambridge: Cambridge University Press, 1997)
Ruggie, John (ed.) (1983) *The Antinomies of Interdependence* (New York: Columbia University Press, 1983)
Ruggie, John and Ernst Haas (eds.) (1975) 'International Responses to Technology', (1975) 29(3) *International Organization* (special issue)
Sahovic, Milan and William Bishop (1968) 'The Authority of the State: Its Range with Respect to Persons and Places', in Max Sörensen (ed.), *Manual of Public International Law* (London: Macmillan, 1968) 311
Salvioli, Gabriele (1932) 'Observations', (1932) 40 *Annuaire de l'institut de droit international* 314
Sartorius, Rolf (1971) 'Hart's Concept of Law', in Robert Summers (ed.), *More Essays in Legal Philosophy* (Oxford: Basil Blackwell, 1971) 131
von Savigny, Friedrich (1949) 'Grundgedanken der historischen Rechtsschule', in E. Wolff, *Quellenbuch zur Geschichte der deutschen Rechtswissenschaft* (Tübingen: Gruyter, 1949)
Scelle, Georges (1932/4) *Précis de droit des gens* (Paris: Sirey, 1932/4)
(1956) 'Le phénomène juridique de dédoublement fonctionnel', in Walter Schätzel and Hans-Jürgen Schlochauer (eds.), *Rechtsfragen der internationalen Organization: Festschrift für Hans Wehberg* (Frankfurt am Main: Klostermann, 1956) 324
Schachter, Oscar (1968) 'Towards a Theory of International Obligation', (1968) 8 *Virginia Journal of International Law* 300
(1984) 'Compensation for Expropriation', (1984) 78 *American Journal of International Law* 121
(1987) 'Remarks' in 'Disentangling Treaty and Customary International Law', (1987) 81 *American Society of International Law Proceedings* 157, 158
(1989) 'Entangled Treaty and Custom', in Yoram Dinstein (ed.), *International Law at a Time of Perplexity: Essays in Honour of Shabtai Rosenne* (Dordrecht: Martinus Nijhoff, 1989) 717
(1991) *International Law in Theory and Practice* (Dordrecht: Nijhoff, 1991)
(1996) 'New Custom: Power, *Opinio Juris* and Contrary Practice', in Jerzy Makarczyk (ed.), *Theory of International Law at the Threshold of the 21st Century: Essays in Honour of Krzysztof Skubiszewsk* (The Hague: Kluwer, 1996) 531
Schmitt, Carl (1934) *Über die drei Arten des rechtswissenschaftlichen Denkens* (Hamburg: Hanseatische Verlagsanstalt, 1934)
Schwartz, Michelle (1993) 'International Legal Protection for Victims of Environmental Abuse', (1993) 18 *Yale Journal of International Law* 355
Schwarzenberger, Georg (1964) *Power Politics* (3rd ed.) (London: Stevens, 1964)
(1965) 'International *Jus Cogens*?', (1965) 43 *Texas Law Review* 455
(1967) *International Law* (3rd ed.) (London: Stevens, 1967) vol. 1

Schwebel, Stephen (1979) 'The Effect of Resolutions of the UN General Assembly on Customary International Law', (1979) 73 *American Society of International Law Proceedings* 301

(1986) 'United Nations Resolutions, Recent Arbitral Awards and Customary International Law', in Adriaan Bos and Hugo Siblesz (eds.), *Realism in Law-Making: Essays on International Law in Honour of Willem Riphagen* (Dordrecht: Martinus Nijhoff, 1986) 203

(1987) 'Ad Hoc Chambers of the International Court of Justice', (1987) 81 *American Journal of International Law* 831

Scott, J. B. (ed.) (1918) *President Wilson's Foreign Policy: Messages, Addresses, Papers* (New York: Oxford University Press, 1918)

Sebenius, James (1992) 'Challenging Conventional Explanations of International Cooperation: Negotiation Analysis and the Case of Epistemic Communities', (1992) 46 *International Organization* 323

Seidl-Hohenveldern, Ignaz (1986) 'International Economic Law', (1986-III) 198 *Recueil des cours* 9

(1987) *Corporations in and under International Law* (Cambridge: Grotius, 1987)

Sepúlveda, César (1990) 'Methods and Procedures for the Creation of Legal Norms in the International System of States: An Inquiry into the Progressive Development of International Law in the Present Era', (1990) 33 *German Yearbook of International Law* 432

Setear, John (1996) 'An Iterative Perspective on Treaties: A Synthesis of International Relations Theory and International Law', (1996) 37 *Harvard International Law Journal* 139

Sgro, Jill (1983) 'China's Stance on Sovereign Immunity: A Critical Perspective on *Jackson* v. *People's Republic of China*', (1983) 22 *Columbia Journal of Transnational Law* 101

Shahabuddeen, Mohamed (1996) *Precedent in the World Court* (Cambridge: Cambridge University Press, 1996)

Shaw, Malcolm (1989) 'Genocide and International Law', in Yoram Dinstein (ed.), *International Law at a Time of Perplexity: Essays in Honour of Shabtai Rosenne* (Dordrecht: Martinus Nijhoff, 1989) 797

(1997) *International Law* (4th ed.) (Cambridge: Cambridge University Press, 1997)

Siegel, Kenneth (1985) 'The International Law of Compensation for Expropriation and International Debt: A Dangerous Uncertainty', (1985) 8 *Hastings International and Comparative Law Review* 223

Simma, Bruno (1984) 'Reciprocity', in Rudolf Bernhardt (ed.), *Encyclopedia of Public International Law* (Amsterdam: North-Holland, 1984) vol. 7, 400

(1989) 'Bilateralism and Community Interest in the Law of State Responsibility', in Yoram Dinstein (ed.), *International Law at a Time of Perplexity: Essays in Honour of Shabtai Rosenne* (Dordrecht: Martinus Nijhoff, 1989) 821

(1994) (ed.), *The Charter of the United Nations* (Oxford: Oxford University Press, 1994)

Simma, Bruno and Philip Alston (1992) 'The Sources of Human Rights Law: Custom, Jus Cogens, and General Principles', (1992) 12 *Australian Yearbook of International Law* 82

Simmonds, Nigel (1990) 'Why Conventionalism Does Not Collapse into Pragmatism', (1990) 49 *Cambridge Law Journal* 63
(1991) 'Between Positivism and Idealism', (1991) 50 *Cambridge Law Journal* 308
Simpson, Brian (1973) 'The Common Law and Legal Theory', in Simpson (ed.), *Oxford Essays in Jurisprudence* (second series) (Oxford: Clarendon, 1973) 77
Sinclair, Ian (1980) 'The Law of Sovereign Immunity. Recent Developments', (1980-II) *Recueil des cours* 113
Slaughter, Anne-Marie (1995) 'International Law in a World of Liberal States', (1995) 6 *European Journal of International Law* 503
Slaughter Burley, Anne-Marie (1993) 'International Law and International Relations Theory: A Dual Agenda', (1993) 87 *American Journal of International Law* 205
Slouka, Zdenek (1968) *International Custom and the Continental Shelf* (The Hague: Martinus Nijhoff, 1968)
Sohn, Louis (1982) 'The New International Law: Protection of the Rights of Individuals Rather Than States', (1982) 32 *American University Law Review* 1
Sornarajah, M. (1982) 'The Extraterritorial Enforcement of US Antitrust Laws: Conflict and Compromise', (1982) 31 *International and Comparative Law Quarterly* 127
Sörensen, Max (1946) *Les sources du droit international: étude sur la jurisprudence de la Cour Permanente de Justice Internationale* (Copenhagen: Munksgaard, 1946)
de Staël-Holstein, Baron (1924) 'Le régime scandinave des eaux littorales', (1924) 3(5) *Revue de droit international* 630
Stein, Ted (1985) 'The Approach of the Different Drummer: The Principle of the Persistent Objector in International Law', (1985) 26 *Harvard International Law Journal* 457
Steiner, Henry and Philip Alston (1996) *International Human Rights in Context* (Oxford: Oxford University Press, 1996)
Stern, Brigitte (1981) 'La coutume au coeur du droit international', in *Mélanges offerts à Paul Reuter* (Paris: Pedone, 1981) 479
Stinchcombe, Arthur (1968) *Constructing Social Theories* (New York: Harcourt, Brace and World, 1968)
Strange, Susan (1983) '*Cave! hic dragones*: A Critique of Regime Analysis', in Stephen Krasner (ed.), *International Regimes* (Ithaca: Cornell University Press, 1983) 337
(1988) *States and Markets* (London: Pinter, 1988)
Strupp, Karl (1930) 'Le droit du juge international de statuer selon l'équité', (1930-III) 33 *Recueil des cours* 351
Sucharitkul, Sompong (1979) 'Immunities of Foreign States Before National Authorities: Some Aspects of Progressive Development of Contemporary International Law', in *Estudios de Derecho Internacional: Homenaje al Profesor Miaja de la Muela* (Madrid: Editorial Tecnos, 1979) 477
Sur, Serge (1990) *La coutume internationale* (Paris: Librairies Techniques, 1990)
(1995) *Relations Internationales* (Paris: Montchrestien, 1995)
Symposium (1994) 'Countermeasures and Dispute Settlement: The Current Debate Within the ILC', (1994) 5 *European Journal of International Law* 20

Sztucki, Jerzy (1974) *Jus Cogens and the Vienna Convention on the Law of Treaties* (Vienna: Springer-Verlag, 1974)

Terz, Panos (1978) 'Zum Jus Cogens im demokratischen Völkerrecht', (1978) 27 *Staat und Recht* 617

Téson, Fernando (1993) 'Feminism and International Law: A Reply', (1993) 33 *Virginia Journal of International Law* 647

Theis, Achim (1986) 'The International Legal Code for Geostationary Radio Satellites', (1986) 29 *German Yearbook of International Law* 227

Thirlway, Hugh (1972) *International Customary Law and Codification* (Leiden: Sijthoff, 1972)

Triepel, Heinrich (1899) *Völkerrecht und Landesrecht* (Aalen: Scientia Antiquariat, 1958)

Trimble, Phillip (1990) Review of David Kennedy, *International Legal Structures*, etc. (1990) 42 *Stanford Law Review* 811

Trooboff, Peter (1986) 'Foreign State Immunity: Emerging Consensus on Principles', (1986-V) 200 *Recueil des cours* 235

Trudeau, Pierre (1970) 'Remarks to the Press Following the Introduction of Legislation on Arctic Pollution, Territorial Sea and Fishing Zones in the Canadian House of Commons on April 8, 1970', (1970) 9 ILM 600

Tunkin, Grigory (1958) 'Co-existence and International Law', (1958-III) 95 *Recueil des cours* 1

Umozurike, Umozurike (1972) *Self-Determination in International Law* (Hamden, CT: Shoe String Press, 1972)

Unger, Roberto (1983) *The Critical Legal Studies Movement* (Cambridge, MA: Harvard University Press, 1983)

United Nations High Commissioner for Refugees (1995) *The State of the World's Refugees 1995* (Oxford: Oxford University Press, 1995)

Vamvoukos, Athanassios (1985) *Termination of Treaties in International Law: The Doctrines of Rebus Sic Stantibus and Desuetude* (Oxford: Clarendon, 1985)

de Vattel, Emer (1758) *Le droit des gens* (trans. Charles Fenwick) (Washington, DC: Carnegie Institution, 1916) (originally published 1758)

Verdross, Alfred (1935) 'Les principes généraux du droit dans la jurisprudence internationale', (1935-II) 52 *Recueil des cours* 191

(1937) 'Forbidden Treaties in International Law', (1937) 31 *American Journal of International Law* 571

(1955) *Völkerrecht* (3rd ed.) (Vienna: Springer, 1955)

(1966) 'Jus Dispositivum and Jus Cogens in International Law', (1966) 60 *American Journal of International Law* 55

Verdross, Alfred and Heribert Koeck (1983) 'Natural Law: The Tradition of Universal Reason and Authority', in Ronald Macdonald and Douglas Johnston (eds.), *The Structure and Process of International Law* (The Hague: Martinus Nijhoff, 1983) 17

Verdross, Alfred and Bruno Simma (1984) *Universelles Völkerrecht* (3rd ed.) (Berlin: Duncker and Humblot, 1984)

Villiger, Mark (1985) *Customary International Law and Treaties* (Dordrecht: Martinus Nijhoff, 1985)

Virally, Michel (1966) 'Réflexions sur le "jus cogens"', (1966) 12 *Annuaire français de droit international* 5

(1967) 'Le principe de réciprocité dans le droit international contemporain', (1967-III) 122 *Recueil des cours* 3

de Visscher, Charles (1957) *Theory and Reality in Public International Law* (trans. Percy Corbett) (Princeton: Princeton University Press, 1957)

(1971) 'Positivism et "*jus cogens*"', (1971) 75 *Revue générale de droit international public* 5

Walden, Raphael (1977) 'The Subjective Element in the Formation of Customary International Law', (1977) 12 *Israel Law Review* 344

(1978) 'Customary International Law: A Jurisprudential Analysis', (1978) 13 *Israel Law Review* 86

Waldock, Humphrey (1956) 'International Law and the New Maritime Claims', (1956) 1 *International Relations* 161

(1962) 'General Course on Public International Law', (1962-II) 106 *Recueil des cours* 1

Waltz, Kenneth (1979) *Theory of International Politics* (New York: McGraw-Hill, 1979)

Walzer, Michael (1983) *Spheres of Justice* (New York: Basic Books, 1983)

Watson, Adam (1992) *The Evolution of International Society* (London: Routledge, 1992)

Watson, J. S. (1977) 'Autointerpretation, Competence, and the Continuing Validity of Article 2(7) of the UN Charter', (1977) 71 *American Journal of International Law* 60

Weber, Max (1921) *Economy and Society* (Guenther Roth and Claus Wittich, eds.) (New York: Bedminster Press, 1968) (first published in 1921)

(1954) *Max Weber on Law in Economy and Society* (trans. and ed. Max Rheinstein and Edward Shils) (Cambridge, MA: Harvard University Press, 1954)

Weil, Prosper (1983) 'Towards Relative Normativity in International Law?', (1983) 77 *American Journal of International Law* 413

Weiler, Joseph *et al.* (eds.) (1989) *International Crimes of State: A Critical Analysis of the ILC's Draft Article 19 on State Responsibility* (Berlin: de Gruyter, 1989)

Weisburd, Arthur (1988) 'Customary International Law: The Problem of Treaties', (1988) 21 *Vanderbilt Journal of Transnational Law* 1

(1995) 'The Emptiness of the Concept of *Jus Cogens*, as Illustrated by the War in Bosnia-Herzegovina', (1995) 17 *Michigan Journal of International Law* 1

Wendt, Alexander (1992) 'Anarchy is What States Make of It: The Social Construction of Power Politics', (1992) 46 *International Organization* 391

Weyrauch, Walter and Maureen Bell (1993) 'Autonomous Lawmaking: The Case of the "Gypsies"', (1993) 103 *Yale Law Journal* 323

Wight, Martin (1966) 'Western Values in International Relations', in Martin Wight and Herbert Butterfield (eds.), *Diplomatic Investigations* (London: Allen and Unwin, 1966)

(1977) *Systems of States* (Leicester: Leicester University Press, 1977)

Wilkinson, Harvie (1979) *From Brown to Bakke: The Supreme Court and School Integration, 1954–1978* (Oxford: Oxford University Press, 1979)

de Winter, L. I. (1968) 'Excessive Jurisdiction in Private International Law', (1968) 17 *International and Comparative Law Quarterly* 706

Wittgenstein, Ludwig (1953) *Philosophical Investigations* (trans. G. E. M. Anscombe) (Oxford: Blackwell, 1963) (first published in 1953)

Wolfke, Karol (1993a) *Custom in Present International Law* (2nd rev. ed.) (Dordrecht: Martinus Nijhoff, 1993)

(1993b) 'Some Persistent Controversies Regarding Customary International Law', (1993) 24 *Netherlands Yearbook of International Law* 1

Wright, Shelley (1992) 'Economic Rights and Social Justice: A Feminist Analysis of Some International Human Rights Conventions', (1992) 12 *Australian Yearbook of International Law* 241

(1993) 'Economic Rights, Social Justice and the State: A Feminist Reappraisal', in Dorinda Dallmeyer (ed.), *Reconceiving Reality: Women and International Law* (Washington, DC: American Society of International Law, 1993) 117

Yanai, Shunji and Kuniaki Asomura (1977) 'Japan and the Emerging Order of the Sea: Two Maritime Laws of Japan', (1977) 21 *Japanese Annual of International Law* 48

Young, Oran (1977) *Resource Management at the International Level* (London: Pinter, 1977)

(1979) *Compliance and Public Authority: A Theory with International Applications* (Baltimore: Johns Hopkins University Press, 1979)

(1989) *International Cooperation* (Ithaca: Cornell University Press, 1989)

(1992) 'International Law and *International Relations* Theory: Building Bridges', (1992) 86 *American Society of International Law Proceedings* 172

Young, Richard (1948) 'Recent Developments with Respect to the Continental Shelf', (1948) 42 *American Journal of International Law* 849

(1949) 'Further Claims to Areas Beneath the High Seas', (1949) 43 *American Journal of International Law* 790

(1950) 'The Continental Shelf in the Practice of the American States', (1950-I) *Inter-American Juridical Yearbook* 27

Zimmermann, Andreas (1993) 'Asylum Law in the Federal Republic of Germany in the Context of International Law', (1993) 53 *Zeitschrift für ausländisches öffentliches Recht und Völkerrecht* 49

Zoller, Elisabeth (1984) *Peacetime Unilateral Remedies: An Analysis of Countermeasures* (Dobbs Ferry: Transnational, 1984)

# Index